—— HOW TO ——
RECONSTRUCT A
NATION

Righteous Principles for National Leadership and Governance

S. Ali McIntosh

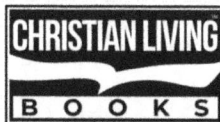

CHRISTIAN LIVING
B O O K S

Largo, Maryland
USA

Christian Living Books, Inc.
P. O. Box 7584
Largo, MD 20792
christianlivingbooks.com
We bring your dreams to fruition.

Hardcover ISBN 9781562293574
Paperback ISBN 9781562293796

HOW TO
RECONSTRUCT A
NATION

Contents

Dedication

To Mommy, The Evangelist & Prophetess

There is nothing quite like a mother's love. Her prayer for me is continuous; her support for me is consistent; her faith in me is steadfast. My mother taught me how to have faith and how to love and care for people. It was my mother, who by example, taught me how to lead. She never ceased to nurture my dreams and made me feel like I could accomplish anything. She is, and has always been, my biggest fan and constant supporter. Mommy, thanks for your unending support. I owe you my life and will always love you.

Response From Mommy

My darling daughter, it is nothing short of God's miracle that you are still alive, and doing what God has called you to do. I am proud to know that you have stood the test of time in holding on to the promises, knowing that you have come this far by holding onto God's unchanging hands. Like Ephesians 6:6 says, 'You are doing the will of God from the heart, not as eye-service or men-pleasers, but from the heart.' So, press on, the race is not over, it has only just begun. Stay calm and humble. My prayers are with you. I love you so much.

*Pastor Dr. Hopeful Jane White 2010 - Mother of the Author
(Photography by Rodger D. Sands – Rodger D Photography,
Nassau, Bahamas)*

Acknowledgments

First, I wish to thank my Co-Author, the Holy Spirit (Divine Intelligence), for making this project a success. Without His inspiration and intellectual expressions, the coordination of all this varied information may have been remiss from this project. I claim no such wisdom alone. Thanks to my family and friends who lent their tremendous support, financial resources and encouragement over the many years; with special mention of Pastor Berkie & Vivian Rolle in Staniel Cay, Exuma; and Apostle Dr. Agnes Glinton, Mr. Brian Rolle, Mrs. Karen & Dr Kevin Moss, Drs. Hasting & Rhea Johnson, and Mr. John J Stuart in Nassau. Special Thanks to Dr. Ruth White, former Principal at Bahamas SDA Academy, whose editing of the original manuscript in 2003 brought grammatical excellence to what was a work in progress. Her editing work was a marvelous teacher, as it taught me how to critique when proofing and correcting my own work over the years.

Special thanks to the personnel at the American University (AU) in Washington, D.C. beginning in 1998 with Ms. Suzanne Groscup, former Academic Advisor and APEL Lecturer, who was my introduction to AU–a wonderful first impression. Thanks to former Presidents, Dr. Benjamin Ladner and Dr. Cornelius Kerwin; the former Dean of the AU School of Public Affairs, Dr. William LeoGrande; and Dr. Robert Tobias, the present Distinguish Practitioner in Residence and Director of the Institute for Public Policy

Implementation, for their advice, referral and direction over the years. Indeed, a special thanks to the entire staff at AU, with whom I have interacted, from Campus Police to the Cafeteria staff. The times spent at the university were the most refreshing times of my entire life. It was a home away from home with each of my three Sabbaticals spent there.

Thanks to my proof-readers and siblings, Prestina and Maria, who assisted during the initial proofing process; and to my final editing team and fact-checkers, associates Mr. Cornelius McKinney, Ms. Dione Pratt and former Parliamentarian Mrs. Veronica Owens, who got the book ready for publishing. And, special thanks to my Publisher, Kimberly Stewart, at Christian Living Books, Inc., who was certain that we had a finished product that is second to none.

And to the Bahamian people, who have allowed me during my entire adult life to be their humble Servant, through my Radio Broadcasting career and ministry on ZNS Inspirational Station; the Prayer Ministries of the Seventh-Day Adventist Church in the Bahamas; the work of the National Committee for Youth Renewal & Revival, the Bahamas Constitution Party and the Josiah Institute for Leadership and Public Policy; serving with some of the most supportive executives, board members and volunteers. Thank you and may God ever bless you all.

Mandate

THE PREAMBLE TO THE CONSTITUTION

WHEREAS, Four hundred and eighty-one years ago the rediscovery of this Family of Islands, rocks and cays heralded the rebirth of the New World;

AND WHEREAS, the People of this Family of Islands recognize that the preservation of their freedom will be guaranteed by a national commitment to Self-discipline, Industry, Loyalty, Unity and An Abiding Respect for Christian Values and the Rule of Law;

NOW KNOW YE THEREFORE:

We, the Inheritors of and Successors to this Family of Islands, recognizing the supremacy of God and believing in the fundamental rights and freedoms of the individual, DO HEREBY PROCLAIM IN SOLEMN PRAISE, the establishment of a free and democratic sovereign nation founded on Spiritual Values and in which no man, woman or child shall ever be slave or bondsman to anyone, or their labour exploited or their lives frustrated by deprivation, AND DO HEREBY PROVIDE by these Articles for the indivisible unity and creation under God of the Commonwealth of The Bahamas."

The Bahamian Constitution

THE BAHAMAS INDEPENDENCE ORDER 1973

(Chapter 1 - Article 1, 2)

1. The Commonwealth of The Bahamas shall be a Sovereign democratic State.

2. This Constitution is the supreme law of the Commonwealth of The Bahamas and, subject to the provisions of this Constitution, if any other law is inconsistent with this Constitution, this Constitution shall prevail and the other law shall, to the extent of the inconsistency, be void.

Preface

"The Constitution is not an instrument for government to restrain the people, it is an instrument for the people to restrain the government - lest it comes to dominate all our lives and interests."

Grosvenor Morris
A framer of the American Constitution

Foreword

I am extremely humbled and honoured to have been asked by Ali McIntosh, my friend and Sister in Christ, to write the Foreword for this book. I thank GOD for His grace and mercy in, and upon my life and for blessing me with His favour.

In 1997, I encountered Ali as I canvassed the Golden Gates Constituency in a single-handed effort to garner support as an Independent Candidate on the Ballot of the upcoming General Elections. I had a team of persons who had expressed their support for me up to the day we were scheduled to begin pounding the pavement and knocking on doors. And true to Bahamian form, no one showed up. I could easily have allowed that predicament to discourage me, but with a sense of peace, I forged ahead. Day after day, I knocked on every door I encountered and delivered my "The Best Man for the Job Is a Woman" presentation to everyone who was gracious enough to listen. As fate would have it, I met Ali.

Ali was a gracious and attentive listener, with many well thought out questions, and comments, which I answered with the passion and conviction that was the driving force behind why I was on a campaign mission, alone. I recognized that Ali and I were both very passionate, and courageous women, but had no clue how our lives would be intertwined in the future.

Ali and I crossed paths ever so briefly down through the years. That day on the campaign trail, I had the feeling of being in the presence of greatness as we exchanged points on our vision for moving our beloved nation forward. I knew I was in the presence of a woman with a GOD ordained mandate to be the conduit for changing the Bahamian political paradigm from corrupt governance to righteous governance, unknowing to me.

Through the years, I have admired Ali's gentle spirit, but tenacious disposition from afar. Her faith in GOD is comforting, refreshing, and endearing. The vision (platform), which I'm convinced was entrusted to her by GOD for the nation of The Bahamas, has brought me to the place where I need no other argument, I need no other plea; and have therefore put my support behind The Bahamas Constitution Party, because whatever GOD is doing in this season, I want to be in the number.

I am excited about Ali's mandate. However, I am doubly excited about what Righteous Governance means for the spiritual growth and development of the Bahamian people, individually and collectively, the economy, and the culture of The Bahamas. The Bahamas WILL see Righteous Governance because GOD is not like man and cannot lie, and Righteous Governance is GOD'S plan for The Bahamas.

I know that this book is part of GOD'S process for Righteous Governance, therefore, it is already a success. I celebrate you, Sis, for your obedience, which I know was not always easy. Nevertheless, you have redefined the meaning of perseverance. Well done!

Mrs. Veronica Owens
Former Educator
Former Member of Parliament (MP)
Former Parliamentary Secretary, Bahamas Ministry of Education

Introduction

A nineteenth Century Scottish Theologian, P.T. Forsyth, is quoted as saying,

> 'You must live with people to know their problems and live with God in order to solve them.'

This statement brings into view, most appropriately, the description of my life's work. Having been brought up by two pastoral parents, and as a youth deeply involved in church work, when I initially felt the call of God on my life for leadership, I obviously assumed it was for pastoral ministry. As I grew and set out to make mental and educational preparations for service to God's people, I was awakened to some very heart-wrenching realities about 'What the call was' and 'Who God's people were'.

The idea of national leadership and governance in the context of God's calling was a very difficult deliberation for me, at first. But, as I further considered the agenda to bring 'righteous order and peace' to society; and the return of The Bahamas to being a 'Christian' nation, in the context of The Bahamas Constitution; I have come to quantify it, as the work of the Kingdom of God.

As I reflect in hindsight, I was under divine consideration from the very early days of my youth. I have spent my entire adult life in the public's view. I got my first job, as a political reporter, at the tender age of twenty, with the governing party's propaganda machinery: the (PLP) Nassau Herald. And over the past thirty-four years, I have been on both sides of the spectrum: either as a talk show host or a guest, or as a newspaper writer or the focus of the story. This has made my public exposure in The Bahamas consistent for more than a quarter of a century.

Additionally, as I reflect on what we shall discuss in this book, I wish to recommend reading a book by Dr. Kelafo Collie of Grand Bahama, who wrote *Reordering the Nation*. This book provides scriptural references for the concept of rebuilding The Bahamas, as a nation called 'under God'.

When I discovered the author and the book, I was delightfully surprised and encouraged by his theories and contributions on the subject. In addition to being an anointed preacher, Dr. Collie is a medical doctor and a Resident Psychiatrist at the government-owned Rand Memorial Hospital in his island home of Freeport, Grand Bahama. He is also a student of the late Dr. Myles Munroe, The Bahamas' foremost teacher on leadership and the kingdom of God. Dr. Munroe's call to The Bahamas and the World has provided 'liberating visions' on this profound subject of The Bahamas being the place 'where God lives'.

Just by sheer association, and by being citizens of The Bahamas, we were all, in some ways, students or mentees of Dr. Myles Munroe, who was never too shy to propagate his message over the mainstream media. I feel an even greater sense of awareness, as I lived in the subdivision at the rear of his church for close to two decades; and the church's property was a passageway for me to and from my home to a bus stop. Also, the church's proximity to my home provided an easy and quick walk to a place of worship whenever I could not attend my own church.

Following my divine encounter in 1998, I began planning, researching, and documenting towards this agenda, and have been making contributions to or rewriting this book over the past eighteen years. At first, I wrote a 62-page research paper at the American University in the Fall of 2001. Over the years, as I have been involved with governance, participating in General Elections, and exposed to the disorder associated with politics in The Bahamas, I have added more and more material. In 2013, I separated the materials into categories, and will publish such in a series of two more books hereafter. In fact, as you will observe, because of my editing and additions, I have provided up to date analysis, with subsequent re-analysis. So please, bear with me.

After analyzing an abundance of both theoretical data and information gleaned from personal participation in political wrangling over the past four General Elections, in my humble opinion, it is safe to say in 2020, that indeed 'the Commonwealth of The Bahamas is in grave crisis on all fronts.'

The Wikipedia online Dictionary describes a Crisis as an 'any event that is going or is expected to lead to an unstable and dangerous situation affecting an individual, group, community, or whole society.' Crises' are deemed to be negative changes in security, economic, political, societal, or environmental affairs, especially when they occur abruptly, with little or no warning. More loosely, it is a term meaning "a testing time" or an "emergency event".

Further to that, my definition of a society in a state of crisis is 'when order and protocol need to be re-established'. A state of crisis is also considered when the social and moral fabric needs to be mended and brought back to an acceptable standard, because it has been broken and torn apart by elements, such as high crime, judicial inequality, illegal migration issues, political anarchy, corruption and failed governance. This clearly describes the state of the

Bahamian society. In fact, according to Sociology, the normalization of crisis is where we sit, constantly on the edge of a burgeoning state of crisis.

This normalization of crisis, and a constant state of a burgeoning crisis is not unique to The Bahamas. Many societies across the world, including the United States of America, also face this threat of endangerment. However, Trust or, too often, the lack of it is one of the central issues of our time, which produces crises in a society. Without trust, institutions don't work, societies falter, and people lose faith in their leaders.

However, when society is in crisis, the people look to the government for leadership out of their economic decline or degradation, and their moral or social maladies. Therefore, any government elected to office must show strong leadership and fiscal restraint, if the society is to survive the trickle-down effect of this 'global economic and moral meltdown'. So, the leaders of the nation during times of crisis must be people with moral character, resolved integrity, and innate spiritual discernment.

Therefore, to set a proper tone for this deliberation, I wish to quote the nineteenth-century U.S. Statesman Henry Clay. In the following statement, he reminds us that "Government is for the people, and by the people" and not the other way around.

'Government is a trust,' said Clay, 'and the officers of the government are trustees; and both are created for the benefit of the people.'

Although the concept of civil governance is considered by some to be secular in nature, the idea of government was actually created by the mind of the Almighty God, for the orderly and proper service to, and on behalf of the masses, for His glory.

Governmental leadership within the life of a nation is supposed to provide political direction, economic and infrastructural development, social justice, equity, stability and peace. Meanwhile, the leaders themselves must 'maintain' a high level of moral influence and inspiration to the people of that nation.

This book brings together a combination of thoughts, ideas, opinions, experiences and divine revelations. It includes some thought-provoking information about how we should govern a society that has long spiraled out of control; what standards we should use to promote institutional integrity; and what core values we should promote for the establishment of moral authority for national leadership.

While I have sought in this book to define the principles of governance for the Bahamian society from the values enunciated in the Preamble of The Bahamas Constitution; these ideals can be used far beyond our local context, to provide concepts that can be utilized in other public sector environments by nations seeking to guide its leadership in a principled and accountable fashion.

Having had the opportunity to garner experiences from my encounter with all of the Bahamian Prime Ministers, both past and present, several founding fathers of the nation, and hundreds of politicians and activists of the modern Bahamas over the past two and a half decades; I have attempted in this deliberation to form an authoritative opinion on what makes and does not make for effective governance in this 21st century Bahamas.

I believe that all persons who desire to be engaged in any category of national leadership, whether it is elected or appointed, should be subject to a Litmus Test, to determine their credibility and integrity to hold the office to which they aspire or are being appointed. This 'vetting' process should be held to a high standard, with consideration given to persons not just for political expediency, but for their personal integrity, joint national vision, and shared national goals.

I hope in this dialogue to articulate how the correct interpretation and application of the values of 'Self-discipline, Industry, Loyalty, Unity, and an Abiding Respect for Christian Values and the Rule of Law' would affect governance and the overall development and well-being of Bahamian society.

It is my desire that the articulation of these theories, add clarity to the Preamble of the Constitution, and set an inspirational perspective to the remainder of its Articles; and that these theories, further qualify the values defined within the Preamble, as substantive and well-grounded criteria for leadership in the national life and governance of the Commonwealth of The Bahamas.

In the future, I trust that the ideas put forward in this book for the reform of our forty-seven (47) year old inherited constitution from Mother England; be considered, observed, and included in the discussion to create a viable new constitution for a proposed Republic of the Commonwealth of The Bahamas. The work of constitutional reform cannot be left only to the Progressive Liberal Party and Free National Movement, or their appointed Commissions; but rather to a wider range of Bahamian citizens, striving for the ultimate reconstruction of the Commonwealth of The Bahamas.

As we explore all these reform ideas in the context of democracy, we must also be clear on the role that the government should play or not play in the lives of the citizenry, and what the people's response to these institutions of leadership should be. We also want to establish the role the Church should play in influencing the governing process and the creation of public policy.

David, the ancient king of Israel, instructed his son Solomon, his successor, that the way to succeed in governance is by upholding godly principles. He recommended divine inspiration when he said this:

'He that ruleth over men must be just, ruling in the fear of God'. 2 Samuel 23:2-4

Subsequently, Solomon, who later compared the role and inspiration of righteous versus wicked leadership, stated this:

'When the righteous is in authority, the people rejoice: but when the wicked beareth rule, the people mourn'.

Proverbs 29:2

This idea of Righteous governance, that I now bring forward to the table again, was first propagated by the Father of the Nation, the late Sir Lynden Pindling and his colleague, the late Sir Randol Fawkes, from the early days preceding Majority Rule in the late 1950s. Therefore, it is not a new agenda in Bahamian politics.

It is clear, however, that somewhere along the way, successive governments have lost sight of the original intent of this 'Righteous' agenda. Thus, the need at this critical juncture or crossroad in our nation's development is to return to the original objectives set forth by the founders of the modern Bahamas.

When I look at the leadership and the recruitment of most candidates for members of Parliament in the major political parties, we appear to be stagnated in our journey towards the intended goals of the founders of this small island state. We are digressing in a fast-forward motion towards losing 'sovereignty and real ownership' of the Commonwealth of The Bahamas.

Notwithstanding the recent 2017 General Elections and the election of a new Free National Movement government, with a seemingly new slate of persons; the country stands poised to remain at a place of imminent crisis. In addition to what political activists and observers view as numerous blunders and missteps by the new government; this FNM Administration passionate pursuit towards globalization, the One World Order, and the Bahamas' ascension to the World Trade Organization (WTO); is creating mayhem and causing massive panic among local activists and segments of the business community, because of their desire for the government to make a greater move towards protectionism for local business interests. For while new faces are out-front, the commitment to the system of oppression and the colonialist-Oligarchy, remains entrenched. Therefore, the divine call for this righteous agenda for governance for the Commonwealth of The Bahamas remains intact.

I hope that this book will enhance the journey of anyone who desires to serve in public office; and that it assists them to clearly identify what their responsibilities should be when making themselves available for service to the nation.

I trust also that upon the completion of reading this book, We the People would undoubtedly have a deeper understanding and appreciation for what the commitment to these values ought to be for the Bahamian people and their elected governments; and what the benefits of that commitment will mean for subsequent generations of Bahamians.

It is my sincerest regards for the longevity and the protection of the Sovereignty of this Independent state, and the strengthening of our national identity, 'Until the Road We Trod Leads Unto Our God – March On Bahamaland.'

I remain, your most humble servant,

S Ali McIntosh, Servant Leader

PART ONE

The Vision and The Mission

How It All Began – My Testimony

When I arrived in Washington, D.C. on the morning of Monday, February 9, 1998, it marked the beginning of the greatest faith walk of my life. My one-way ticket from Nassau, and the thirty dollars I started the journey with the evening before, had all expired. Left with seventeen (17) cents in my wallet and holding onto a divine promise of great accomplishment in this city, I was similar to most immigrants arriving in the United States for the first time, with nothing left and no choice, but to 'go forward'.

Several months prior to this, in late September, I was forced to close the office of the National Committee for Youth Renewal & Revival, and the Light for Life Youth Resource & Counselling Centre because of a lack of funding, and the tremendous pressure placed upon me by the Free National Movement/Ingraham administration. I felt rejected and unappreciated, that the planning and lobbying for youth initiatives had gone unrecognized, and even more so, unrewarded.

I had been pondering for several days how to start over, even though I had just failed weeks prior. What was I supposed to do?

At thirty-two years old, and no work, no home, no money and a government which did not value my potential contribution to youth development and nation-building. While I could not understand why at the time, I believe that the government were a little intimidated by my candid speaking and my seemingly growing popularity, gained through my years as a radio broadcaster and newspaper journalist, and as a new emerging voice for youth empowerment.

Within a few days after closing my office, I was invited by some friends – Ed Smith and his wife – to operate from their business establishment on East Street near downtown, so that I could continue to canvass and galvanize for the youth work. Amidst my daily intercessions, Heaven responded to me.

It was the final week in October 1997, and I laid on the couch in my sister's house, somewhat discouraged and despondent. It had been only days before that I had moved out of my own rented apartment and had to move in with Monique and her family, in order to avoid being evicted. It was there, after everyone had gone to bed, that I lay silently, allowing the tears to flow down the sides of my face; as I reminisced on the two years of constructing, planning, and undertaking the work of national youth development for my beloved Bahamas.

As I recall the tedious hours of work, and the personal monies spent to host various youth leaders on a weekly basis for almost a year, I felt unrewarded and destitute. Amidst this feeling of sadness, I suddenly felt an overwhelming presence of peace, which seemed to have enveloped me and lifted me slightly off the sofa, in a most comforting moment of encouragement. In that moment, I heard a sweet voice say to me, 'It will not all be for loss.'

In an instant, I was back on the couch. I began to weep again. Not for sorrow, but for joy, that my prayers and concerns had come before the throne of Heaven, and I had gotten an answer. It was all I needed to cheer myself up, so I could begin looking for ways to continue the work. Within days, I was given further instructions for my life in a dream. This was not the first time I had encountered what I had come to know as the 'Heavenly Messenger' with divine instructions.

In a vision on the early Saturday morning of November 1, 1997, I saw papers which signified the completion of a document called 'The Phoenix Connection'. My activities at the Institution and the completion of that project were so historic that I was invited to visit the President of the United States. Then I heard the voice of a man say to me...

'Go to American University and study Psychology, and I will send someone to help you.'

The voice assured me that I would enter the university through a special programme that was only a few months long. The Messenger's final instruction was given in the tone of a warning, 'Do not be disobedient to the call.'

As soon as the weekend was over, I investigated the details of the instructions in the dream. I made some inquiries and found from reference materials in the Library at the College of The Bahamas, that there was indeed an 'American University' nestled in the suburbs of northwest Washington, D.C. While my findings comforted me, three days later I received stronger confirmation, that I was living out the divine plan set out in my vision when a South Korean man walked into my makeshift office housed in Edward Smith's business establishment on East Street north.

I was invited by this man to attend an 'all expenses paid' trip, as an Observer Delegate to a Conference in Washington, D.C., hosted by Youth Federation for World Peace, the international Youth arm of the Sun Young Moon organization. I accepted the invitation, and three weeks later, I traveled to the United States' capital to spend the Thanksgiving holiday weekend among hundreds of international delegates attending eight (8) different conferences hosted simultaneously by them.

Following the youth conference, I capitalized on being in Washington and visited the campus of the American University at 4400 Massachusetts Ave, N.W., Washington, D.C. While I was not certain what I was going to do when I got there, I went expecting to find what I was looking for.

Upon arriving on the AU Campus, I inquired at the Student Enrollment Department, the most logical place for enrollment into the university. As I began to indicate what I wanted to do, I was immediately referred to the McKinley Building, where I met an Academic Advisor, a lovely middle-aged woman named Suzanne. After a short interview, she readily enrolled me in the Assessment for Prior Experiential Learning (APEL) program, a one (1) semester-long, non-degree course. She instructed me to send them my high school transcripts and the relevant fee, which was only twenty-five (25) dollars. She advised me that if I wanted to start the program, I would have to return to Washington, in six (6) weeks, when classes would begin for the Winter term, in mid-January.

I left the campus less than an hour after I arrived. I was shocked but delighted that I was already enrolled in the university, despite having never made contact with them before that very hour. I was excited and stunned all at the same time. The instructions of the night visions proved to be true to a detail. Therefore, I knew I had to follow through to see what would happen next. Upon my return to Nassau, I immediately returned the pertinent documentation and fee that the American University requested.

The eight weeks prior to leaving for Washington was the most disconcerting time of my life. Despite my recent discoveries of the authentic details of the vision, I experienced tremendous doubt, fear, and procrastination. The lack of visible funding to attend American University only added stress to the already heavy burden I was carrying.

As it grew closer to the scheduled time to leave, I was planning yet vacillating daily. The mounting conflict within me of whether to follow through with traveling to the United States or not was somewhat abated, as I continually reflected on the final warning in the night vision of November, 'Do not be disobedient to the call.'

Receiving my I-20 Form from the university in early January, served to remind me that the time was quickly approaching, and I still hadn't found a sponsor to go to the American University. Finally, by the first week of February, it became clear that if I was going to go, I must do it quickly before I totally changed my mind.

Early in the morning on Saturday, February 7th, I called a friend whose family owned a travel agency, Arrow Travel & Tours, and credited a one-way ticket to Washington for the next day. Since I was scheduled to begin my journey on Sunday, I arranged a stop-over flight to Atlanta Georgia and an early flight from Atlanta to Washington, D.C. on that Monday morning. I left Nassau that Sunday afternoon with thirty dollars in my wallet, and the conviction, that because God sent me, He would authenticate the call by opening every door needed for my sustenance.

My sisters who lived in Atlanta, housed me that Sunday evening and made sure I had warm clothes, medicine, and other items for the trip. Since I was trusting God for the authentication of this assignment, I did not confide in any of them that I had less than fifteen dollars left in my wallet after paying the Departure tax in Nassau. I was convinced that if they knew, they would have tried to persuade me to change my mind and not follow through.

Subsequently, the journey that began when I arrived in Washington that sunny, but blisteringly cold Monday morning, was the greatest faith walk I have ever taken, and yet my most spiritually enlightening experience. I was walking in strong faith with all fingers crossed, hoping in the God that I had served all of my life; that He would prove faithful as He had promised.

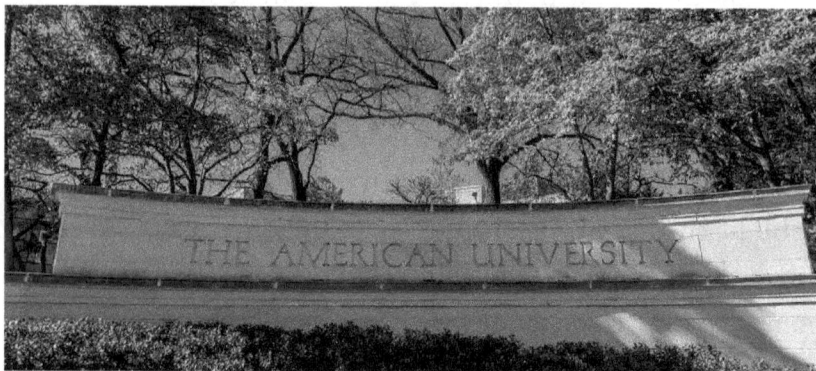

American University Entrance in Washington, D.C.

Washington Monument

The BCP Vision for the Nation

There was a miracle waiting for me in Washington, D.C. that day, a testament to the scripture:

> 'Behold, to obey is better than sacrifice, and to harken than the fat of rams.' 1 Samuel 15:22

And every day after that, there was a miracle at almost every encounter. Every need was met with God's provision; through unexpected sources sent by God to supply it.

I had spent only seventeen miraculous days in Washington, D.C. when I came face to face with the most profound assignment of my life. On the morning of February 25, 1998, I awoke early as I always do, prayed, and went back to sleep. When I awoke again around 9:30 am, it took me a few minutes to regain my composure. The more I gained my composure, the more I realized that I had been in a vision. It was magnanimous and so explicit that I held my head and walked around the room for a few minutes, allowing the instructions of the strange vision to flow back into my mind. I began to cry. I fell to my knees and slowly allowed my body to fall completely to the floor as I began to moan repeatedly, 'No! No! No!'

I moaned not because of what I had seen, nor because of what I had heard, but because of who was speaking. It was the same voice that spoke to me four months earlier and told me to go to Washington, D.C. It was the same voice that spoke to me three years prior and told me to form a service for young people. It was the same voice I had heard so many times before, when I needed comfort, when I needed strength, when I needed encouragement when I needed instructions. So to hear that voice again, telling me the things I had heard, was more than I could fathom, because of what it all meant! I was mandated!

The vision was clear and concise. Only three simple commands formed the instructions:

1. Run 39 candidates under the banner of The Bahamas Constitution Party.

2. Ask Christian men and women to make themselves available to serve.

3. Go to Sir Lynden Pindling and 'exact' from him the original intent of the Preamble of the Constitution.

I did not stop crying for what seemed an inordinate amount of time that morning. And for many more days, I questioned God as to what I was supposed to do with the information I had received. I walked around the campus puzzled and meditative for weeks, wondering to whom I should tell this information. There was nobody in Washington I could confide in, and I dreaded calling home with such a preposterous suggestion. I felt like I had been entrusted with some national security secret. However, it required some further clarification as to the way forward. Therefore, I was literally troubled daily over the instructions in the vision.

One day as I pondered on them, the Lord reminded me about a prophetic word I had received eleven (11) years earlier in 1987. The memory of that prophetic word squashed the troubling conflict in my mind. The prophecy was given to me in October 1987 during the Annual Fall Revival services, by Prophet Dr. S. D. James, a former Professor/Scientist, the Bishop and Founder of the Evangelistic Pentecostal Churches Worldwide, the World Leader of my former church.

In reflection, the year 1987 had been a very difficult one for me. Personal and employment issues, coupled with a near nervous breakdown, had left me barely holding on to my self-esteem and my confidence. However, maybe due to my vulnerable state resulting from the myriad of negative experiences I suffered during the course of that year when Prophet James called me out and gave me 'the word,' I accepted, on faith, that his encouraging words were authentic, and from the Lord.

The Prophet's favourite opening greeting, 'Be not dismayed whatever betide, God will take care of you' was the encouragement the Lord used to comfort my grieving spirit. He noted that even though he was unaware of the details of the personal situations going on in my life at the time, the 'tragedy' that I had experienced was not meant to destroy me, but to take me to the next level.

The Prophet S D James said that God told him that He was going to use me to do something 'special, spectacular, and dynamic' in the nation. And although he didn't know specifically what it was – because God did not reveal it to him – he was sure that whatever God was going to do with my life, would be a 'great and significant' accomplishment. However, Prophet James was able to confirm to me, that when the Lord was ready to use me to do this 'great thing', that I would 'enter' or be enrolled in an institution of higher learning. And at that time, God would reveal to me what it was He wanted me to do.

While this recollection helped me to understand that the Lord was preparing to use me, my thoughts were continuously on the vision of February 25th, and the magnitude of the awesome national responsibility that it laid upon my young life.

(NB - Chief Apostle Samuel D James passed away on November 15, 2020 in Banks, Alabama after more than 50 years of Prophetic Ministry to the nations of the World, and more than 40 years of visitations to the Bahamas.)

CHAPTER TWO

Divine Revelation For The Bahamas

F ive weeks after the February vision, on the sunny morning of April 3, 1998, while in my morning devotions, the Spirit of the Lord began to bring revelations to me concerning national leadership and governance in The Bahamas. These revelations were obviously meant to clarify my constant questioning, as to why it was necessary to create a new political machinery in The Bahamas, and how it was all going to come to fruition.

As I opened my Bible, it rested on Ezekiel chapter 40 verses 1-5. As I read it, it spoke to me strongly and emphatically, regarding the situation in Bahamaland. The message in the scripture admonished:

> 'You should see with your eyes, Listen with your ears, Set your heart on the things that I would show you; which was the reason I brought you to this place.'

Thus, it immediately got my attention.

As I continued reading, the Spirit of the Lord began to speak to me through the word and made me understand that in the twenty-fifth (25th) year of The Bahamas' Independence (which was in 1998), He had sent His Heavenly Messenger to examine the condition of the Commonwealth of The Bahamas. He made me understand upfront, that the reason He had brought me to Washington, D.C. was to make known to me the things that He was about to tell me. He insisted that I should make it a matter that warranted my most urgent attention and consideration, and that it should be kept close to my heart, as of utmost importance. And that all the things that He would speak to me, would have to be declared to the Bahamian people.

As I read through the book of Ezekiel chapters 40 - 42, I wondered what the scripture meant. It seemed so repetitious, talking about the measurement of every aspect of the house and the temple in such detail. Yet, I was consoled that God was attempting to convey a message I did not yet understand. I remained patient and continued reading.

By the time I got mid-way into the reading of Ezekiel chapter 43, the Lord began to bring 'revelation' to me beyond anything I had ever experienced up to that point in my life. It was as if my mind was opened into a new dimension of knowledge and revelation. It was clear that the Spirit of the Lord had given me access into the mind of God regarding the matters that had transpired openly and behind closed doors in The Bahamas.

In order to relate to you what was being revealed, you need to understand the political situation in The Bahamas during the time that I was in Washington, D.C., in April 1998. It was thirteen (13) months after the March 1997 General Elections, in which the Free National Movement, under the leadership of Prime Minister Hubert Ingraham, was overwhelmingly returned to power for the second term.

The Progressive Liberal Party (PLP), which had governed The Bahamas for twenty-five (25) consecutive years prior to the FNM taking office in 1992, seemed near defunct, because they had won only six seats in Parliament in the General Elections. The PLP was further demoralized, when the former Prime Minister, the late Sir Lynden Pindling was forced by Prime Minister Hubert Ingraham to resign his Kemp's Bay seat in the Summer of 1997, in order for Sir Lynden to receive the Prime Minister Pension & Retirement Package.

Within the first few months of the FNM's second term, industrial unrest had begun to brew in many sectors. Meanwhile, other Public Sector unions like The Bahamas Public Services Union (BPSU) and the Trade Union Congress (TUC) – who were responsible for the majority of government employees – were also threatening industrial action with concerns about job security. These concerns were based on how the Ingraham administration had been handling the proposed privatization of The Bahamas Telecommunication Corporation (BATELCO).

Additionally, the new multi-billion-dollar investment by Sol Kerzner, Sun International, had practically changed the entire moral and social model of the country, particularly in Nassau. Although the investment was economically viable, and translated into apparent prosperity and many jobs, the Sun International project had demanded and received a level of loyalty from Prime Minister Ingraham and his administration – and many sectors of the society – that could only be compared to idolatry.

The Kerzner-Sun International Resort was given the 'Most Favorite Nation' Status by the Ingraham administration, which entitled them to the largest group of incentives of any investment that had ever been facilitated in The Bahamas to date. So, once Sun International became the single largest employer in the country outside of the Public Service, it appeared that everything Sol Kerzner wanted, Sol Kerzner got. This included the re-routing of the two main thoroughfares in downtown Nassau, Bay and Shirley Streets, which was redirected to accommodate Sol Kerzner's idea of an easy route from the airport straight to the new hotel.

In addition to the mounting massive industrial unrest, the government gave permission for 'gay' cruises to frequent the Port of Nassau, creating quite a stir from within the local religious community. The Christian community's reaction to this was led by my fellow broadcaster and now Member of Parliament, Pastor Vaughn Miller; my NCYRR colleague and Leader of Save The Bahamas Campaign Pastor Mario Moxey, and The Bahamas Christian Council. The Gay- Cruise ships issue was provoking almost vehement responses between the FNM Government and the Church leaders. While I was unaware of what was going on in Nassau, the Lord began to reveal to me His disgust against the government of the day and political leadership in The Bahamas.

The revelation on the morning of April 3, 1998, changed my whole perspective of contemporary political events taking place in the country. I was astonished to discover how differently we saw things versus how God saw them.

The Revelation Specific To Government

In the revelation of that day, I learned that the situation and all that had transpired 'politically' between the former Prime Minister Sir Lynden Pindling and the current Prime Minister Hubert Ingraham, had come up before the Lord and had displeased him greatly. He equated it to me as Hubert Ingraham 'touching' Sir Lynden Pindling. Quite like the reference in the scriptures 'Touch not my anointed' – Psalm 105:15. He confided that He had 'ceased' to hold in high regard the government of Prime Minister Hubert

Ingraham, because of all that he had done in forcing Sir Lynden Pindling to retire from public life before he had finished his duties.

While the Spirit of the Lord had recognized and taken note of any or all actions, wrong doings, or indiscretions by Sir Lynden Pindling, He had not given the authority to former Prime Minister Hubert Ingraham or anyone else to eliminate Sir Lynden from the political scene in the country at that time. It was to be His work and His work alone when the time was right.

The Lord caused me to understand that the late Sir Lynden Pindling was His servant, called forth to do a special work in the country. He said that He had used Sir Lynden to begin a work in The Bahamas to 'free the Bahamian people from colonialism and establish an Independent Christian nation; and that this Sovereign nation would represent His purpose on the earth in the Western Hemisphere in the End times'. And that the effort by former Prime Minister Hubert Ingraham to politically 'slay' Sir Lynden ahead of God's time, was a direct attempt to circumvent God's purposes for the Commonwealth of The Bahamas.

The Lord reflected that in the days of Colonialism, in the early twentieth century and into the 1950s, the disenfranchised people of the Colonies of the Bahama Islands had cried unto Him concerning their 'slavery and mistreatment' by their Colonial bosses. He said that He had heard their prayers and their moaning and was ready to respond.

However, He (God) took special note of the prayers of our forefathers and mothers, when they began to make Him promises concerning specific things. In particular, when they requested:

'God, if you would give us our land and our freedom so that we could live in dignity in our own homeland; we would give you back the nation as a Christian nation and would give our children and the generations that follow, as a pledge.'

Correspondingly, He (God) heard the vows and the many prayers over the years by the leaders of the people; namely community and Church leaders, and all who were considered both mothers and fathers in the nation. These were the prayers of a people in a post-slavery era, yearning to be free; People, yearning for dignity in the place where they were born; People of colour, who were former slaves and children of former slaves, residing in the Colonies of the Bahama Islands.

God confided to me that in the 1940s, He began the process to deliver the people of the Colonies of the Bahama Islands; and in the early 1950s, He raised up a young man named Lynden Oscar Pindling to facilitate the work of leading the people to freedom and accomplishing this agenda for nationhood.

The young Pindling was chosen to lead the people. The young Pindling was to hear God's instructions as to what to do to deliver the people from 'colonialism' and bring them to Majority Rule and Independence. This arrangement in the rise and work of Sir Lynden Pindling was to facilitate God's answer to the prayers of the Bahamian people; and for the young Pindling to follow through on the promises and pledges made by the people. This was the work of the late Sir Lynden Oscar Pindling.

The process and attainment of Majority Rule in January 1967, and the attainment of Independence in July 1973, were direct answers from God to the prayers of the Bahamian people. God answered those prayers based on a promise by our forefathers to give the nation back to Him. This was a commitment between God, the government, and the people of the Commonwealth of The Bahamas, led by Sir Lynden Pindling.

The Lord told me that The Bahamas is His nation; and that the Preamble of the Constitution is a contract that commits 'the Bahamian people to Him, and He to the Bahamian people' in a binding legal fashion.

Here are the 'Tenets of the Contract' made in the Preamble of the Constitution:

Tenet 1: AND WHEREAS, the People of this Family of Islands recognizing that the preservation of their freedom will be guaranteed by a national commitment to Self-discipline, Industry, Loyalty, Unity and An Abiding Respect for Christian Values and the Rule of Law;

Tenet 2: NOW KNOW YE, THEREFORE: We, the Inheritors of and Successors to this Family of Islands, recognizing the Supremacy of God and believing in the fundamental rights and freedoms of the individual,

Tenet 3: WE DO HEREBY PROCLAIM IN SOLEMN PRAISE, the establishment of a free and democratic sovereign nation founded on Spiritual Values,

Tenet 4: WE DECLARE THAT, In which no man, woman or child shall ever be slave or bondsman to anyone, or their labour exploited or their lives frustrated by deprivation,

Tenet 5: AND WE DO HEREBY PROVIDE by these Articles for the indivisible Unity and Creation under God of the Commonwealth of The Bahamas.

This Contract was Sealed and Ratified between God and the Government of The Bahamas and the Bahamian people, with the two significant achievements of Majority Rule in 1967 and National Independence in 1973; both of which occurred without bloodshed.

The intricate political movements and accomplishments were later called by Bahamians, the 'Quiet Revolution', memorialized in a book of the same name by the late Senator and Mother in the Nation, Dame Dr. Doris Johnson.

However, this was not just a Quiet Revolution. It was the fulfillment of the terms of the agreement by God to our forefathers. This entailed:

- God gave the Bahamian government of the day and that generation, the land and their Freedom, through Majority Rule and Independence.

- In return, the Government of The Bahamas, made the Commonwealth of The Bahamas, a Christian nation, by proclamation in the Preamble.

God began to declare to me out of the scriptures that day in 1998, that twenty-five (25) years after Independence in 1973, He had sent his Heavenly Messenger to evaluate whether the Bahamian nation was indeed in compliance with its original Declaration of Independence, regarding its pledge to Christian nationhood. And further, whether the commitment He had made with the Government and the people of the Commonwealth of The Bahamas, at the inception of the nation, was still enforced. He was concerned that He could not see or discern the original pledge, in the operation of the governance of the nation at that time in 1998. And it was His desire to see reflected in the nation, the values enunciated in the Preamble Contract.

His words and His demeanor indicated to me that He was disgusted with the national leadership disregard for sacred things; that is, they were substituting the things of God with their ways, in an attempt to bring God's standards down to their own. This exercise and attitude of leadership in the nation, He insisted, had permeated throughout the entire nation, and had contaminated to some degree, every level and every sector in the society, including the Christian church.

He told me to advise the nation that they must remove the 'dead carcasses of their kings' out of the high places; far from Him, so that He might dwell in the midst of them forever.

He explained to me, that His use of the term 'dead carcasses of kings' mentioned in the Ezekiel scriptural reference, referred primarily to two (2) things:

1. Specifically, to the government of the day under the leadership of former Prime Minister Hubert Ingraham, and

2. Generally, to the Bahamian people's recognition of partisan political leadership being supreme in their lives, interests and affairs above God's will for theirs.

Both of these implications have resulted in the diminishing of Godly principles and values in the lives of the people, and the idolization of partisan political leadership (party politics) within the nation.

He implied that He (God) wanted to govern The Bahamas through men and women who would allow Him to govern through them. And if He cannot govern the nation through men and women who would allow His will in the Commonwealth of The Bahamas, then He would judge the nation, and take the Sovereignty back, just as He did to ancient Israel. He warned me that as a nation, we must return to our national commitment to honour the Almighty God, which is articulated and recognized in the Preamble of the Constitution.

At the pronouncement of these things on my bed that April morning, my whole 'world' had begun to shake. I began crying and became confused as to why the Lord would entrust me with this significant information. I suddenly became totally aware that if He was telling me these things, my life was mandated to declare them.

At that moment of recognition, I became so overwhelmed, I jumped up from the mattress where I sat, and ran through the kitchen to the living room, hoping to leave the revelations behind me. I shouted for Him to stop talking. Almost immediately it ceased. I could absorb no more of His voice in my head at that moment.

For more than twenty minutes, I sat in the living room, attempting to regain some sense of calmness in my mind. I was afraid to return to the mattress in the small dining area where I sat. However, I was convinced that the Spirit of the Lord was not quite finished speaking yet. So finally, after gaining enough courage, I returned to the room, took the Bible from the bed, and sat at my desk, and prepared myself to hear what else He would say. When I was ready to listen, He spoke to me in the clearest terms and caused me to understand the process by which He would test the Bahamian people.

The Lord told me to speak to the nation and tell them to examine the Constitution and see whether they are ashamed concerning the things that are written therein, relative to the lives they were living, and the direction the country was headed. He said, that 'if the people acknowledge their obligation articulated in the Preamble of the Constitution', then I must reveal to them all that He has spoken to me.

He further indicated that once the Bahamian people go back to the polls to elect a new government, it would indicate their choice and allegiance either to God or man. However, based upon the choice made by them, it would be His prerogative to respond in kind, as He so chooses.

I was very guarded from that point on, in any further inquiries to Him, regarding how and why these things were necessary and how they would possibly come to fruition. Responding, almost immediately to the inquiries in my mind, He encouraged me that, when the time was right, the new political machinery would win the hearts of the people through divine favour, and valiantly defeat the FNM and the PLP.

This new political machinery, He indicated, would provide important techniques and a strategic direction to lead the Bahamian people in a national effort to adopt righteous principles in all facets of the society, as is indicated in the Constitution's Preamble.

In response to my questioning as to why this was necessary, He baffled me when He indicated that this was to prepare a people for Himself, to be ready for the day of the Lord. You ask, what is the day of the Lord? It is the day when the Lord makes all things right. Many aspects of the revelation were confirmed a few days later, when I received several e-mails in Washington from the new Internet Editor of The Nassau Guardian newspaper, informing me, and invoking my response about the dilemma transpiring in the country, between the church and the government, regarding the gay cruise ship issue.

I was glad to read that while the Lord was speaking to me in Washington concerning The Bahamas and the Constitution, unbeknown by me, several of my ministerial colleagues were in Nassau waving the Constitution in the face of the government, for their own consideration. This confirmed for me that surely the Almighty God was speaking and making ready 'the apparatus' with which He would eventually judge the nation of the Commonwealth of The Bahamas.

As Mary's disposition in the visitation of the Angel Gabriel, all my questions were answered, and every resistance rebuffed. For that reason, I submitted to the Purpose and Will of the Heavenly Messenger with Mary's response:

"Behold the handmaid of the Lord; Be it unto me according to thy word." Luke 1:38

Barring any caution, I had concerning my ability to carry forth this agenda, I began to write down the vision and to prepare a platform for the proposed new political machinery called The Bahamas Constitution Party (BCP).

It could possibly take many more pages to adequately articulate all that He revealed during those morning hours of April 3, 1998. However, what we need to consider can be adequately derived from examining, defining, and applying the values articulated in the Preamble of the Constitution, to matters of governance and national leadership.

It is also clear, in the context of this revelation, that what God requires of the Bahamian people and their elected and appointed political leadership, is a commitment to the promise of recognizing God in the governance of the nation, and by extension in their own personal lives.

I returned to Nassau on April 15, 1998, questioning how I was going to orchestrate an examination of the Constitution before I was scheduled to return to Washington two weeks later. As I was preparing to leave Nassau at the end of April, the Bar Association, in conjunction with the College of The Bahamas, announced the joint sponsorship of Colloquium 2000, a series of town meetings examining certain aspects of the Bahamian Constitution. That announcement became my queue to give directions that same week in my weekly newspaper column, 'Answering the Call', as to what the nation should consider in examining the entire Constitution, and specifically the Preamble of the Constitution.

Interpretation & The Implication

To add my interpretation to the revelation, I wish to refer to the Prophet Ezekiel highlighting the Sovereignty of God (Yahweh Elohim), the Covenant-Maker and the Covenant-Keeper. According to Matthew Henry Commentary of the Entire Bible (Hendrickson Publishers 1991); the ancient Prophet noted, in contrast, that it is God, who 'judges and comforts', 'kills and makes alive', and 'wounds and heals'. The implication is that the same God whose hands can 'destroy'; we must look to for 'deliverance'. The concept is confirmed in scripture when it states that 'He has smitten and He will bind us up.' (Isaiah 61:1, Hosea 6:1). It is the work of the Messiah.

It is in this context, the Lord has sent the word to the Commonwealth of The Bahamas, to offer both 'Judgement' and 'Deliverance.' His offer of the renewal of the Covenant in the Preamble of the Constitution is clear. Despite our initial and long-standing assertions that The Bahamas is a Christian nation, it is sad to see that the government has brought contempt on the religion they themselves professed. And it has become clear, that their worship of 'things' they have positioned in 'high and honourable' places, has become 'loathsome and abominable' to God.

Since successive governments have set up their altars to idols, this has established a wall of separation between them and God and has actually stemmed the flow of 'favour' for the nation. They have set up their own devices, making them comparable to divine institutions, and urged everyone to comply with them, as if they are of equal authority to God's. This consistent flow of idolatry has brought contempt on the nation of The Bahamas. For whenever God's ordinances are profaned, His name is polluted. And when His name is polluted, people fall under His displeasure.

God now calls for National Repentance and Reformation in the governance of the nation, thus the agenda of the Bahamas Constitution Party. This work of The Bahamas Constitution Party is like the message of Elijah to the nation of The Bahamas: to return the hearts of the children to the fathers and the hearts of the fathers to the children – a Day of Reconciliation and Renewal.

The implication of the message here is clear. 'He that hath an ear let him hear what the Spirit says unto the Church and the nation.' God has called for the people to 'know' their duty, and to do what is right, so that the nation would be blessed.

The Preamble of the Constitution calls for a recognition of 'Christian Values' and the 'Rule of Law'. The Christian Values come from Biblical morality (the Ten Commandments); and the Rule of Law is referred to from the Constitution. Therefore, if the Bahamian nation is to invoke the 'favour' of God, they must submit to or accede to the 'Law of the House' – which is the Constitution.

My submission is, if the 'Law of the House' directs you to the 'Law of God', then it suggests, that the people of The Bahamas should allow Biblical morality to govern the land. The Ten Commandments or Biblical Morality brings Holiness to everything. It will not only bring 'Holiness' or 'Righteousness' to the holy places or holy things but 'Righteousness' to the whole land, in essence, the governance of the entire nation. This causes Righteousness to bring wholeness and equity to all the people, no matter who they are. Righteousness brings exaltation to the people of the nation, not reproach.

Reflecting on contemporary Bahamian history, on Black Tuesday (April 27, 1965), Sir Lynden Pindling threw the Mace out of the window of the House of Assembly, into Rawson Square, where the people were gathered. It was the day that the Lord identified to Sir Lynden Pindling and those in the PLP, that the Mace was the 'Symbol of Oppression' of the people of the Colonies of the Bahama Islands.

Just for clarification, the Mace, which sits in front of the Speaker in the House of Assembly is not the 'Power of the People', it is the 'Power and Authority' of the Speaker. The Speaker in his/her authority has the power to suppress the voice of the people, by shutting down any conversation by any Member of the Parliament, if he or she deems it to be invalid, including suspending their presence from any sitting of Parliament.

So, when the Mace was thrown outside the window by Sir Lynden Pindling and was broken into pieces, the symbol of the people's oppression was broken, and therefore, Majority Rule was achieved not long thereafter. However, when the PLP government came to power in 1967, that 'Symbol of Oppression' should have been permanently removed from the Parliament and replaced with a symbol that gave 'Power and Freedom' to the Bahamian people; such as a Bible or a monument of the Ten Commandments.

With respect to this notion, no one can expect the protection of the law, who does not submit to it. Therefore, whatever one submits to, yields to them its protection. If we as a people continue to yield to the Mace – the Symbol of Oppression – we continue to do what has always been done, 'Oppress' the people. Thus, Majority Rule and Independence has only provided the Bahamian people with 'New Rulers, but the same System of Oppression'. The players have changed, but the game remains the same.

Consequently, if we submit to the Law of God, we would engender the divine protection, and favour of the covenant-making, covenant-keeping Yahweh Elohim, who is the original Architect of the Commonwealth of The Bahamas.

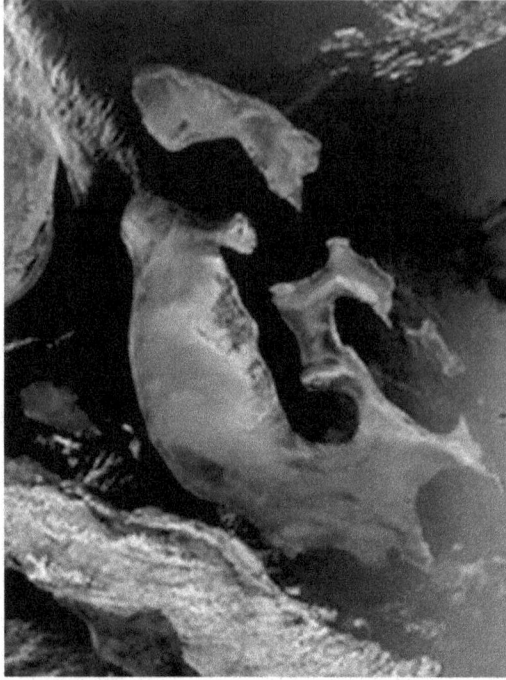

Photo of the Islands of The Bahamas (Photographer Unknown)

The Implication For The Nation

You may ask the question, what does all this mean for the nation?

Over the past twenty-two years, I have had many opportunities during my involvement in the political life of the nation, to consider what all this meant. Even at this point, and subsequent to every General Election results, I would ask this same question, 'Lord, Is this vision and revelation still valid?' I continued to be redirected to the following question: What does God really require of the Bahamian people and its elected government?

In 2013, on the threshold of the fortieth (40th) anniversary of The Bahamas' Independence, and forty-six (46) years after the attainment of a Majority Rule government, I began serious re-evaluation as to where we were as a nation. I had come to the conclusion that The Bahamas had come full circle. After 40 years as a nation, we seemed to have returned back to where we started prior to 1967 and 1973. Symbolically, we have spent one full generation in the wilderness, still standing outside the Promise Land, and looking back at Egypt.

I understood by comments and interviews made in 2013, as we celebrated the 1st Majority Rule Holiday, that in the years leading up to the 1967 victory, everyone did their part to help the PLP to obliterate the 'iniquitous' situations existing in the country, by their work and their vote. This massive effort was to bring about 'Righteous' governance and break the economic and social chains off the masses and cause them to be freed from the bondage of Colonialism.

The former Governor-General, Her Excellency Dame Marguerite Pindling, wife of the late Sir Lynden Pindling, indicated in a television interview during celebrations for the forty-sixth (46th) anniversary of Majority Rule in January 2013; that the pursuit of Majority Rule made the people felt like they were 'somebody' because they could see victory and freedom in sight. She alleged that the people were happy, and Majority Rule was their struggle, for themselves and for their children. She reflected on the work and sacrifices of her husband Sir Lynden Pindling and the PLP leadership at the time; that what they had accomplished in their early struggles could not possibly be equated to any dollar value amount.

She quoted this:

'The people were unified; they were pure in their pursuit;
And they rallied around the leadership of the PLP to achieve what they thought, and many exclaimed that God was in the workings.'

I wish to concur with her sentiments and conclude that their work was a work that God orchestrated, God defended, and in time, God brought to fruition. Everyone did their part, everyone made their sacrifices, but God did what He promised; to bring the Bahamian people to Majority Rule and Independence, so that the Bahamian people would be His people and He would be their God. This work by the men and women who led the PLP at the time was accomplished without bloodshed for a reason: so that no one could claim the glory or take the credit. It was for God's Glory and to God's credit.

This was amplified in many examples, but more so, when those who opposed the work of Independence, failed in their attempt to kill Sir Lynden because God was in the making. The country achieved these significant accomplishments for a specific purpose: A purpose which cannot be frustrated, a purpose which time has not diminished.

And so it was, that when the former Prime Minister Hubert Ingraham forced the late Sir Lynden Pindling, the Father of the Nation to resign in the summer of 1997, he 'touched' a matter that was not quite finished. Sir Lynden lost the Election in 1992 after twenty-five (25) years in office, and then again in 1997 with an even greater margin. He lost the government but held on to his seat once again.

He still had a binding and pending obligation, which was why he was elected again to Parliament in 1997. He was elected again so that he might 'Repent' for the wrongdoings of the government led by the Progressive Liberal Party. He was to articulate to the Bahamian people, from the floor of that honourable House of Assembly where he had spent his entire career, what needed to be said concerning the matters that I have articulated regarding the obligation of the Government and the people of The Bahamas. Following Sir Lynden

Pindling's resignation, there was no National repentance on behalf of the PLP Government.

We can all pontificate as to why Sir Lynden Pindling and the PLP lost the government in 1992. Needless to say, many editorials have indicated as much. Some have indicated that Sir Lynden was corrupt, and some have said that he had tolerated too much misbehavior and corruption among the members of his government and had therefore reaped the consequences. But despite the many opinions, my sincerest belief is that Sir Lynden failed to adequately articulate the awesome responsibility of the entire nation, to uphold the principles that were placed in the Constitution's Preamble Contract, on the attainment of Majority Rule and Independence.

Those principles and core values in the Preamble were placed there as a binding pledge for every administration, to uphold 'Righteousness' in the governance of the nation. It was not only the responsibility of the first Pindling Administration, who attained Majority Rule and Independence, but thereafter, all successive governments of the Commonwealth of The Bahamas.

So now, God wants His nation back...!

In the earlier revelation, He said to me that 'We can give it back to Him, or He will take it back'.

What does that look like? How do we give it back? Or what will the 'take back' entail? Will it entail the return of oppression to the Bahamian people similar to the days of Colonialism prior to Majority Rule and Independence? Could it be economic recession, or international financial or social pressure against our Sovereignty?

Initially, I could not imagine that what God was implying could possibly happen. But, in the next chapter let us look at the reality of what was, what is, and what could possibly come, based on our financial state. Let's look at the real statistical data on the state of the nation's finances.

CHAPTER THREE

Editorial On The Real Statistical Data

I n 1998, when the Vision and revelations were first given, the nation seemed economically secured with booming prosperity. The National Debt was under control at about ($1.76 B), Crime and Unemployment seemed manageable, and the Middle class was in a relatively comfortable prosperous position. As I will show hereafter, my evaluation of the economy over the term, to bring us forward to our present reality.

Bahamas Government - Actual Data, Historical Chart of 1975 - 1998

In my research, I wished to show the real statistics of Bahamas Government Operation and the National Debt up 1998, when this revelation was given. Then compared to where we have come in 19 years. The charts below show the growth of The Bahamas Economy and Government Operations, Financing, and the National Debt from 1975 – 1998. No Data charts for the years between 1998 to 2006 were available during my online research.

	1975	1976	1977	1978	1979	1980	1981	1982
1. Revenue & Grants (a+b+c+d)	**118.3**	**137.3**	**136.8**	**164.0**	**202.1**	**244.1**	**282.2**	**273.5**
a. Tax Revenue	96.3	116.3	118.7	139.9	175.6	201.2	207.7	207.8
b. Non-Tax Revenue	22.0	21.1	18.1	24.1	26.5	43.0	74.5	65.7
c. Capital Revenue	---	---	---	---	---	---	---	---
d. Grants	---	---	---	---	---	---	---	---
2. Expenditure (d+e+f)	**132.2**	**160.6**	**164.5**	**197.0**	**210.3**	**251.9**	**344.4**	**351.7**
d. Current Expenditure	113.8	128.4	136.0	157.6	178.8	208.1	243.7	262.0
e. Capital Expenditure	13.8	28.3	23.7	28.3	26.3	38.8	45.6	40.3
f. Net Lending to Public Corps.	4.6	3.8	4.9	11.1	5.2	5.0	55.1	49.4
Fiscal Deficit (1-2)	(13.9)	(23.3)	(27.7)	(33.0)	(8.2)	(7.8)	(62.2)	(78.2)
Fiscal Deficit (as % of GDP)	-1.3%	-2.0%	-2.3%	-2.4%	-0.5%	-0.5%	-3.7%	-4.6%

	1983	1984	1985	1986	1987	1988	1989	1990
1. Revenue & Grants (a+b+c+d)	**298.2**	**333.4**	**376.8**	**398.9**	**436.3**	**432.6**	**448.0**	**489.3**
a. Tax Revenue	244.7	266.4	318.2	339.1	380.2	383.5	394.2	430.0
b. Non-Tax Revenue	53.5	67.0	58.6	59.7	56.1	49.1	53.9	59.3
c. Capital Revenue	---	---	---	---	---	---	---	---
d. Grants	---	---	---	---	---	---	---	---
2. Expenditure (d+e+f)	**366.6**	**350.0**	**405.2**	**411.1**	**450.8**	**519.0**	**550.7**	**549.0**
d. Current Expenditure	293.7	324.5	354.3	365.6	397.4	437.1	470.8	474.5
e. Capital Expenditure	20.6	18.8	51.7	54.5	64.5	76.8	90.9	57.7
f. Net Lending to Public Corps.	52.4	6.7	(0.9)	(9.0)	(11.1)	5.2	(11.0)	16.8
Fiscal Deficit (1-2)	(68.4)	(16.6)	(28.4)	(12.2)	(14.5)	(86.4)	(102.7)	(59.7)
Fiscal Deficit (as % of GDP)	-4.0%	-0.9%	-1.4%	-0.5%	-0.6%	-3.4%	-3.4%	-1.9%

	1991	1992	1993	1994	1995	1996	1997	1998
1. Revenue & Grants (a+b+c)	**490.4**	**534.2**	**531.5**	**609.9**	**669.1**	**686.4**	**729.4**	**761.4**
a. Tax Revenue	424.0	481.0	476.0	544.9	594.8	615.3	658.2	681.4
b. Non-Tax Revenue	66.4	53.2	55.5	60.9	60.9	70.6	69.9	79.5
c. Capital Revenue	---	---	---	0.5	9.3	0.0	0.8	0.5
d. Grants	---	---	---	3.6	4.1	0.5	0.5	---
2. Expenditure (d+e+f)	**604.1**	**614.7**	**622.0**	**642.7**	**682.6**	**749.7**	**865.0**	**842.2**
d. Current Expenditure	504.9	523.9	531.4	556.7	588.2	650.0	699.1	724.8
e. Capital Expenditure	60.9	68.4	50.8	48.8	70.3	69.6	130.4	82.0
f. Net Lending to Public Corps.	38.3	22.5	39.8	37.2	24.1	30.1	35.5	35.4
Fiscal Deficit (1-2)	(113.7)	(80.6)	(90.5)	(32.8)	(13.5)	(63.3)	(135.6)	(80.8)
Fiscal Deficit (as % of GDP)	-3.7%	-2.6%	-2.8%	-1.0%	-0.4%	-1.7%	-3.4%	-2.0%

Research Department, Central Bank of The Bahamas, A. Gabriella Frazier - The Monetary & Fiscal Implication of Achieving Debt Sustainability – Appendix #3 - Chart of Government Operations & Financing, 1975 - 1998

B$M	1975	1976	1977	1978	1979	1980	1981	1982
1. Direct Charge (a+b)	**127.2**	**149.8**	**184.1**	**202.5**	**234.9**	**243.1**	**281.0**	**351.7**
a. Foreign Currency	64.0	56.3	69.4	59.9	53.9	40.8	87.7	147.9
b. Bahamian Dollar	63.2	93.4	114.6	142.6	181.0	202.3	193.3	203.8
2. Contingent Liabilites	**22.3**	**22.7**	**34.7**	**30.4**	**40.4**	**58.8**	**78.8**	**92.0**
National Debt (1+2)	**149.5**	**172.5**	**218.7**	**233.0**	**275.2**	**301.8**	**359.8**	**443.7**

	1983	1984	1985	1986	1987	1988	1989	1990
1. Direct Charge (a+b)	**426.5**	**443.4**	**478.2**	**528.9**	**527.9**	**574.4**	**670.3**	**773.2**
a. Foreign Currency	162.2	155.1	146.7	168.2	144.2	130.6	131.5	139.3
b. Bahamian Dollar	264.2	288.3	331.5	360.7	383.7	443.8	538.7	633.9
2. Contingent Liabilites	**78.8**	**68.4**	**67.3**	**81.4**	**78.7**	**86.5**	**117.4**	**146.0**
National Debt (1+2)	**505.3**	**511.9**	**545.5**	**610.4**	**606.6**	**660.9**	**787.6**	**919.2**

	1991	1992	1993	1994	1995	1996	1997	1998
1. Direct Charge (a+b)	**870.5**	**952.4**	**1,064.7**	**1,136.3**	**1,165.8**	**1,235.1**	**1,374.7**	**1,431.5**
a. Foreign Currency	147.4	145.9	167.3	148.8	155.6	133.4	144.7	133.7
b. Bahamian Dollar	723.2	806.4	897.4	987.4	1,010.3	1,101.8	1,230.0	1,297.7
2. Contingent Liabilities	**303.9**	**342.1**	**350.9**	**342.7**	**329.0**	**313.8**	**318.6**	**332.9**
National Debt (1+2)	**1,174.4**	**1,294.5**	**1,415.6**	**1,479.0**	**1,494.8**	**1,548.9**	**1,693.4**	**1,764.4**

Research Department, Central Bank of The Bahamas, A. Gabriella Frazier - The Monetary & Fiscal Implication of Achieving Debt Sustainability - Appendix #4 – Chart of National Debt of 1975 – 1998

Bahamas Government Debt to GDP - Explained

Government Budget is an itemized accounting of the payments received by government (taxes and other fees) and the payments made by government (purchases and transfer payments). A budget deficit occurs when a government spends more money than it takes in. The opposite of a Budget Deficit is a Budget Surplus.

The Gross Domestic Product (GDP) measures of national income and output for a given country's economy. The gross domestic product (GDP) is equal to the total expenditures for all final goods and services produced within the country in a stipulated period of time.

Debt To GDP Ratio 1991 - 2016

The Bahamas recorded a government debt equivalent to 77.90 percent of the country's Gross Domestic Product in 2016. Government Debt to GDP in The Bahamas averaged 40.68 percent from 1991 until 2016, reaching an all-time high of 77.90 percent in 2016 and a record low of 23.20 percent in 1991.

BAHAMAS GOVERNMENT DEBT TO GDP

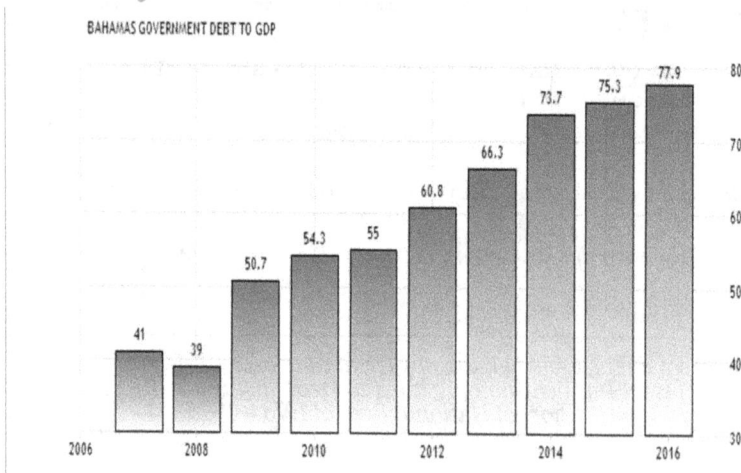

Graph - Bahamas Debt to GDP 2006-2016. Source: Trading Economics Online / Central Bank of the Bahamas

Analysis of 2012 - 2016 Financial Crisis

Between 2012 and 2013, Moody's Credit Agency and Standard & Poor's Agency, which provides Credit Ratings for countries had downgraded The Bahamas on several occasions, on both its Investment Rating and Sovereign Rating. These downgrades in such rapid succession began to place pressure on the entire financial prospects of the country regarding its burrowing potential. And yet, the prospect of further downgrades was imminent.

In the 2013 -2014 Budget year, the Christie administration and the Internal Monetary Fund (IMF) projected a two-point seven (2.7%) percent growth in the Bahamian economy. Despite this, the IMF and the other credit rating agencies had determined that the projected growth levels would not be sufficient to help the government out of its financial woes before something critical would have to be done. This was due to the fact that the country's Debt to GDP ratio was approaching the critical range of sixty to ninety percent (60-90%); which would begin to raise a red flag and give cause for concern, regarding the country's credit ratings and its burrowing power.

The Christie administration had already projected that they would raise the debt up $1.2 billion in its first two years in office, which took the government's debt, including local and foreign indebtedness, to five and a half ($5.5) billion dollars by the end of the 2013-2014 fiscal year. This figure pushed the Debt to GDP ratio nearer to the sixty percent (60%) level, (with the Recurrent deficits already in the hundreds of millions), due to Out-of-Control spending by the Christie Administration in its early 2012 term; coupled with staggering overruns accumulated from Road projects of the former Ingraham administration 2007-2012 term.

In the meantime, on the local scene, the banks were cautiously lending, and thousands of mortgages were in critical delinquency;

with the majority of Bahamians assets heavily financed, coupled with very little personal savings. Many Bahamians were living in a state of what we call 'hand to mouth', a term used to equate that a person is 'only two salaries away' from financial crisis or ruin. At the time, the suggestion and consideration of the International Monetary Fund (IMF) to devalue the Bahamian dollar in the eighteen to twenty-four (18-24) months (leading up to June 2014), would have placed Bahamians financial prospects in a most precarious position.

The foreign debt of the Bahamian government was considered moderate to high, with much of it being contributed by loans from the People's Republic of China, whose presence in The Bahamas was becoming ominous, with almost four ($4) billion dollars investment in Baha-Mar Development on Cable Beach. In addition to that investment, the country had obtained loans from China for infrastructure projects like the Airport Gateway Project, and others across the country. Both the Tourism industry and the PLP Administration had high expectations, with the Cable Beach Baha-Mar Resort's scheduled opening for December 2014. However, the delay of both the completion and opening of the Baha-Mar Resort continued to put pressure on both the government's revenue and the overall economy.

Despite attempts at reductions, government spending was still too high, and government revenue projections were far below expectations. And it was doubtful, and speculative by some, whether the implementation of Value Added Tax (VAT), would change the dynamics of the government revenues, in the short term, in order to make a dent in the indebtedness of the Bahamian economy. The commitment of the Administration was to use the implementation of VAT at seven (7%), specifically to reduce the National Debt. However, while the implementation of Value Added Tax (VAT) by the PLP government in Budget 2015/2016, provided an immediate and good source of Revenue for the government; it had proven to do 'almost nothing' to reduce the continued vehement rising of the National Debt and the Debt to GDP ratio.

The continual slide into the danger zone is noted in online articles by the Tribune's Business Editor, Neil Hartman. The links below show the condition of The Bahamas economy by the Central Bank of The Bahamas at the end of 2015 and 2016.

https://www.tribune242.com/news/2015/may/04/national-debt-breaches-70-danger-threshold/
https://www.tribune242.com/news/2016/sep/30/bahamas-total-debt-over-90-gdp/
https://www.tribune242.com/news/2016/may/24/govt-adds-16bn-national-debt-over-three-years/

Real Data on Bahamas Government Economic Situation – as of July 2017

Bahamas Government Debt to GDP - actual values, historical data, forecast, chart, statistics, economic calendar, and news. Bahamas Government Debt to GDP - Actual data, historical chart, and calendar of releases - was last updated in July 2017. (Information obtained from Trading Economics website on July 25th, 2017.)

The statistical data obtained online as of July 2017 will give you the reader an indication of how far we have come, and how critical our economic situation presently is. The statistics listed below shows where the Economy was at the time the FNM Administration was presenting its first budget as a new 2-month-old Administration.

List of Statistical Data Reported

Tuesday July 18th 2017
Bahamas Interest Rate at 4.00 percent
The benchmark interest rate in the Bahamas was last recorded at 4 percent.

Sunday July 16th 2017
Bahamas GDP per capita PPP at 21481.70 USD
The Gross Domestic Product per capita in the Bahamas was last recorded at 21481.70 US dollars in 2016, when adjusted by purchasing power parity (PPP). The GDP per Capita, in the Bahamas, when adjusted by Purchasing Power Parity is equivalent to 121 percent of the world's average.

Wednesday July 12th 2017
Bahamas GDP per capita at 20568.30 USD
The Gross Domestic Product per capita in the Bahamas was last recorded at 20568.30 US dollars in 2016. The GDP per Capita in the Bahamas is equivalent to 163 percent of the world's average.

Monday July 10th 2017
Bahamas GDP at 9.05 USD Billion
The Gross Domestic Product (GDP) in the Bahamas was worth 9.05 billion US dollars in 2016. The GDP value of the Bahamas represents 0.01 percent of the world economy.

Friday July 07th 2017
Bahamas | Credit Rating at 65.00
Standard & Poor's credit rating for Bahamas stands at BB+ with stable outlook. Moody's credit rating for Bahamas was last set at Baa3 with a negative watch outlook.

Friday July 07th 2017

Bahamas Money Supply M0 at 282.00 BSD Million

Money Supply M0 in the Bahamas increased to 282 BSD Million in March from 271 BSD Million in February of 2017.

Friday July 07th 2017

Bahamas Money Supply M1 at 2430.00 BSD Million

Money Supply M1 in the Bahamas decreased to 2430 BSD Million in March from 2483 BSD Million in February of 2017.

Friday July 07th 2017

Bahamas Money Supply M2 at 6587.00 BSD Million

Money Supply M2 in the Bahamas decreased to 6587 BSD Million in March from 6654 BSD Million in February of 2017.

Friday July 07th 2017

Bahamas Money Supply M3 at 6885.00 BSD Million

Money Supply M3 in the Bahamas decreased to 6885 BSD Million in March from 6957 BSD Million in February of 2017.

Monday July 03rd 2017

Bahamas Social Security Rate at 9.80 percent

The Social Security Rate in the Bahamas stands at 9.80 percent.

Monday July 03rd 2017

Bahamas Social Security Rate For Companies at 5.90 percent

The Social Security Rate For Companies in the Bahamas stands at 5.90 percent.

Monday July 03rd 2017

Bahamas Personal Income Tax Rate at 0.00 percent

The Personal Income Tax Rate in the Bahamas stands at 0 percent.

Monday July 03rd 2017

Deposit Interest Rate in Bahamas at 1.40 percent

Deposit Interest Rate in the Bahamas decreased to 1.40 percent in 2015 from 1.42 percent in 2014.

Monday July 03rd 2017

Ease of Doing Business in Bahamas at 121.00

Bahamas is ranked 121 among 190 economies in the ease of doing business, according to the latest World Bank annual ratings. The rank of Bahamas deteriorated to 121 in 2016 from 120 in 2015.

Monday July 03rd 2017

Bahamas Corporate Tax Rate at 0.00 percent

The Corporate Tax Rate in the Bahamas stands at 0 percent.

Monday July 03rd 2017

Bahamas Corruption Index at 66.00 Points

Bahamas scored 66 points out of 100 on the 2016 Corruption Perceptions Index reported by Transparency International.

Monday July 03rd 2017

Bahamas Corruption Rank at 24.00

Bahamas is the 24 least corrupt nation out of 175 countries, according to the 2016 Corruption Perceptions Index reported by Transparency International.

Monday July 03rd 2017

Bahamas Current Account at -171.80 BSD Million

Bahamas recorded a Current Account deficit of 171.80 BSD Million in the fourth quarter of 2016.

Monday July 03rd 2017

Bahamas Current Account to GDP at -11.40 percent

Bahamas recorded a Current Account deficit of 11.40 percent of the country's Gross Domestic Product in 2016.

Monday July 03rd 2017
Bahamas Balance of Trade at -557.30 BSD Million
Bahamas recorded a trade deficit of 557.30 BSD Million in the fourth quarter of 2016.

Monday July 03rd 2017
Bahamas Bank Lending Rate at 12.39 percent
Bank Lending Rate in Bahamas decreased to 12.39 percent in December from 12.92 percent in November of 2016.

Monday July 03rd 2017
Bahamas Building Permits at 304.00 Units
Building Permits in Bahamas decreased to 304 Units in the second quarter of 2016 from 310 Units in the first quarter of 2016.

Monday July 03rd 2017
Bahamas Consumer Price Index Cpi at 103.27 Index Points
Consumer Price Index Cpi in the Bahamas decreased to 103.27 Index Points in March from 103.83 Index Points in February of 2017.

Monday July 03rd 2017
Bahamas Exports at 99.50 BSD Million
Exports in Bahamas decreased to 99.50 BSD Million in the fourth quarter of 2016 from 99.90 BSD Million in the third quarter of 2016.

Monday July 03rd 2017
Bahamas Foreign Exchange Reserves at 958.60 BSD Million
Foreign Exchange Reserves in the Bahamas increased to 958.60 BSD Million in April from 920.30 BSD Million in March of 2017.

Monday July 03rd 2017
Bahamas Government Budget at -3.50 percent of GDP
Bahamas recorded a Government Budget deficit equal to 3.50 percent of the country's Gross Domestic Product in 2016.

Monday July 03rd 2017
Bahamas Government Debt to GDP at 77.90 percent
Bahamas recorded a government debt equivalent to 77.90 percent of the country's Gross Domestic Product in 2016.

Monday July 03rd 2017
Bahamas Imports at 656.70 BSD Million
Imports in Bahamas decreased to 656.70 BSD Million in the fourth quarter of 2016 from 685.60 BSD Million in the third quarter of 2016.

Monday July 03rd 2017
Bahamas Inflation Rate at 2.70 percent
The inflation rate in the Bahamas was recorded at 2.70 percent in March of 2017.

Monday July 03rd 2017
Bahamas Inflation Rate MoM at -0.50 percent
The Consumer Price Index in Bahamas decreased 0.50 percent in March of 2017 over the previous month.

Monday July 03rd 2017
Bahamas Population at 0.38 Million
The total population in the Bahamas was estimated at 0.4 million people in 2016, according to the latest census figures.

Monday July 03rd 2017
Bahamas Private Sector Credit at 6143.49 BSD Million

Private Sector Credit in the Bahamas decreased to 6143.49 BSD Million in April from 6152.88 BSD Million in March of 2017.

Monday July 03rd 2017
Bahamas Social Security Rate For Employees at 3.90 percent
The Social Security Rate For Employees in Bahamas stands at 3.90 percent.

Monday July 03rd 2017
Bahamas Visitor Arrivals at 606.40 Thousand
Tourist Arrivals in the Bahamas increased to 606.40 Thousand in December from 536.30 Thousand in November of 2016.

Monday July 03rd 2017
Bahamas Unemployment Rate at 14.80 percent
Unemployment Rate in the Bahamas decreased to 14.80 percent in 2015 from 15.70 percent in 2014.

Monday July 03rd 2017
Bahamas Sales Tax Rate at 7.50 percent
The Sales Tax Rate in the Bahamas stands at 7.50 percent.

Monday July 03rd 2017
Bahamas GDP Annual Growth Rate at 0.60 percent
The Gross Domestic Product (GDP) in the Bahamas expanded 0.60 percent in 2016 from the previous year.

BAHAMAS CURRENT - Gross Domestic Product 2019 - 2020 & Beyond

The Gross Domestic Product (GDP) in the Bahamas was worth 12.83 billion US dollars in 2019, according to official data from the World Bank and projections from Trading Economics. The GDP value of the Bahamas represents 0.01 percent of the world economy. source: World Bank

GRAPH - Gross Domestic Product Rate 1960 - 2019

Actual	Previous	Highest	Lowest	Dates	Unit	Frequency	
12.83	12.42	12.83	0.17	1960 - 2019	USD Billion	Yearly	Current USD

Source: Trading Economics Online / Central Bank of the Bahamas

GRAPH - Bahamas GDP Annual Growth Rate 1960 - 2019

Last	Previous	Highest	Lowest	Unit
0.90	1.60	7.90	-4.20	percent (%)

Source: Trading Economics Online / Central Bank of the Bahamas

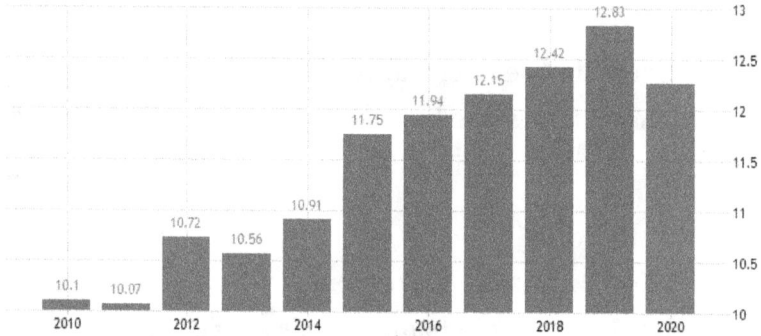

Source: Trading Economics Online / Central Bank of the Bahamas

Bahamas Main Indicators for 2018 - 2022

Main Indicators	2018	2019 (e)	2020 (e)	2021 (e)	2022 (e)
GDP *(billions USD)*	13.02e	13.58	11.56	12.28	13.23
GDP *(Constant Prices, Annual % Change)*	3.0e	1.2	-14.8	4.6	5.5
GDP per Capita *(USD)*	34	35	30	31	33
General Government Gross Debt *(in % of GDP)*	61.0	58.8	68.7	82.0	80.2
Inflation Rate *(%)*	2.3	1.3	1.8	2.1	2.4
Current Account *(billions USD)*	-1.49	0.08	-2.03	-1.96	-1.62
Current Account *(in % of GDP)*	-11.4	0.6	-17.5	-15.9	-12.3

Source: IMF - World Economic Outlook Database - October 2020

My Concluding Analysis

The Bahamas produces little, in comparison to our consumption. We grow about nine to ten percent (9-10%) of what we eat, as the country continues to accrue an Import bill of over eight hundred million dollars a year for food. This is coupled with the fact that ninety–seven (97%) percent of the consumables in the country are also imported. We can do better in growing more food and producing more consumables or finish products by creating industries from our abundant natural resources.

And while it appears that successive governments only attribute the value of Sun, Sand, and Sea, by their superficial benefit to the Tourism Industry; they have by far seemed to underestimate their intrinsic value, as Light Industries, in and of themselves.

Over the years, successive administrations have left the most lucrative of our Natural Resources namely Sand, Aragonite, Calcium carbonate, Limestone, Silicone, Solar salt, Precious stones, and Oil, in the hands of foreign investors and foreign sources. This list of over twenty-six (26) Natural Resources also includes an abundance of Sea vegetables and life-saving algae, Mangroves, Alkaline Mud; in addition to the commonly known seafood like Fish & spiny Lobster.

Successive governments, from Hubert Ingraham's 'Government in the Sunshine' in 1992, to Perry Christie's 'Hope & Help' administration in 2002; did not appreciate the intrinsic worth and value of The Bahamas' vast natural resources inventory, and the strategic position of the country; and the tremendous benefit that both of these together could contribute to the future economic development of the nation and the prosperity to the Bahamian people. Rather, they have accommodated foreigners and their interests in the country's abundant natural resources, to the detriment of the Bahamian people.

The best effort of both the FNM and PLP administrations are

that they seemed prepared to sell the nation to foreigners, with systemic oppressive Initiatives such as, the extension of the Hawksbill Creek Agreement in Freeport, Grand Bahama; the sale and exploitation of the Cays & the Marine Reserve parks in Exuma; thousands of Mayaguana beachfront property for pennies on the dollar; Oil exploration leases at the exclusion of Bahamian ownership; the sale of BATELCO for mere pittance, and the privatization and out-sourcing of Government-owned utility companies to foreign sources; the 30 year Tax-exempt status for Baha-Mar Resorts in Cable Beach; the Disney Lighthouse Point Project in Eleuthera with (Most Favoured Nation Status) at the exclusion of Bahamian entrepreneurship, and the lease of the seabed for fifty (50) years; the exclusive leases for the mining of Billions of dollars of Aragonite, Salt and Sand, for pennies on the ton; and finally the tremendous public and private sector investment of the People Republic of China and its state-owned agencies.

None of these high-ticketed projects by successive FNM & PLP Administrations are yielding or expected to yield any significant empowerment for the Bahamian masses, the Bahamian entrepreneur, or significant Revenue to the Government in taxes and benefit, to the extent that it can possibly produce. It is true that we can grow the economy, but by which measure, and for whose benefit. If the increase of the Gross Domestic Product only benefits the foreign investors; then the illusion of growth is a false perception for local empowerment.

There are no acceptable excuses for the former PLP and FNM administrations' or the present FNM administration, regarding long-standing leases and commitments that disenfranchise the Bahamian people. In 2019, the government was still committing to thirty and fifty (30 & 50) year agreements, despite the protest of the Bahamian people, which is expected to further disenfranchise, yet another generation of the Bahamian people. It appears that after fifty-four years of black 'majority' government, and forty-seven years of Independence, not much has changed.

The Bahamas' regime remains a tyrannical system, facilitated by both the PLP and the FNM administrations, to bring the majority of Bahamian people back under economic oppression, in another form of Colonialism. The true Bahamian Economy with the ideals of Bahamianization, conceptualized by the Pindling era, has long been lost beneath the ideals of Foreign Direct Investment and political expediency.

Regrettably, as we seek to move the nation forward, the unemployment rate is in the double digits, in Nassau, (even higher among youths); with now staggering rates also in Grand Bahama and Abaco since the destruction brought on by Hurricane Dorian in September 2019 and the extenuation situation affecting businesses, employment brought on by COVID-19 continuous Shutdowns, Quarantines, and Curfews during 2020.

The illiteracy rate remains high, and an inordinate number of students graduating from public high schools are reading below their grade level, with some high school graduates reading as low as grade seven. While the potential for technical and vocational training is promising to prepare a higher level of workers, there are not enough seats to accomplish that agenda. However, the potential of Bahamian children is vast but requires a greater investment from the government in developing the creative potential of the next generation.

Recent statistics also show, that less than twenty (20%) of persons graduating from both public and private high school each year, choose to or cannot afford to attend college; meanwhile, the other half of the eighty percent (80%) enter the job market, with less than required literacy and numeracy skills. Coupled with that grim reality, the overwhelming statistics are confirming that the majority of those who leave The Bahamas for a university education are choosing not to return to the country, causing a tremendous 'brain drain' of prospective younger, educated professionals in the nation for future development.

In the interim, serious crimes such as armed robberies and murders have risen at a staggering rate per capita over the past decade, resulting in fear among the populace. And even now, as the Police seek to get serious crime under control; the fear of crime and diminishing economic opportunities for the masses, brings clear what the prospects for the future really are.

In retrospect to all I have felt compelled to give an analogy on, the corrupted actions of the Christie led PLP Government during its 2012 - 2017 term, with the weak and embattled seventy-three (73) year-old Prime Minister, an oversized Cabinet encumbered by most who had either scandal-ridden pasts or numerous conflicts of interests; had brought the nation as close to the term 'failed governance' as it had ever been in its modern history. And without a doubt, the moral and social fabric of the country began to crumble right before our eyes, as 'covetousness and greed' of a sitting, lame-duck administration had reared its ugly head in magnanimous proportions.

The convoluted and conflicted actions of the PLP government regarding the defeated January 2013 Referendum on the Gambling Industry and its eventual Legalization; and the 2016 defeated Constitutional Referendum, where the government campaigned with the might and money of the Public Treasury on behalf of a positive result; brought the integrity and moral authority of the Christie-led PLP administration to almost naught in the eyes of the Bahamian people, and indeed the world, that their word was no longer credible. Widely considered to be devoid of any righteous principles and laden with compromises, the PLP administration continued in office with no clear mandate prior to 2017 General Elections.

Concurrently, the Official Opposition the Free National Movement itself lacked Moral Authority and Integrity, giving the people no clear indication as to where they intended to take the nation should they be elected. The FNM Parliamentary leadership altered its official position on the 2016 Constitutional Referendum, voting Yes unequivocally in Parliament, and changing to a No stance, once they saw where the third parties and the people were leaning. Additionally, the abrupt overturn of the FNM leadership in Parliament became an even greater concern as to whether the Bahamas could survive the defeat of the PLP to an FNM administration. The state of the entire political leadership in the nation was in a Crisis and a position of failed governance.

However, just prior to the 2017 General Elections, hoping to secure a positive legacy, the Christie-led PLP government attempted to redeem itself, by overseeing the opening of the multi-billion-dollar Baha-Mar Resort in Cable Beach, despite several technical, logistic, and financial concerns.

In its compromised and conflicted negotiations with the PRC government-owned China EXIM Bank, the former PLP government agreed to atrocious terms and conditions for the completion and sale of the foreclosed property from the original owner and developer Sakis Izmirilian; that conceded both the Bahamas' economy and its sovereignty to PRC and its agencies and putting it at a greater risk for complete failure. This whole issue of placing 'all your eggs in one basket' for The Bahamas, placed the Bahamian economy at risk for default, making it possible for the full colonialization of the Bahamian economy by the People's Republic of China. Indeed, a return to economic, social, and cultural slavery! This begs to conclude, that if the People's Republic of China with its predatory economic practices takes control of the Bahamian economy, there is no getting out, for the foreseeable future.

Therefore, for the Bahamian people, when as a society, we have returned to where we were prior to Majority Rule in 1967, and Independence in 1973, both socially and economically; then we must know that we are in trouble. It is abundantly clear that we must now go in a totally different direction.

2017 And Beyond – The Need for New Type of Government

Regarding Election results, we love to reiterate the statement that says, 'The Voice of the people is the Voice of God'. I wish to declare that, Certainly, it is not!

The voice of the people is the voice of the people. And sometimes, God permits the people to have their way. And with their way, comes the benefit or the consequence, of their desire.

In the General Elections of May 2017, the Bahamian people elected the Free National Movement back into office, under the new leadership of Prime Minister, the Honourable Dr. Hubert A Minnis. Certainly, much has been said by the people and political pundits that, 'The Bahamian people did not vote the FNM in, they voted the PLP out!' However be it, the leadership of the Commonwealth of The Bahamas marches onward.

And in concurrence, we observed that five short years ago in 2012, the Bahamian people voted the FNM out for perceived corruption. In 2017, they voted the PLP out for perceived corruption. But in reality, nothing ever changes. New government, new faces of new people, but the same system, and the same oppression continues! And no new policies to change the direction of our economic decline. Just the continuation of this 'Spend and Burrow' idiotic policy, that has compromised the stability of the Bahamian economy over the years, sending it further into the downward spiral to the present dilemma we are now facing.

The Hon. Dr Hubert Alexander Minnis, Prime Minister of Commonwealth of the Bahamas since May 11th 2017 (Photography by Bahamas Information Services (BIS) Nassau, Bahamas)

As I conclude my editorial on all that I have seen over the past four General Elections, including 2017, I am of the opinion that the Free National Movement (FNM) and the Progressive Liberal Party (PLP) are cut from the same political cloth, and their Economic policies come from the same ideologies of the Ingraham-Christie-Davis clan. And incongruence, the Bahamian people continue to elect governments based on Party-lines – No real policies, No salient agendas, just Party lines. PLP-FNM!

Like the age-old saying in The Bahamas goes, 'To make a long story short,' the borrowing continues, growing the National Debt, to even more staggering and almost paralyzing, debilitating levels.

With Moody Agency on its heels for another downgrade of its Sovereign Credit rating, the new Minnis administration in its first budget committed to borrowing seven hundred and twenty-two ($722,000,000) million dollars, to facilitate its 2017-2018 Budget.

Upon this consideration by Moody, austerity measures were promised by the new Prime Minister, Dr. Hubert A. Minnis, in his maiden address to the nation on July 26th 2017, he promised the following:

> 'A reduction in spending that would go into effect at a rate of ten (10%) percent across all government ministries; a halt on all public-sector hiring; and a slowdown on government traveling, and other services, except essential services.'

To this point, with no announcement from the new government of plans for the creation of major industrial sector jobs, the economy must settle for the continuation of more low-paying and tentative hotel and tourism-related employment, like maids, bartenders, bellmen, space-cleaners, customer service representatives, and others; mostly dependent upon the China-Financed mega-resorts Baha-Mar Resorts and The Pointe on the island of New Providence; and the proposed purchase and reopening of The Grand Lucaya property in Grand Bahama.

It's unfortunate though, that all we the Bahamian people ever receive from our governments is the talk of austerity measures. Any serious government needs a plan for the reconstruction of the economy, for growth of the industrial sector during the austerity period. If austerity measures are only to save money, then it is useless and has no real objective. Investment in real Industries must accompany Austerity measures if the growth of the economy is to be realized on the other end of the Austerity period.

Additionally, with the proposed Ascension of the Bahamas to the World Trade Organization still weighed in the balance, and the recently gazetted Commercial Enterprises Bill 2018, the prognosis for real economic empowerment for the masses seemed even more fleeting. Economic Colonialism is at the door knocking...by nations far greater and stronger than us. And I am of the strong opinion, as are many persons in the country, that the Bahamas Ascension to the WTO should not be forwarded, as it represents the greatest form of Economic Colonialism that can possibly endanger the Commonwealth of the Bahamas.

As the Bahamian masses are concerned, we will not survive a full Ascension to the World Trade Organization, or the long-term effects of China's predatory lending and investment practices in the Bahamas. There will be no difference between the effects of the WTO or China's Investments in the Bahamas; as they both want their giant stake in the country based on the particular natural resources they are interested in, leaving the Bahamian masses the crumbs to fight over.

So, now, where do we go from here? A devalued dollar? A failed Bahamian-owned economy? Or a massive infiltration, manipulation, or take-over of the economy by China? In my estimation, a total economic annexation by the People's Republic of China seems possible, based on our high indebtedness to them, and the massive Chinese investments in the country.

Meanwhile, the rich get richer, and the poor get poorer. Our newly elected politicians, who have promised relief during the campaign, are afraid to touch the 'Holy Grail' of any significant income to the Public Treasury coming from our abundant natural resources like Sand, Aragonite, and Calcium Carbonate. For the moment, the Natural Resources continue to remain in the hands of the Oligarchy. And as most FNM and PLP Members of Parliament and politicians before them, the present Members of Parliament will continue to collect a good salary, eat well, get prosperous, and keep their mouth shut, regarding the exportation of the Natural resources to the tone of Billions of dollars, with nothing for the Treasury or the Bahamian people.

Conversely, with Value Added Tax (VAT) having been increased to twelve (12%) percent, it continues to mount on the poor, wages continue to drop for the poor, and there is an ever-increasing, bleaker economic outlook for the real empowerment of the Bahamian masses.

And in so far as the political leadership, they seem unwilling and unable to navigate and negotiate a greater stake in our own local economy for the Bahamian masses. Therefore, considering everything that I have inferred from the facts and statistical data regarding our present situation as a nation, 'The Bahamas is Indeed in an Economic and leadership Crisis!

However, if the Bahamian people will ever be empowered, they will have to go God's way. If the Bahamian people and their government choose to go God's way, He will bring them back from the brink of economic collapse and a return from the projected and prospective economic colonialism facing us with the consequences of globalization proposed by the WTO and the People's Republic of China for this Bahamaland.

The people always have a choice, but God always has a plan! The plan for God's people is for a new political agenda and protocol for real economic development and prosperity, through the development of all the Natural Resources inherent in these islands, and the development of the talents of the Bahamian people.

However, the choice still lies with the people. It is only a matter of whether or not the people want to see God's plan for their lives come to fruition. It is whether the people want what God wants for them. Whatever happens – benefits or consequences – the people still must choose. It is up to them. It is truly the People's time!

CHAPTER FOUR

The Father of The Nation

The Father of the Nation - The Right Honourable Sir Lynden Oscar Pindling, LL.B., KCMG, Prime Minister of the Commonwealth of The Bahamas from 1967 to 1992. (Photo Courtesy of Sir Lynden Pindling family Foundation)

The late Sir Lynden Oscar Pindling was born on the twenty-second day of March in the year of our Lord, 1930. While his birth as an only child was a gift to his parents Arnold and Viola Pindling, it was also a symbolic gift to the Colony of the Bahama Islands. Privileged to be given the best education in Nassau at the Government High school, and a college education in London, Sir Lynden became an Attorney at Law by the time he was twenty-two years old.

Returning home in 1953, he immediately became involved in the newly formed, fledgling political party, the Progressive Liberal Party. He was able to secure a seat in the House of Assembly in 1956. He became the PLP leader in the House of Assembly and eventually became its leader after all of the party leaders failed to gain their seats in subsequent elections. He served in Parliament for eight consecutive terms, forty-one years, until his retirement from active politics in 1997.

Sir Lynden, as he was affectionately referred to, led the fight against Colonial oppression from Great Britain, and became the first black Premier of the Bahama Islands in 1967, when the PLP won Majority Rule over the United Bahamian Party (UBP), also known as the Bay Street Boys. He became the first Prime Minister of an independent Bahamas in 1973 when the islands were renamed the Commonwealth of The Bahamas. He served as the Prime Minister until 1992, when the Progressive Liberal Party lost the government, after holding political power for twenty-five (25) years. Sir Lynden was the longest-serving Member of the Bahamian Parliament at the time of his retirement and was considered the Father of the House. However, he shall always be esteemed and remembered as the Father of the modern Bahamas – the 'Father of the Nation'.

A Second Look at Sir Lynden Pindling

The vision I saw on February 25th and the subsequent revelations I received several weeks later on April 3, 1998, in Washington, D.C., forever changed my perspective of Sir Lynden Pindling. Like many persons, I was somewhat confused as to what to think of the slander, aspersions, innuendoes that were unabashedly levied against him over the years, after losing the government in 1992. While I held this Bahamian hero in high regard, it was mind-boggling, regarding the accusations hurled at him from all quarters in the new Free National Movement government, and in particular, from its leader Prime Minister Hubert Ingraham. It brewed a conflict in my mind since I did not have any significant information to disprove the accusations.

Despite the rumors that were being circulated about his imminent departure from The Bahamas, to spend all the money he was accused of gaining from drug trafficking and the likes, Sir Lynden kept proving them wrong. He remained in The Bahamas, except for the occasional travel, and cancer treatments at John Hopkins University. This gave me comfort that there might have been some untruths and possibly just political mischief in all the things that were being said.

Once I returned to The Bahamas from Washington, D.C. on April 15, 1998, I immediately made contact with Sir Lynden's law firm, Pindling & Company. I telephoned and was able to speak with him almost immediately. He was courteous, and when prompted, he quickly agreed to a meeting and invited me to come to his office two days later. He did not inquire why I wanted to see him, he just made himself available to meet with me.

I recall heading to the meeting with Sir Lynden that early morning around 7:30 am. I was walking west on Bay Street near the Sheraton British Colonial Hotel, when a local photographer Franklyn Ferguson, famous for wearing an old straw hat stopped me and inquired,

'Where are you going so early in the morning?'

Before I could speak, he answered his own question.

'You could only be going to see Sir Lynden!'

He was right. I was told that Sir Lynden was known to be an early bird and was prompt in his office for early morning appointments, after his usual 5:00 am jog on the beach and breakfast with his family. I arrived on time and was ushered into his office by his secretary. I remembered sitting across the desk from him, nervously attempting to ask him questions about the Constitution without revealing the dream and revelations that I had received.

Sir Lynden spoke very candidly to me regarding his assessment of the situation in the nation. He readily admitted that as a nation, we had not achieved the society which we 'initially' intended to create. He eagerly disclosed that we were not necessarily on our way either, based on where the FNM government was intent on taking the country. He evaluated it as a more 'liberal – secular' stance.

I asked Sir Lynden whether the founders of the nation intended to create a Christian nation; and if they did, what that would have meant for the country. He evaded that question at first, but instead gave me a quick lesson on different concepts of governments around the world, and challenged me to consider two things:

1. What the founding fathers could have meant concerning the establishment of The Bahamas as a Christian nation; and

2. In what sense was the country considered Christian, whether fundamental or literal.

From his brief lesson, I got the impression that, to some degree, he did not wish to take any responsibility at the time. He gave me some other issues to think about and research for myself.

Finally, I confided in him that I had a dream and in it, I was given instructions to 'exact' from him the original intent of the Preamble of the Constitution. I indicated to him that I was not at liberty to reveal much more, but if he could leave the 'door' open, I would return at another time and tell him more. I was not certain why I did not tell him anything else then, except for the fact that I was a little bit intimidated and knew very little of what I was speaking about, and I needed to acquaint myself with more details.

We ended the meeting with his commitment to 'leave the door open' for me to return, whenever I was ready to talk. Within the next few days, I purchased a copy of The Bahamas Constitution, which became my constant companion from that point on. I returned to Washington, D.C., and finished my initial platform, with the aid of the material gathered from reading the document legally referred to as The Bahamas Independence Order 1973.

My second meeting with Sir Lynden was two months later in June of 1998. Sir Lynden was the first person to whom I spoke, other than my family and closest colleagues. Although I had a little more knowledge and confidence at the time, it was still somewhat intimidating to speak with this 'political giant' concerning my plans to begin the work towards a new political party in the country. I minced words for a few minutes, and then I simply stopped talking and handed him the document. It was the first draft of a proposed platform for the new political machinery called The Bahamas Constitution Party (BCP).

As he read, he grunted softly, while spreading his lips and nodding his head periodically in apparent agreement. He was obviously a speed-reader. It took him possibly less than ten minutes to peruse the twenty (20) pages. When he raised his head, I was not sure what to expect. He stopped my obvious nervousness when he congratulated me for making such a commendable effort. I breathe a sigh of relief. I thought he might have spoken to the contrary; after all, he was a lawyer and the Prime Minister for twenty-five (25) years... he obviously knew much more about those things than I.

He said that he was impressed that I had invested the time to write the paper, and confided in me that most people he knew, who have spoken of starting a political party never made the effort to draft a proposed platform. He commended my tenacity and challenged me, that 'if I could find ten persons who were prepared to stand with me' I should proceed with the formation of the party.

You can imagine what that encouragement meant to me: Sir Lynden had encouraged me to continue the work to establish the political party. And ten people! That was his favourite number – 10. I guess, in his estimation, anything could be forwarded with ten persons. I was very relieved and strongly encouraged by that second meeting. I left the office elated.

I contacted him on several occasions over the next two years. He would always personally return my telephone calls. I would see him periodically at a church service or social function and remind him that I still needed to sit and talk about the Constitution, to which he always agreed. We were members of the same religious denomination, the Seventh-Day Adventists Church.

After Sir Lynden left politics in 1997, he had pursued an entirely different spiritual path, and was re-baptized and returned to the Seventh-Day Adventist Church where he had been brought up. It was a momentous occasion for Sir Lynden and the church, resulting in a new celebrated spiritual experience during the final three (3) years of his life.

Early in the year 2000, I officially requested an interview with him for my publication, The New Spectator Magazine, and waited patiently for his response. Between his weekly trips to Freeport and his cancer treatments, I had all but grown despondent that I would be able to get an interview for the magazine before the scheduled press time in the summer.

Acknowledging that the information I needed from him was urgent, Sir Lynden called me himself about ten weeks before he died and consented to the last public interview he gave to a newspaper. He knew that he was losing his fight with prostate cancer, so he decided to share with me what he thought I needed to know about the original intent of the Preamble of The Bahamas Constitution. The private interview was conducted three days later on June 13, 2000, in the radio studios of the Broadcasting Corporation of The Bahamas.

Meeting Sir Lynden Pindling for the Last Time

I fondly remember meeting Sir Lynden at the door in the lobby of the Broadcasting Corporation of The Bahamas and gasped slightly when I saw him. Before I knew it, it had come out of my mouth that his head was white. He laughed at my obvious surprise. He looked frail, but as always, he was in good spirits. He apologized that he did not get back to me sooner. He quickly perused my list of questions and returned the sheet of paper to me. It seemed as if it did not matter what I asked him, he was ready to answer. Accompanied by his security detail, Sir Lynden and I went quietly with the Technician to the studio, alerting no other staff at the station that the former Prime Minister was in the building.

As we walked, I recalled fond memories of this political giant, who stood only a few inches over five feet. When I was a rookie reporter for the PLP newspaper, the *Nassau Herald* back in 1986, Sir Lynden gave me an experience that I would not soon forget.

Early into the General Election campaign, I was appointed as part of the Press entourage that accompanied Sir Lynden as the Leader of the PLP during the 1987 campaigns. So, it was not unusual for me to be assigned to cover any function he was attending. However, on this occasion, he personally requested that I travel with him to his constituency to cover the South Andros Homecoming. This was because he had recently learned that I was the 'newly discovered' niece of the late Dully Neymour, his closest friend and Campaign General in the South Andros constituency, he represented in Parliament.

The day before we were scheduled to go to South Andros, I received a message that Sir Lynden had requested that I come over to his office in the Churchill building to see him. Before I could get the message, everyone else in the Parliament building had already heard of this request and was looking quite impressively at me, when I arrived at the Parliament to cover the Annual Budget Debate that morning. Based on the comments from the Parliament staff, politicians, and other Press people who were in and near the building that day, I became increasingly aware that it was quite a 'big deal' for the 'Chief' to send for you. I was somewhat alarmed and anxious as to why the Prime Minister of The Bahamas wanted to see me.

I immediately made my way across the street to the Churchill Building and was ushered into his office by his secretary Mrs. Smith. It was just a few nervous minutes of waiting, as I sat across the desk while he was on the telephone, wondering what I could have done to be summoned to the Prime Minister's office, so early in the day. After all, I was a twenty-year-old rookie reporter, with no status and very little experience under my belt. I figured that whatever the message was, he could have sent it with a staffer or any number of persons he had at his disposal.

He finally looked up from the telephone and exchanged some pleasantries. I relaxed. I was not in any trouble. He apologized that he would not be able to attend the South Andros Homecoming because of some other pressing engagements, but that he had made arrangements for me to travel to Andros and that his secretary would 'see to getting them to me' later that day. He apologized again and sent me on my way.

I breathed a huge sigh of relief as I exited his office. I could not figure out why it was necessary for him to call me to his office to apologize for not being able to attend the Homecoming. After all, he was the Prime Minister of the country and a very busy man. However, I felt honoured, to be given a privilege that was not necessarily available for even some of his most loyal political supporters. I truly believe that at that time, he was attempting to create a special memory for me, as he did on many more occasions for other young Bahamians. He was intent on making memories of the man he was for the next generation: Sir Lynden Pindling, Prime Minister – a man, a local icon, and a national hero!

The Final Interview with Sir Lynden

During that final interview that June morning in 2000, and what would be the last conversation I had with him, we walked briefly through his political career and talked about his burning desire to bring about political equality and social justice for the coloured people in The Bahamas in the 1950's and 1960's. Sir Lynden identified to me some of the obvious iniquitous situations that existed in the islands during those times.

Some of those included the multiple votes afforded rich men, with each business owned was accorded a separate vote as an individual during a General Election. He noted that black men who owned no property could not vote, and women could not vote. So, he and others in the PLP began the fight to bring freedom to the black masses, with the process geared towards Internal Self-governance for the Colony of the Bahama Islands. Prior to that, the government, or the Legislative Council as it was called, was basically run by the Bay Street Boys, who also ran and owned the Economy.

The political struggle of the Progressive Liberal Party resulted in the establishment of the first Bahamian Constitution in 1963, which mandated Internal Self-governance for the Colony of the Bahama Islands. This accomplishment was intended to eventually render equity, dignity, and basic human rights to black people, and bring the country closer to Majority Rule and Independence. Once Internal Self-governance was achieved, the Bay Street Boys had to form themselves into the United Bahamian Party, in order to facilitate the new political agenda, and the new legislative machinery created by that action in the country. In that new political environment, the PLP was made Her Majesty's Official Opposition in the House of Assembly.

Sir Lynden gave me a quick education on the importance of a Constitution and explained how the Constitution should represent the nation's commitment to effective self-governance and nation-building.

In layman's terms, Sir Lynden explained that, and I quote:

'The Constitution was the blueprint of the rules you agreed to be governed by, and how you agreed to do that. And how challenges to the status quo were to be made, and how they were to be adjudicated. Through the Constitution, everybody would get to know what the rules of the games were, like rules of engagements during a war, so you know, just how to proceed. That's what the Constitution did, it gave form and substance to what was a feeling.'

When questioned about the process of educating the Bahamian people concerning the Constitution and Independence, he noted that the process of education was a continuous one, which began from the formation of the Progressive Liberal Party (PLP).

'Once we began to talk about the change of the franchise, we had to explain what the franchise was, or a political party is. Once we started talking about votes for women, we had to explain why that was important. Once we started to talk about Majority Rule, we had to explain what Majority Rule was; and once you had it, what you can do with it, and what you can't do without it. So the process continued from day to day, year to year, and the end product was Independence, which was the pathos of the movement. Majority Rule and Independence were the pathos of the movement.'

His Royal Highness Prince Charles & Prime Minister Lynden Pindling look on during the celebrations of the Bahamas Independence on historic Clifford Park on the morning of July 10th 1973. (Photographer Unknown)

When we first turned our thoughts to the Preamble of the Constitution, I did not even have to ask Sir Lynden a question. By the time I had read the last word of the Preamble, Sir Lynden stopped me and began to educate me on the process of the Preamble.

'Now let me tell you something you did not know. That Preamble appears in the Independence Constitution. It is a Preamble that was prepared for the 1969 Constitution, after the introduction of Majority Rule. We knew where we were heading afterwards. We thought that expression of feelings needed to be up front in the '69 Constitution. We were told by the Colonial Office in London, that it was not appropriate to have it in a Colonial Constitution, it would have to wait until we got to writing our Independence Constitution. The Preamble was much longer than that. This would have been the only thing that was wholly Bahamian from Concept to Introduction in the Constitution. The words were actually penned by Arthur Foulkes.'

'Arthur did the original draft, which he shared with us, essentially the leaders of the PLP, the Cabinet and Members of Parliament at the time, when we were preparing the document for submission to the Colonial office. We told the Colonial office that this is what we wanted. We were coming to a Conference, and this is what we wanted to see in the final document. We put a little thing here and took out a little thing there, and the piece we submitted, which was much more than that. But just those three or four paragraphs finally appeared in the Independence Constitution.'

Sir Lynden's response made everybody laugh when I asked him whether he thought the Preamble was a mission statement. By then, persons had begun to gather in the Production studio, beckoning to me and asking why I did not let them know he was in-studio. Although he was serious, everyone couldn't help laughing, when he repeated 'No!' about seven times, stammering as he spoke.

'No! No! No! No! No! No! No! You young people always get it mixed up with these modern concepts. Mission!... Like you are going to the moon or something. No, no, no! The Preamble is a statement of historical and psychological fact. It is a statement of historical achievement. The generation that brought about this, were the inheritors of and successors to all who have gone before us. And the statement was a recognition of former Bahamians, a statement of fact, that, having gotten this far, we pledge to go much further.'

'What it says is that we who existed in 1969 and 1973, having inherited and succeeded to these Bahama Islands - agreed to be bound by spiritual values, in which every man, woman and child could grow - having never to be a slave or bondsman again, which recapitulated our history. We will be subject to no man, no matter where he comes from.'

> 'Those are the principles the founding fathers thought had brought us to that particular point. These principles, having brought us to that particular point - we commend them to subsequent generations, worthy of consideration. Because, if they can bring one generation to this point and lead them successfully, perhaps they could do the same for subsequent generations and lead them successfully. These would have to be determined and practiced by every generation that follows.'

There was a point in the interview that was a bit tedious when I struggled to conceptualize what else I needed Sir Lynden to tell me. I wasn't quite sure how to articulate those concerns, but I knew he had the information. That was an awkward moment for me as a journalist. While I thought I knew what I wanted to ask him, I still did not completely understand the subject of the matter I was seeking from him. I didn't want to push him, but I sense there was more he could tell me. By stalling, Sir Lynden forced me to try to articulate it.

After he sensed my determination to press him, he decided to identify the information for me. The information spoke to the responsibility of the Bahamian people in preserving their own freedom. He explained:

> 'It means that the people themselves will demonstrate a desire to preserve their freedom and offer the guarantee. And how serious they are in that, will be determined by their commitment to self-discipline, industry, loyalty, unity and their respect for Christian Values and the Rule of Law. In other words, the Bahamian who thinks that somebody is going to come along and do all the work for him, and he is going to reap all the benefits ...it is not going to happen. He will lose his freedom in the process. He is going to have to go out, and by his own self-discipline, loyalty, industry and unity, guarantee the freedom he wants to have in place in his own country.'

In that regard, Sir Lynden obligated the government to uphold the core values of the Preamble in the governance of the nation and confirmed the government's responsibility to 'lead the people' towards those core values. Sir Lynden stated:

'It is very important that the things that the government do, and how they do it, give high priority to these areas. The government can't expect to succeed, if it's not going to abide by the Rule of Law – it's absolutely fundamental. If you abandon the rule of law, you introduce anarchy - and that negates the very first point of self-discipline. It's all enshrined there.'

'The policies and programmes of the government should be those that enhance self-discipline, industry, loyalty, unity and respect for Christian values and the Rule of law. And if the policies and programs detract from those things in any significant and material way, we will erode and will subsequently lose our freedom'

Sir Lynden was eager to affirm the collective sentiments of the founding fathers regarding their desire for The Bahamas at its inception. He confirmed in his conclusion on the subject, that in following the values in the Preamble, it would be difficult for the nation to falter under such virtuous practices. He said:

'Those were the principles that guided the founding fathers in the establishment of the new nation, and it was our hope and desire that it would be the guiding feature for future generations and governments. If you wish to maintain a free democratic sovereign nation founded on spiritual values, enshrining that no man, woman or child is enslaved or lives deprived – then you can't go wrong! You can't go wrong!'

I was somewhat satisfied by the information I got from Sir Lynden that day. I knew I could have gotten more, but I was pleased with the assessment of the Preamble by the man who had stood at the helm of creating the modern Bahamas: He himself had believed that the Preamble's core values were necessary for effective governance in the Bahamian nation, far into the future.

Prime Minister Hon. Lynden O. Pindling and Mrs. Marguerite Pindling greets HRH Prince Charles on his arrival to the Bahamas on his visit for the Independence Declaration in July 1973. Also shown is Bahamas Governor Sir Ralph Grey & Lady Grey, and local Royal Bahamas Police Force Officials (Photographer Unknown)

Concluding Thoughts On Sir Lynden

The first half of the interview was printed in my newsmagazine, *The New Spectator* in the August 2000 Summer Edition. The interview was transcribed to include all of the comments that were made, including his usual keen sense of humour. When I was preparing to print, Joe Gibson, a veteran Public Relations and Marketing professional, responsible for marketing at the *Nassau Guardian* newspaper at the time, suggested that I spread Sir Lynden's face across the entire front of the magazine with the words, 'Father of the Nation'. Without any rebuttal I did it. It was the perfect idea.

We printed sixteen thousand copies which were inserted in the *Nassau Guardian* on August 16th, 2002. That same week, I called his son Obie to bring the magazine to Sir Lynden's attention. I had heard that he was ill, and I wanted to be certain that he saw the publication. Prior to this, it seemed that no newspaper or magazine in the country was eager to print Sir Lynden on the front page, much less as a full cover.

The newsmagazine was published only ten days before Sir Lynden died. We did not know that he would die so soon afterward. However, I gave Sir Lynden what he needed to see before he died! This must-have meant so much to him. The Memorial Publication of the recognition of him as the Father of the Nation! This was a closing validation of him and his work on behalf of the nation: The validation that his work was not in vain.

In closing, I want to share a dream I had on the morning of August 26th, 2000, the day that Sir Lynden's life journey ended. The day he died.

I dreamt that I was given a 'governmental' assignment, to lead a high-level delegation on an overseas trip to the State of New York for a period of three months. The arrival scene seemed a bit chaotic as we were surrounded by many police officers and security personnel.

It seemed a quieter moment when the group was taken by bus to see where we would 'reside' during the trip. Although we were supposed to be in New York, it seemed that we were actually still in The Bahamas. The female tour guide announced when we arrived in front of an old building, 'This is Sir Lynden Pindling's building'.

The building was in need of some repairs and paint. She opened the first apartment door and showed us inside. I said to myself,

'These people should keep this building better than this, knowing that this building belongs to Sir Lynden Pindling.'

She showed us inside the second apartment, and then the third. When she got to the third door, she said,

'This one is Sir Lynden Pindling's personal apartment. He just left.'

She only opened the door half-way. I could see clear water leaking from the ceiling onto the floor. I pressed past her, opened the door fully, and went inside. The room was royally furnished and clean, although it was worn by time. Everything was in order, except that the curtains, the carpet, and the furnishings were faded in different places from exposure to the sun streaming through the windows. The carpet was clean but was soaked from the clear water still dripping from the ceiling. Although this unit showed signs of age and deterioration, it was beautifully adorned, furnished, and clean.

In the midst of this aged surroundings, there sat a brand-new framed photograph on the mantle above a fireplace. I went over to see the photograph that he had placed there before he left. The photograph was of Sir Lynden and I, both elegantly dressed in black, sitting as if in a conversation. On the left, next to the fireplace was a small table. There were scores of photo albums piled high with thousands of photographs. The photographs were on both the table and the floor beside it. I held my hand to my mouth. I was baffled and surprised that of all the photographs he had to choose from, he chose that one with us to place on the mantle.

I was engrossed in that thought until our tour guide drew my attention to something else Sir Lynden had done before he left. I turned to my right and saw on another small table near the door we came through, scores of framed photographs of children; ones I knew and ones I did not know. They were photographs of Bahamian children. While I thought of all the things he could have chosen to do before he left, the tour guide pointed to the children's photos and said:

'He left them for you.'

The loud ringing of the telephone on the nightstand beside the bed woke me from my sleep and the dream I was having. I picked it up to stop the ringing. I could hear the person on the other end shouting to me to turn on the television. The person on the phone shouted:

'Sir Lynden is dead.'

The news brought me back to full consciousness. I quickly turned on the television. It was true! Sir Lynden was dead! He was gone from this earth. He had certainly left!

I watched the multiple newscasts which continued throughout the morning. Then the programming turned to documentaries about the former Prime Minister, the Father of the Nation through-out the day and into the night. Even after I left the house later in the day, I could not stop thinking about it all. For days afterward, I kept wondering what the implication of the message in the dream meant. It was interesting that the dream was so timely placed within hours of Sir Lynden's death.

As I considered it, I realized that during my interaction with Sir Lynden, he never sent me a message, except to say call him or come to see him. He always told me personally what he had to say, even if it was to apologize or to say that he would get back to me later. It was ironic, that even in death, it was no different. And while he had clearly died throughout the night while I was asleep; before anyone could tell me that he was gone, he got a message to me himself, 'I am gone, but I remember you!'

It was quite the experience for me to be remembered by someone while they were dying. And to know it. I shared the dream with a friend who was at Sir Lynden's home that early Saturday morning during his passing and immediately afterward. The young man shared with me that the scene was quite as I described it in my dream, with policemen and security all over the place. He noted that before he left the Pindling's Residence, he observed on a small table in the living room, a copy of The New Spectator, my newsmagazine, featuring the full front-page photograph of the Father of the Nation.

Sir Lynden was the Father of the Nation and a father to us all. And I believe that 'in so far as' nation-building and governance, he passed something on to me when he left. He implanted a seed for the recruitment of the next generation of Bahamian leaders.

In retrospection, I am certain that he was convinced that there are some of us in this generation who are prepared to continue the fight for the longevity of this Bahamian state, with the passion of those who have gone before us, and with the purpose for which we originally obtained Nationhood. Therefore, politically speaking, I am actually the 'child' of his old age.

While my big brothers Perry Christie and Hubert Ingraham claim to be Sir Lynden's only protégé; I have been mentored by him. What he couldn't say to them, and certainly what he didn't say to them, he told me. Metaphorically, he whispered in my ear before he left,

'Don't forget the children, the next generation. I leave them in your care.'

I wish to express my profound gratitude to Her Excellency Dame (Lady) Marguerite Pindling, the wife of the Right Honourable Sir Lynden Pindling, and former Governor General of the Commonwealth of the Bahamas.

'Madam, I wish to thank you for lending your husband to our country. The spirit of his work and the contributions of his life will never be forgotten. Your contribution and your support of this giant of a man, through all the good times and bad times, the popularity and the poverty; you and your children's sacrifice will always be imprinted as the essence of his legacy. On behalf of the next generation of Bahamians, Thank you!'

I believe that quite like the Apostle Paul in the scriptures, Sir Lynden could say to the very end, 'I have fought a good fight, I have kept the faith, I have finished my course.'

May the soul of our father, the Father of the nation, of this our great Bahamaland, Sir Lynden Oscar Pindling, Rest In Peace!

CHAPTER FIVE

What The Founding Fathers Envisioned

His Excellency Sir Arthur Foulkes, the former Governor-General of the Bahamas April 2012-2014 and framer of the Preamble of the Constitution. (Photography by Bahamas Information Services (BIS) Nassau, Bahamas)

During my final interview with Sir Lynden in June of 2000, he referred me to speak with Sir Arthur Foulkes, regarding the

Preamble of the Constitution. I was unable to sit with Sir Arthur until September 2000, shortly after Sir Lynden's funeral.

A newspaper journalist by profession, Sir Arthur Foulkes became entrenched in the movement to bring freedom and Internal Self-governance to the Bahamian people, when he joined the PLP in the early 1960s. He left his job as a writer for *The Tribune* newspaper and made personal sacrifices to his own family's maintenance, in order to publish the Progressive Liberal Party's newspaper, *The Bahamian Times*.

His writing talent gave him the opportunity to assist in the compilation of many documents and public communications for the movement, including the various Constitutional Conferences with Britain in the 1960s; and the Memorandum to the United Nations in 1965, about Irregular and Unfair voting practices in The Bahamas.

Although he left the PLP in the 1970s to form the Free National Movement with Sir Cecil Wallace-Whitfield, Sir Arthur has been consistently involved in public service to the Bahamian people as a Politician, a Statesman, and a Diplomat for almost forty years. Subsequently, he received a Knighthood in 2001 from Her Majesty Queen Elizabeth II. Sir Arthur was installed as the Governor-General of the Commonwealth of The Bahamas on April 14, 2010 and served until July 7, 2014.

His Excellency, the Governor-General Sir Arthur Foulkes & Lady Joan Foulkes, & the Prime Minister Hubert Ingraham & Mrs. Delores Ingraham receives His Royal Highness, Prince Harry on the occasion of his Royal Visit to The Bahamas in March 6, 2012, on the 60th Anniversary of HRH Queen Elizabeth II Coronation. (Photo by Bahamas Information Services)

When I met with him at his home on the western end of New Providence, we had a very cordial and jovial time of fellowship. It was as if we were long-time friends. Obviously, a lover of the arts, Sir Arthur shared with me the personal stories of all the artists of the paintings which adorned the wall at his home.

During the informal interview with this veteran journalist and diplomat, he shared some of the same sentiments that Sir Lynden did on the Preamble of the Constitution; but added some additional inspiration, that could only have come from the heart of the man who had similarly envisioned and wrote the poetic words of the Preamble.

Sir Arthur confirmed to me, like Sir Lynden did, that the original Preamble statement was a far lengthier one than what was actually placed in the 1973 Constitution. He noted that the original statement actually recalled the origin of the islands, slavery, colonialism, and the emergence of a people who attained freedom, Majority Rule and Independence, peacefully without bloodshed. He noted that although it was originally written for the 1969 Constitution, the Colonial Office in London suggested that it was not appropriate for a Colonial Constitution; and that it would have to wait to be included in the document for an Independent Bahamas.

> 'The Constitution', Sir Arthur noted, 'was not meant to be just a lifeless piece of paper, but a living entity, representing who we are, how we agreed to govern ourselves; and the basic law of what makes us Bahamian, and what defines a Bahamian'.

According to Sir Arthur, the legalistic language needed something poetic 'to express the aspirations of the people'. He said that it needed to be upfront in the Constitution, and that 'the Preamble of the Constitution represents those aspirations of the Bahamian people and their recognition of those values'.

He acknowledged that the general Bahamian population confesses to being Christian because of their basic belief in Jesus Christ. However, he added that the nation's 'recognition of' and 'obligation to' the Preamble, is what makes The Bahamas a Christian nation.

Further noting that while,

> 'This view does not lead towards Theocracy; it does lead to the observance and respect for Christian principles within the governance of the nation.'

Sir Arthur was eager to articulate that

> 'Modern Christianity acknowledges the right of others to exist and have their own religion. In that sense, having a country tolerant of all religions, where freedom of conscience is maintained and each person having access to information and making up his own mind is what Christianity is, or what being a Christian nation is about.'

He indicated that Democracy from which most Western societies evolved is based on Christianity. This view gives way to 'tolerance for freedom of religion' within the country, with Christianity being the principal religion in The Bahamas.

While he agrees with the separation of Church and State, he referred to the American society, which is supposed to be a Christian nation but has gone too far with the concept of separation of Church and State, by the removal of prayers and the Bible from the public school system and other public institutions.

In recognizing and affirming the government's responsibility towards the Preamble, Sir Arthur echoed a resounding confirmation, like Sir Lynden did, that the Bahamian government should lead the Bahamian society in observance of these Christian and Spiritual values contained in it.

He quoted:

> 'The government should fully recognize the role of the Church, and see the Church as a partner in working for God's people; the Church facilitating the spiritual component, and the government doing what makes for prosperity and peace, to enable the people to flourish and prosper in material and spiritual things.'

Sir Arthur further noted that:

> 'While I do not think that politicians should be Christians or non-Christians, but when making their judgment, that must be a great part of their thinking, a part of their being. Government should not go out and draft a law that is non-Christian. Government must create an environment that encourages and allows Christianity to flourish, and the freedom of religion to exist.'

Sir Arthur indicated that although the Preamble does not have the force of law in the Constitution as the other Articles do, those Articles should reflect the Preamble, as 'an evolutionary, yet perpetual thing'. He feels strongly that even 'if the words of the Preamble changes, the principles and spirit should not change'.

In concluding our interview, Sir Arthur referred to one of Sir Winston Churchill's famous statements.

> 'Democracy is imperfect, waste of time and resources, and cumbersome, but we have nothing better.'

He concluded that:

> 'In a democratic society when a government ceases to do what they are supposed to do in governing the people the way the people have agreed to be governed, the people must exercise their franchise, and remove that government from power.'

Sir Randol F. Fawkes, KT (1924 -2000)
The Father of Labour in The Bahamas

Attorney Sir Randol Francis Fawkes, in the 1960's. (Courtesy of The Sir Randol Fawkes Family Foundation – wwwsirrandolfawkes.com)

Recalling my teenage years in the 1980s, I remembered seeing Sir Randol Fawkes strutting down Bay Street with his brief bag under his arm, hailing everyone as though he knew them personally. For what I had heard of him, he was a Bahamian National hero; one of the persons responsible for the freedom the younger generation enjoyed and took for granted.

I first became acquainted with Sir Randol Fawkes shortly after returning from Washington, D.C. in June 1998. I saw him strutting as he usually did, up Parliament Street towards the Post Office. I took the opportunity to stop him and introduce myself and finally met up close, this giant political hero. And like Sir Lynden, he too was of short stature.

When I introduced myself, I was surprised that he was very familiar with my name and my work. He noted that he had often read my column, 'Answering The Call' and had observed the many articles I had published in the local newspapers. He said that I too was a 'Freedom Fighter.' Of course, I blushed at such a compliment. He asked for my address and encouraged me to 'keep up the good work' and went on his way. I was excited to be complemented by a real 'Freedom Fighter'. I felt elated and humbled as I walked away.

Several weeks later, I received a package in the mail. It was Sir Randol's book *The Faith that Moved the Mountain*. Inside it was autographed, 'To Miss S. Ali McIntosh, a Fellow Freedom Fighter. Continue to do well! From Sir Randol Fawkes 10/07/98' The autograph in the book was dated for July 10, 1998, the 25th Anniversary of The Bahamas' Independence.

Amidst the tremendous amount of writing and studying I was engrossed in, I read the book. It was like one of those great novels, I could hardly put it down. I devoted a time each day to complete the book, which I finally did by the end of that month. Before reading Sir Randol's book, I had never read a book on Bahamian history that was so profound, with such literary power. I concluded, at the time, that it was a book that any person who was interested in the governance of our country should read.

I did not hear from Sir Randol again until one year later. In May 1999, I was on the Steve McKinney Talk Show, 'You Make The Call' after the announcement of the formation of The Bahamas Constitution Party. Several days later Sir Randol appeared on the show also. I called into the show and suggested that, in my estimation, his book was one of the greatest literary treasures of The Bahamas and should be included in public schools as part of the curriculum on Bahamian history.

Several days later, I heard from Sir Randol by phone to thank me for the compliment. I was delighted, and he was overwhelmed that I had made such a compliment on the radio about his book. After that phone call to the radio station, we spoke often. He would call my pager/voicemail and simply say that he was on his way over to my home office in Pinedale. There was no negotiating with Sir Randol. So, if I was out, I would find my way home immediately. Whatever I was doing, I would just make myself available and ready to talk to Sir Randol.

While together, he would talk about the country, both past and present. Although approaching the end of his life, he was still very much consumed with nation-building. It was as if he was not quite finished. So, whenever we spoke, he would talk to me and pour out whatever he had left. He taught me about what made The Bahamas great and how we got there. He would tell me how we got started as a nation, and how they held Prayer meetings on Windsor Park back in the early days of the struggle. How they sang and prayed and talked about what it will take to get free. He was my teacher, and I was his student. He was my Mentor, and I was his mentee.

When the lesson time was up for the day, he would just get up to leave, even if I thought we had more to discuss on the issue. He would say, 'We will talk again, probably tomorrow. I will call.' It always made me laugh when he did that. It was as if he operated on an internal bell or timetable, that reminded him that class was finished for the day.

Sir Randol attended several of the planning meetings of The Bahamas Constitution Party. He told the young people in attendance how important it was for them to get involved in the political life of their country. At one meeting, he gave each of them a copy of his book and told them to read it and donate the funds to the work of the BCP.

Sir Randol was one of the great giants of our time, who cared about the pursuit of justice and fair play more than anything else, even reputation and money. He was generous with his advice and his compliments. He simply spoke his mind. He was courageous, and a man of faith, who expressed confidence towards the agenda of a new political machinery. And for those who knew Sir Randol best, knew he would not have missed the opportunity to have suggested that the BCP be a Labour party. His recommendation was for me to rename the party, The Bahamas Constitutional Labour Party, one of his last requests. He encouraged me immensely.

Sir Randol Fawkes was an amazing and exceptional leader. He was one of the catalysts for social and political change in the 1950s, in his portfolio as the leader of The Bahamas Federation of Labour. In 1967, he was one of two Independent elected Members of Parliament, who joined forces with the Progressive Liberal Party (PLP) to give the Bahamian people Majority Rule, (the General Election results were split down the middle with the PLP and the UBP both obtaining eighteen (18) seats). The entire story was told in his book, *The Faith that Moved the Mountain.* I recommend it highly.

The story was told how Sir Randol was offered a blank cheque by the late Sir Roland Symonette, the then Premier, to choose how much money he wanted to side with the United Bahamian Party (UBP), so that they could maintain the government. Well, Sir Randol refused the cheque, and 'all the riches of the world' to give freedom to the Bahamian people. This was the greatest gift that he could have given us – the gift of Majority Rule.

Sir Randol and Lady Jacqueline Fawkes walk across Parliament Square to the House of Assembly on the Opening of Parliament on February 9th 1967 (Courtesy of The Sir Randol Fawkes Family Foundation – sirrandolfawkes.com)

This great giant of a man, a genuine Bahamian hero, is considered 'The Father of Labour', because of his indelible contribution to the Labour movement in The Bahamas and the rights of the Bahamian worker. His work can never be erased, and his contribution must be etched into Bahamian history in his honour. It is my suggestion, that Sir Randol should be memorialized with no less than a 'Bronze Bust statue in a significant place, possibly Parliament Square; or the renaming of Wulff Road between Blue Hill Road and Collins Avenue as 'Sir Randol Fawkes Way'; and the continued celebration of 'Sir Randol Fawkes Labour Day', celebrated the first Friday in June of each year.

In this regard, I am pleased that the year 2014 marked the first time that the country celebrated the Sir Randol Fawkes Labour Day. Legislation was finally placed before Parliament to rename Labour Day as Sir Randol Fawkes Labour Day. This indisputable leader of men was truly one of the founding fathers of the modern Bahamas.

Retracing his life and work back to the 1940s in his book, The Faith that Moved the Mountain, Sir Randol showed us that the faith that sustained him was part of the values he used to help build the nation through personal campaigns for equitable labour laws and the protection of the fundamental rights and freedoms of the Bahamian worker. His religious faith was not separated from his social and political involvement and action. It gave me courage, that if the 'founding fathers' were sustained by such dedication to spiritual values during the inception of the nation; then the continuation of the next generation needed some 'Freedom fighters' with comparable faith.

Sir Randol's book recorded the days and times in which the Bahamian people endured hardship in a post-slavery, pre-Independence colonial era, and what the movement to free them really meant. These sentiments, outlined in his book, express so vividly those historic times and prayerful days of the peaceful 'Quiet Revolution'. These recollections provide us with a glimpse of the aspirations of the beautiful spirit of our founding fathers and mothers, and the inspiration which in turn motivated them to fight, and obtain freedom and liberty for, the ensuing generations of Bahamian children.

The book, *The Faith that Moved the Mountain*, must be read as an inspiration to awaken in each of us the spirit of the founding fathers and freedom fighters of the modern Bahamas.

- I highly recommend it to students at the high school through college levels

- I recommend it to every leader who believes that he or she is called to leadership in The Bahamas

- I recommend it to every Bahamian who wants to make a difference in their nation.

- Read it to your children, share it with your family and renew your acquaintance with what made us a great people, and the people who made it happen – the founding fathers and mothers of the nation

- Go online www.sirrandolfawkes.com for a historical journey into his life and work

In this regard, Lady Jacqueline Fawkes, the late widow of Sir Randol, of whom he spoke so highly of in his book, told me several weeks after his death in June 2000; that 'I knew about a year after we were married, that I would have to share him.' And certainly, sharing him brought great blessings to The Bahamas.

I wish to express my profound gratitude to the late Lady Jacqueline and her children:

'Madam, thank you for lending your husband to our country. The spirit of his work and the contributions of his life's work will never be forgotten. Your contribution and your support of this giant, through all the good times and bad times, the popularity and the poverty; your and your children's sacrifice will always be imprinted as the essence of his legacy. On behalf of the next generation of Bahamians, 'Thank you!'

I wish to convey my sincerest honour, to the man who taught me that service to God and country are inseparable. For the life of Sir Randol Fawkes, the 'Man whose Faith moved the Mountain.' May he rest in peace, till our Lord comes again when He will say, 'Arise, Sir Randol!'

Conclusion Thoughts on the Founding Fathers

In concluding these thoughts on the founders of the modern Bahamas, I wish to suggest the following items for your earnest consideration:

First, I believe that the founding fathers accepted as true that a high standard of personal morality is required for persons aspiring for national leadership.

Second, I believe that the founding fathers wanted the role of the Church and the counsel of spiritual and Christian leaders to be an integral part in nation building and their influence to be vital in the formation of public policies.

Third, I believe that the founding fathers of this nation also accepted as true, that the integrity needed for leadership, directly relates to the recognition and belief in the fundamental rights and freedoms of the individual; and that the aspiring leader has a commitment to upholding and protecting these rights for all the citizens of the country.

And Fourth, I believe that the founding fathers accepted as true, that the rights and freedoms of the Bahamian people could only be guaranteed, if the people who govern the nation, maintain a belief in the Supremacy of God, and have an abiding respect for Christian and Spiritual Values and the Rule of Law; thereby ordering their policies to reflect the core values articulated in the Preamble of the Bahamian Constitution.

The First (1st) Majority Rule Cabinet led by Premier Lynden O. Pindling in January 1967, following the swearing-in of the first Pindling-led Cabinet by Sir Ralph Grey, the then Governor of the Colonies of the Bahama Islands. In photo from left to right:- Arthur D Hanna, Minister of Education; Cecil Wallace-Whitfield, Minister of Works; Milo B. Butler, Minister of Health Welfare; Clement D Maynard, Minister without Portfolio in Senate; Clarence A Bain, Minister without Portfolio; Randol F Fawkes, Minister of Labour & Commerce; Lynden O Pindling, Prime Minister & Minister of Tourism; Sir Ralph Grey, Governor of The Bahama Islands; Jeffery Thompson, Minister of Internal Affairs; Dr Curtis McMillian, Minister of Communications; Warren Lavarity, Minister of Out Islands Affairs; Rev. Carlton A Francis, Minister. (Courtesy of The Sir Randol Fawkes Family Foundation – wwwsirrandolfawkes.com)

Delegates to the 1972 Constitutional Conference for the Bahamas Independence. Seen from Right to Left: Labour Party Leader Randol Fawkes; Arthur D. Hanna; Orville Turnquest; Paul L. Adderley; Lynden Pindling (PLP Leader and Prime Minister) (Courtesy of The Sir Randol Fawkes Family Foundation – www.sirrandolfawkes.com)

Those 'Freedom Fighters' like Sir Lynden Pindling, Sir Randol Fawkes, Sir Arthur Foulkes, Sir Milo Butler, the Honourable Arthur Hanna, Clarence Bain, Dame Dr. Doris Johnson, Sir Henry Milton Taylor, Sir Orville Turnquest, Sir Cecil Wallace-Whitfield, Rev. Carlton Francis, and all the Signatories to the Bahamian Constitution; in addition to the hundreds of others whose names history does not even record; they fought, struggled and even died for the freedoms that exist in The Bahamas today. Their dreams will always live on in us. And I believe that because that spirit was captured in the Preamble, we as a people should desire to keep its lasting values for all times.

PART TWO

Defining the Values of The Preamble

— CHAPTER SIX —

An Overview Of The Preamble

'Whenever you have lost your way, go back to the original purpose, and start again!'

This was the suggestion put forward by renowned Christian motivator Laura Beth Jones, in one of her motivational workshops on 'Finding your Life's Mission', when visiting Nassau more than two decades ago.

Confirming this same principle, world-renowned author and Bahamian preacher, the late Dr. Myles Munroe, cites three keys to successfully fulfilling your destiny in life: *Purpose, Potential and Principles.* He noted that understanding these three 'Life Laws' determines whether you fail or succeed.

In a further clarification of the meanings of these three keys, in his 1993 book *Becoming a Leader*, Dr. Munroe wrote:

'Purpose as the original intent, tells you why you exist; Potential as the inherent ability, tells you what you can do; and Principles as the inherent laws for function, tell you how to do it.'

The Preamble of the Constitution, which I have determined was the articulated Mission Statement of the Commonwealth of The Bahamas at its inception in 1973, outlines and states the Purpose, the Potential, and the Principle of the government and people of The Bahamas.

When we look at the Core Values articulated in the Preamble, if applied correctly, they were designed to bring us to our intended destiny as a new nation. Therefore, the measure of our success as a nation will be realized only by the actual completion of our God-given assignment, rather than just any good set of ideas or plans. Success is therefore determined by the fulfillment of the 'original' purpose and intent and is measured not by what we have done, but by what we should have done.

In this chapter, I want to give you an overview of what I perceive the Preamble wishes to say to us. I will highlight certain themes, which I hope should merit your most earnest consideration.

The First Refrain of The Preamble
The first refrain of the Preamble states that:

> 'The People of this Family of Islands 'recognize' that the 'preservation of their Freedom' 'will be guaranteed' by a 'national commitment' to Self-discipline, Industry, Loyalty, Unity and An Abiding Respect for Christian Values and the Rule of Law.'

In analyzing this, I wish to first explore the word Recognize. This word is in the present tense. It specifies that the recognition of the thing that follows, which is the 'preservation of their freedom', is 'ever in the present' and has an always 'present' connotation. As it was the 'present recognition' of the generation in 1973, it is 'our present responsibility', and will be the 'present responsibility' one hundred years from now. This infers that the government of the day and the people of this Family of islands will always have the same responsibility as those before them.

The reason that word 'Recognize' continues to be in the present tense is that it is not 'something' that has happened, but it is something that continues to happen; and it will continue to be in the present, as long as there exists a democratic sovereign state called The Commonwealth of The Bahamas.

Secondly, when we speak about the 'Preservation of their Freedom' as it relates to the verb 'recognize'; it then implies that the people admit that the 'preservation of that freedom' hinges on the recognition of something very important. That very important 'something' that has to be 'recognized', is the need for the 'provision' of a guarantee.

So, the phrase 'will be guaranteed' does not simply imply the present need, but the implication of a future need, to continue to provide a guarantee. In this admission, the government and people of The Bahamas have determined that in order for their freedom to be preserved, there must be a guarantor. And that Guarantor is every one of us; every Bahamian must provide the guarantee – both the people and the government.

You may ask again, how does the entire population guarantee that the freedom in the country is preserved for each one of us? How do we guarantee that freedom will always be afforded to each of us, by each of us?

The answer to the question, in terms of how we guarantee freedom, and to what extent do we offer our guarantee, lies in the next theme 'a national commitment to'. These words most powerfully express the height of our responsibility as a people. We, therefore, have two great obligations concerning the 'guarantee of the preservation of our freedom'.

The first obligation is for the people to demand of the government, its adherence to this 'national commitment'; and the second obligation is for the people to adhere to this 'national commitment'.

Each individual who submits themselves to being a citizen of the Commonwealth of The Bahamas has a solemn responsibility and a part in this obligation. Each person by mere citizenship becomes a signatory to the Constitution. In fact, when you become a citizen, even by Naturalization, you submit yourself to the Constitution of The Bahamas and thereby become responsible for providing a 'guarantee' for the 'preservation of freedom' in the nation.

Let me reiterate this fact, if the 'people and the government' must offer the guarantee, then every citizen has a personal responsibility to both 'uphold' their portion, and 'demand' that the government upholds its portion of responsibility, regarding this 'national commitment'.

I want to draw your attention to what the most extensive on-line version of the Oxford Dictionary states concerning these words 'National Commitment'. I think that most people have varied interpretations of what these words mean, but during my research, I came to realize that while the Encyclopedia and Dictionary both gave different references in regard to the origin and periodic use of the words over the past several hundred years, the meanings always refer back to the same implication.

The primary definition of the word 'National' states: 'belonging to a nation, or affecting or shared by the nation as a whole'. The secondary definition refers to being 'peculiar to, and characteristic or distinctive of a people of a particular country' & 'devoted to the interest of the nation'.

The primary definition of the word 'Commitment' states: 'the action of entrusting, giving in charge of, or engaging of oneself to a particular course of conduct'. The secondary definition refers to it as, 'an absolute moral choice of a course of action; or the state of being involved in political or social questions, as in furthering a particular doctrine or cause'.

What I wish to establish is, that when the Preamble states that the people of this Family of Islands, 'Recognize that the preservation of their freedom will be guaranteed by a national commitment', it simply means,

> 'That they have a moral obligation to preserve the nation's freedom by offering their personal guarantee by their commitment to the values of 'Self-discipline, Industry, Loyalty, Unity and An Abiding Respect for Christian Values and the Rule of Law in their lives. Additionally, it means that they will further demand of the government of the day, that these values are also observed in the governance of the nation.'

Therefore, the connotation of a 'national commitment bonds successive governments and successive generations, to build on the founders' initial philosophy and continue to create an environment in the country which promotes these core values as national values.

- It means that these core values should always be a commitment of the government of the day
- It means these core values must always be a national concern to all the citizenry
- It means these core values must always be on the national agenda

- It simply means that the people of The Bahamas must, and can always expect their government, to lead out in unifying the people of The Bahamas in these core values and the philosophy of the founding fathers

You may ask how can almost 400,000 people mandate that these values be embedded in the life of the nation and the governance of the people?

The answer is simple: We go to the polls during the General Elections and vote.

Voting is a solemn duty and privilege, in order to guarantee your voice in the selection and regulation of the government. I wish to refer you to a statement in my introduction that states:

> 'Government is a trust, and the officers of the government are Trustees, and both are created for the benefit of the people'.

Therefore, when 'We the People' elect officers also known as Members of Parliament, who in turn are responsible to appoint all other forms of national leadership, we entrust to them the mandates to which, we as a people, have already committed ourselves. Essentially, because we all cannot go to Parliament to make the decisions of governance, we make it when we elect our Members of Parliament. Voting is how we mandate our wishes in the governance of the nation.

So, the Constitution and its Preamble, both give and obligate each Bahamian, the right and responsibility to mandate, through their voting, that their freedom is preserved, and that their individual rights are protected.

Therefore, any government that is elected to serve in the Commonwealth of The Bahamas, must be committed to the maintenance of these core values stated in the Preamble, in the governance of the nation. And subsequently, the promotion of these core values should be part of their actions and behaviour, for the continued growth and development of the nation. Consequently, the reverse will also be true. If the government is not committed to the Preamble and what it demands, the freedom of the people will be eroded, and ultimately, the loss of the country's democracy and sovereignty may be the result.

What should these values mean to the life of the nation? What are the benefits of applying them to governance and national leadership? Are we as a people obligated to demand that the people who wish to govern us qualify for leadership by their adherence to these core values or principles?

'BE IT THEREFORE RESOLVED, THAT FOR THESE REASONS, THE CORE VALUES ARTICULATED IN THE PREAMBLE OF THE CONSTITUTION ARE CRITERIA FOR NATIONAL LEADERSHIP AND GOVERNANCE IN THE COMMONWEALTH OF THE BAHAMAS'.

The Second Refrain of the Preamble

The second section of the Preamble speaks to the proclamation of the government and the citizens, on the most auspicious Declaration of Independence. It is not accidental that this section begins with the phrase, NOW KNOW YE THEREFORE.

'We, the Inheritors of and Successors to this Family of Islands, recognizing the supremacy of God and believing in the fundamental rights and freedoms of the individual, DO HEREBY PROCLAIM IN SOLEMN PRAISE, the establishment of a free and democratic sovereign nation founded on Spiritual Values and in which no man, woman or child shall ever be slave or bondsman to anyone, or their labour exploited or their lives frustrated by deprivation, AND DO HEREBY PROVIDE by these Articles for the indivisible unity and creation under God of the Commonwealth of The Bahamas.'

This was meant to declare for all and sundry, that the people who took possession and responsibility for The Bahamas on July 10th, 1973, had certain desires for the establishment of the new nation called the Commonwealth of The Bahamas.

This Declaration further acknowledged, that the Government and the people, (the Inheritors of and Successors to this Family of Islands), 'recognizing the Supremacy of the Almighty God (Yahweh Elohim), and believing in the Fundamental Rights and Freedoms of the Individual', is a vital 'part and parcel' of the intended vocation of this new Sovereign State.

I believe it was necessary to establish upfront to the World in 1973, that the new environment that was to exist in The Bahamas thereafter, would be predicated on certain basic tenets and principles. The first founding principle which is Spiritual Values would predicate social justice, political fairness, and economic opportunities for every citizen of the Commonwealth of The Bahamas. The basic tenet also spoke to the creation of an environment in the nation, that encourages the general citizenry to be committed to fostering a 'My Brother's Keeper' mentality. This was in order to guarantee that, 'no man, woman or child is ever enslaved or made a bondsman again, or their labour exploited, or their lives frustrated by deprivation' by anyone; no matter where they come from or how much wealth they bring.

This founding principle was meant to ensure that in the environment where God is recognized, and the people's freedom and fundamental rights are protected and preserved; all citizens would be industrious and would occupy themselves with the concept of making opportunities available, and having opportunities made available to them. This new environment would hold the government accountable for the provision of economic opportunities for all the citizenry, despite their political and religious persuasion. This new environment would also guarantee that no child would ever have to go to bed hungry in this new nation. It does not necessarily mean that the government will be responsible to feed every child, but that the climate and attitude encouraged by the government will encourage citizens to help each other, whenever that is possible.

I believe that the concepts and core values set forth in the Preamble should give inspiration to the other thirty-seven (37) articles of the Constitution, and should provide for 'indivisible Unity' of our people in this 'Righteous' state called The Commonwealth of The Bahamas.

And finally, as I close this analysis, in his Analects, Confucious puts the matter concisely, when he wrote:

> 'The Master said, 'Guide them by edicts, keep them in line with punishments, and the common people will stay out of trouble and have no sense of shame. Guide them by virtue, keep them in line with the rites, and they will, besides having a sense of shame, reform themselves.'

———— CHAPTER SEVEN ————

The Value of Self-Discipline

The first core value we will look at is Self-discipline. I believe that this is key to understanding what the founding fathers anticipated would be one of the finest attributes of good governance for this new nation. Having been oppressed by Colonialism and then engaged in the subsequent fight for universal suffrage, women's suffrage, fair labour laws and standards, Majority Rule, and finally Independence; the leaders and the people were moved to recognize that 'Self-discipline' was one of their perpetual responsibilities in the security of the future of the nation. The concept of self-imposed restraint simply demonstrated their commitment to ensuring the security of the community as a whole, over personal selfish gain.

The Oxford Online Dictionary describes the word Discipline as 'to chastise or to inflict penitential discipline upon'. It speaks further to the idea of 'the training to habit of order, and the training of prompt action in obedience to command'.

The Webster Dictionary, which does not define the word Self-discipline, instead defines the words Self-denial and Self-control, which can be used synonymously. The term Self-denial is defined as, 'the readiness to forego gratification to further a cause, or to help another person'. The term Self-control is defined as 'the ability to restrain one's impulses of expressions or emotion'. Both of these terms are similar to the initial suggestion of Self-discipline.

As we relate the core value of Self-Discipline to the functions of national leadership, I wish to refer to the idea we shall discuss in more detail in the Chapter on Servant Leadership. The idea of servant-oriented leadership is no new concept. It was introduced by the world's exemplary teacher on leadership – Jesus Christ when He instructed His disciples:

> 'Whoever wants to lead or exercise authority over the others, must be the servant and minister to the others first.' Mark 10:43

Jesus demonstrated the ultimate example of servant leadership in John 13: 1-17, which recounts His performance of washing His disciples' feet. In verses 14 – 17, Jesus instructed His disciples:

> 'If I then, your Lord and Master, have washed your feet;
> ye also ought to wash one another's feet, for I have given
> you an example that ye shall do as I have done to you.'

National leadership, in democratic environments, gives power and authority, through legitimate elections, to men and women to exercise influence over others; with the implication, that the power surrendered 'by the people to the leaders' are for the purpose of the 'leaders rendering service to the people' before rendering it to themselves.

When the government of a nation exercises self-discipline and self-control within the exercise of its public duties, its example, authorizes its citizenry to consider the exercise of self-restraint in its daily duties also. It further encourages the citizenry to consider acts of volunteerism of time, resources and finances, towards charitable, religious, and non-profit institutions as conduits for their benevolence. As the government does, so do the people.

The exercise of self-discipline in national leadership is seen in how the government's overall economic development plans and vision for the country are implemented. The value placed on the long-term development of the country versus the immediate gratification of superficial economic activities, speaks to the character of the leadership. When presented with choices of economic opportunities for the country, governments with strong characters should seek to discern the most beneficial choices for the nation. Not simply, whether it is right or wrong, or whether it is good or evil, but whether those developments, over the long term, would be for the greater good and the betterment of the society into the future.

The government's consideration should not only be of an economical value, but the significance to the environmental, social, intellectual, and spiritual advancement of the community. When decisions are made solely due to economic considerations, to the detriment of all other concerns, the leader is clearly losing or has lost his sense of self-discipline.

The handling of money matters and fiscal management also shows explicitly the level of discipline within the thinking of the nation's leaders. By both secular and biblical standards, the exhibit of good stewardship is primarily related to how we handle money and those things relating to financial resources.

Many parables told by Christ speak to these issues, for example, the Rich Young Ruler, the Woman Who Lost Her Coin, the Prodigal Son, the Woman with Two Mites, and the Parable of the Talents. In each story, the person's response to money was illustrated, and the consequence or reward based on their particular reaction high-lighted. These stories speak to a higher purpose and exemplify the innate ability in man to be greedy, selfish, deceitful, foolish, or sacrificing. These stories are also meant to demonstrate that the financial resources of any person, institution, or government belong to God first; thereafter they must be used for service to mankind.

Only submission to the core value of Self-discipline will cause a leader to 'seek out' the choice of 'service above self'. This attribute cannot be simply gained by desire, but by a recognition of the individual, of their need to be of service to others first. This will then be followed by the commitment to exemplify the core-value of self-discipline in every aspect of the leader's public duty.

Examples of Undisciplined Government

As we seek to identify and evaluate manifestations of the loss of self-discipline in government, we can turn to these few examples for consideration. When the government's preference is more focused on physical development and beauty, rather than the development of people, the government is clearly losing focus on priorities. While these are only my opinion, I believe they warrant some consideration.

This illustration is based on the FNM administration's initial decision to borrow fifty-eight ($58) million dollars in 2001 for road reconstruction and expansion. Although some major work was warranted, much of it I deemed at the time to be for political mileage. At the same time, a local doctor's request for assistance with one million ($1M) dollars to build a local children's hospital, which was needed to expand the treatment of childhood and adolescent cancer patients, was unacceptable to the government. They had clearly lost focus on the exercise of self-discipline. The expenditure of the people's money should be primarily on the development of the people and secondarily, on the development of the physical environment.

Regarding the roadworks, since 2001, both the PLP and the FNM governments have borrowed additional monies to complete this same New Providence roadwork project, which was estimated to be completed with the original $58 million loan from the Inter-American Development Bank (IDB). After five years of PLP borrowing in 2002 - 2007; the FNM government returned to power in 2007 and borrowed an additional two hundred ($200) million in 2009 (called 'stimulus money'), to complete the same roadwork project, which was still not 100% completed when the FNM left office in 2012.

In early 2013, the New Providence Road Work was finally completed by the Christie administration. The cost to the Bahamian taxpayers totaling more than two hundred ($206) million dollars. The project had cost overruns of more than one hundred ($100) million dollars, attributed to by both governments, particularly the Ingraham administration's poor budgeting on the project. In essence, the project was twelve (12) years in the making and $148 million over the original estimate of fifty-eight ($58) million dollars.

This complaint was not intended to express or imply that we do not appreciate the roadworks. However, much of this squandering of the people's money by both governments, have been due to incompetent international and local contractors, and companies, who to a great degree, were mostly friends and supporters of various Parliamentarians, who in turn, benefitted through mismanagement and kickbacks. Although it was intimated by some, that the rising cost of fuel had escalated the cost of the overruns. While this could be somewhat true, the overruns were astronomical, to say the least.

Former Prime Minister Right Honourable Hubert Ingraham, PM 1992-2002, 2007-2012 (Photography by Bahamas Information Services (BIS) Nassau, Bahamas)

Lest I am judged as unpatriotic, I wish to remind us of the following quote, credited to Mark Twain; 'Patriotism is supporting your country all the time, and your government when it deserves it.'

Therefore, Bahamians should demand to know if there is anyone accounting for the astronomical mismanagement of the people's money by our governments. Bahamians deserve to know who will be held responsible. Does the idea of self-discipline and restraint play a part in the fiscal management of the people's resources? They talk, but are they 'Walking the Talk?'

Another illustration of the lack of self-discipline is the development and preservation of The Exuma Cays. The government's decision to sell or allow the sale of many of the cays in the Exumas for 'pocket change' to billionaire investors, who could afford to pay much more than the asking price, in my opinion, was considerably short-sighted. Consider that these billionaires were purchasing undisturbed land in 'Paradise'. I am of the opinion that if you want to buy a piece of Paradise, you have to pay the price to live in Paradise.

As a result of the sale of the majority of the smaller, uninhabited cays, many of the residents of the larger Exuma Cays (such as Farmers Cay, Staniel Cay, Black Point) have been disadvantaged by their inability to continue to harvest the 'Top-plants' from these small cays, which grow the plant in abundance, another one of our listed Natural Resources. This practice of harvesting 'Top' and plaiting straw has been used for decades, as an industry to earn a living for many poor residents in the cays. This natural material is used for making the beautiful straw bags which are sold at the world-famous straw market in downtown Nassau, as well as throughout the islands of The Bahamas. While I am all for development and progress, it must happen without losing the indigenous culture of a people. This is possible.

I have been informed that some of the managers and developers of the cays have actually put the dogs at the residents, who were attempting to gather 'top' from the backside of the various cays. Consequent to this lack of these raw materials, many of the indigenous craft have been replaced by souvenir imports from China.

Both the FNM and PLP governments were somewhat responsible for the negative economic fallouts in Exuma. It is my opinion that governments should always be aware, that when a decision is made, it sometimes causes an equally opposite reaction and consequence. Therefore, decisions made by the government must not be made in haste, without adequate considerations for the long-term consequences or benefits.

In this regard, and in the first instance, the PLP government during their first term in office in 2002 – 2007, had encouraged the 'Buy and Ship' from China agenda, in conjunction with the

Bahamas Chamber of Commerce, causing Straw goods to lose some popularity and sales to subsequently dwindle, leading to them being replaced by Chinese souvenirs, which were cheaper. The FNM government, during their 2007 - 2012 term, attempted to rectify the matter by putting in place a program to encourage the making of straw craft by these same Exumians. The government hoped that the program would have eliminated the abundance of crafts in the world-famous Nassau Straw Market with labels reading 'Made in China.'

Consequently, the selling of our resources, like the cays in Exuma (for what I consider a small bowl of pottage, compared to the hundreds of millions that are being further invested and resale for), are considered undisciplined actions of the government. If you must sell what I consider valuable assets, you should at least attempt to get commitments for something that will represent that same level of security in the nation. But what do we get in return for the selling of the country's inheritance? Jobs! Not even permanent jobs, just temporary construction jobs, and other domestic, temporary jobs, NO real ownership of development by Bahamians!

Some of these developments, for the most part, are not sustainable over the long term and are pegged to enrich the developer primarily, and not the community at large!

For example, I will refer to the tourism-related project on mainland Exuma, which had been in receivership for two years, as the workers had to be paid by the government, prior to its recent sale. The project was too large, for a small island like Exuma, in the first place. In addition to a large hotel, the project included a Townhouse development, a Marina, a Golf course, a Casino, and an Employee housing unit.

In order for a project of that magnitude to survive, the developers had to bring in the majority of its workers and provide housing.

The huge influx of new people to Exuma, just to service the hotel, led to an increase in the level of crime and criminal activity in the small island pristine communities. Even to the present, the new owners of the development are still struggling to survive, because of the cost to run a project that size on an island too underdeveloped to accommodate it.

This is also similar to the project in Bimini, and a proposed investment in Mayaguana and the Disney Project in Eleuthera. These and other 'anchor projects' proposed by the PLP in its first Christie administration in 2002-2007, and others entertained by the Hubert Ingraham led FNM in 2007 -2012, and the present Minnis lead Administration; are set to change our once beautiful paradise: with real and proposed heavy dredging to the local shorelines by some of these gigantic projects, has raised serious environmental concerns.

The World Bank Report for 1998 - 1999 refers to the need for small and developing countries to invest more in human capital, than just infrastructure. While the report spoke of knowledge and education, I believe it also refers to all aspects of physical, social, and intellectual development. Investment in human capital accounts for that part of economic growth that cannot be explained, but which is measurable in the long term, by the development of the workforce, which accounts for productivity.

My concern is that the government is attempting to develop primarily opportunities for domestic and menial labour for the majority of our people, through the establishment of tourism projects such as hotels and casinos. I wish to propose that we seek to develop our workforce with more intellectual development through meaningful industries, which do not pose such significant threats to our pristine environment.

The Right Honourable Perry G. Christie, former Prime Minister of the Common-wealth of the Bahamas 2002-2007, 2012-2017 (Photography by Bahamas Information Services (BIS) Nassau, Bahamas)

Harvest the Exuma Park

Since the 1950s, the Bahamas Government and the Bahamas National Trust have overseen a protected part of the waters of the Exuma Cays called the Exuma National Park Land and Sea Reserve.

The government has entertained and allowed 'special interests' millionaires and billionaires, who have purchased the smaller Exuma cays, to carry out full-scale dredging in and around the Land and Sea park, which has served only to enrich themselves, in direct contradiction, and in detriment of the very 'environment', they propose to protect.

In addition to this, I believe that the time is coming for there to be periodic farmings of the Reserve Park in the Exuma Cays. In fact, the government must consider that every few years, harvesting (meaning mass fishing) should be allowed to take place in the park, with regulations, and for a predetermined season. I believe that once the park becomes overpopulated as it is now, there should be some 'way' to alleviate the overcrowding of Conch and fish species in the area. If, as argued by the National Trust, the Exuma Land, and Sea Park is a breeding ground for all species, then it would mean that responsible fishing can take place, because the species breed in abundance in the area. This will allow the residents to fish responsibly in the reserve and make a living. It is my belief that it is necessary to put people first, particularly in adverse economic conditions.

Personal Behaviour of Leaders

Before I conclude this chapter, I want to touch on the aspect of personal self-discipline in the lives of leaders. I have heard many concerns as to whether the personal conduct or moral behaviour of persons in leadership should matter to the people they represent. This question has been causing many people to vacillate, whether to judge a leader's worth based on his or her moral character or evaluate his or her leadership based simply on the job he or she is doing.

When we were planning the original objectives of the Bahamas Constitution Party (BCP), we coined or adopted a phrase as part of the fundamental principles of the organization that says,

'Integrity more noble than expediency is never negotiable.'

The reason we had determined that 'Integrity' should be non-negotiable was, because without 'personal' integrity the leader may not be able to exercise 'institutional' integrity within the context of his or her political office. In the framework of politics, there are many variables, and in instances where 'political expediency' seems to be most urgent, leaders must already have in place a moral framework to choose 'Integrity over Expediency'.

A leader's ability to exercise or impose self-discipline will determine whether their character will withstand tests of moral fortitude against political corruption. The leader's ability to restrain themselves against personal gratification, and their ability to consider moral and social implications in their own life, before making choices, will determine what kind of choices he or she will make as a leader when managing the people's resources.

If an individual's personal life is lacking the moral standard necessary to be a role model, and a good steward of the people's money: should it matter that he or she may have the education background to execute a job? Would not such an individual's lack of integrity make him or her more of a threat to the office? I am of the opinion that he or she would have the knowledge of how to manipulate the system, which is more of the same thing we are trying to rid ourselves of. Additionally, the office could possibly serve as a cloak for an unprincipled, corrupt-minded individual, and therefore result in corruption and malfeasance in public office.

Just as an example, in late 2007, the brutal murders of two of Nassau's leading citizens: A College of The Bahamas Professor, and a world-famous straw-handbag designer, brought to light a disturbing arrangement of some of Bahamas' elite men called 'The Gentleman's Club'. The club organized, hosted, and entertained at a distinguished residence near downtown, including a secret list of some thirty-seven (37) of Nassau's elite homosexual & bi-sexual gentlemen as members.

What is interesting about all this, is that it was alleged that on this 'secret list' were included several high-ranking members of the Christie administration, several pastors and priests, several bankers, doctors, high-ranking members of the Royal Bahamas Police Force, among other public officials.

The threat of exposing the 'List of the Gentlemen's Club Members' had sparked such controversy among the nation's leadership, that in a debate in the House of Assembly following those murders; a former member of the Perry Christie Cabinet, then in opposition, threatened the governing FNM Ingraham administration, that he would reveal the names of the 'sweethearts' or extra-marital affairs of all the FNM Members of Parliament. In turn, the then Prime Minister Hubert Ingraham threatened to expose the names on the 'secret list' of the thirty-seven (37) members of the Gentlemen's Club.

In response, Perry Christie, former Prime Minister and the then Leader of the Opposition, was quick to pull the PLP Member of Parliament in order, so that his actions would not 'tempt' Prime Minister Hubert Ingraham, to expose the secret list, which many believed contained the names of several prominent members of the PLP Parliamentarian caucus at the time.

Can you imagine, the Parliament or rather the entire political leadership of The Bahamas at that time, morally compromised by some dirty little secret or the other? How do we anticipate that the leadership of our country can be sustained with 'compromised' reputation? How do we expect genuine governance in an environment sustained on lies, cover-up, plots, and immorality? How can we expect that both the FNM government and the PLP leadership in Parliament are working for the greater good of The Bahamas when their 'dirty secrets' are holding them at bay from reporting such on each other? Is this all they are covering up or are they using other compromising situations to prevent each other from governing in truth and honesty on behalf of the people of The Bahamas? Certainly, we the people deserve better than this!

Somewhere I once read that, 'Marital fidelity or faithfulness to one's spouse is one of the greatest tests of integrity'.

When you really think about it, possibly ninety (90%) percent of the moral impropriety that brings disrepute on leaders, relates to sexual impropriety, or infidelity in marriages or relationships. The writer is totally correct and right on point, because due to the need to conceal sexual improprieties, many more sins are committed, such as lying, conspiracy, stealing, and the like.

Therefore, I insist that people must consider the leader's worth based not only on his or her ability to do the job well but their ability to exercise moral character, strength, and integrity. The judgment of the leader based on their moral temperament will determine how committed he or she is for the long term, and how committed they are to the greater good of the people and the institutions they represent.

Therefore, Self-discipline as a criterion for national leadership is essential for service-oriented or servant leadership. Without a commitment to this core value in the government or the individual who holds public office, the result will be the disintegration of the trust of the people, and the erosion of the confidence that the people have placed in that administration.

Quoting from a Long hand-written note on May 14, 1934, by Judge Harry S. Truman, a former President of the United States asserted that:

> 'In reading the lives of great men, I found that the first victory they won was over themselves. Self-discipline with all of them came first.' (Harry S. Truman Presidential Library – President's Secretary's Files)

CHAPTER EIGHT

The Value Of Industry

This second core value, Industry, speaks to the recognition of ourselves, and the kind of people we have committed to becoming. Our two main industries, Tourism and Banking are service-oriented. Our most strategic location in this Western Hemisphere sets us up to cater to travelers from all around the World, and to service their needs, no matter how varying and complicated.

Whenever I travel, I have often met people from different countries around the world. It seems as if it is the dream of the majority of them to someday visit The Bahamas. For some of them, it seems almost a fantasy, a marvel, to encounter someone from a country, that almost everyone in the world wants to visit within their lifetime. For The Bahamas and for Bahamian people, it speaks volumes and is a good indication of the industriousness of our people, who are mostly dedicated to serving and pleasing the millions of visitors that come to our shores each year.

We make jobs and companies of services that seem nonsensical anywhere else in the world. From the multi-millionaire client that wants first-rate personal service by the hotel management; to the little girl who just wants to get her hair braided; to the child who is dying and who just wants to swim with the dolphins or the pigs; to the old European guest who wants to sit and look at the beautiful waters from the porch of their cottage; to the couple who want to get married bare feet overlooking the ocean; and to guests who return for their 'thirtieth year' to go fishing. These varied tasks that are requested by guests from all across the world, make the industriousness of the Bahamian people even more relevant if the country is to survive as a service-based economy.

The word Industry has many definitions but infers primarily to the 'application of skill, intelligence, diligence, ingenuity, cleverness or assiduity to whatever the designated task'. It further speaks to the 'systematic and habitual employment in some useful work, or profitable occupation, or a trade; especially in the production of the arts and manufactory'. The word also refers to the 'scholarly or diligent study of a subject'.

Some of the more animated words which are also used to describe the applications of Industry or Industrious are, 'to busy oneself in, to seize the opportunity, to rouse oneself, make haste, have hand in, trouble oneself about, zeal, vigilance, perseverance, earnestness, and devotion'.

When applying the meaning of the word Industry to national leaders and governance, it can apply both to the individual politician and the government as a whole. Persons who aspire for local political office and the high post of national leadership, should not be individuals who are lazy and idle. If we elect lazy and idle people to public office, we will have lazy and idle leaders. This substantiates my belief that political parties should not go looking for people to run for office, but instead, they should or may simply endorse people who are already working in their communities. When the political party machinery goes in search of persons to give a Nomination to because they have been a party loyalist, they end up selecting persons who are simply there for the ride, because the party machinery is behind them.

Individual Politician Productivity

Firstly, we must seek to identify within persons aspiring for public office, a determined career path. Even if the person is not presently employed in their career, there should be productivity that is visible, to determine their industriousness. The person who aspires for positions of national leadership must be diligent and industrious in whatever field he or she finds themselves. This not only refers to the elected official or politician, but to the civil servant, the diplomat, the senator, or whoever else is paid from the public purse.

Even the key personnel in governmental posts must be persons who do not subscribe to a slothful and lazy attitude and behaviour. I believe that the government must not measure the advancement of a person in the civil service on how long the person has been in that office, but whether that person is productive, industrious, and hardworking. We must begin to elevate our thinking as to how we determine who becomes the Director, or the Supervisor, or the Manager within the Civil Service.

I believe that the idea of 'political favours' and 'who you know' to continue to keep persons employed in the Public Service, must be dispensed with immediately. There is no justification for funding personal agendas, nepotism, and political 'cronyism' with the Public purse. It is simply Corruption. It would be just as if you stole the money from the Public Treasury and gave it away to your friends or supporters. National leaders must encourage industrious labour, in addition to the behaviour and the attitude of excellence within our service-based economy, in the public service, as well as in the private sector.

When identifying the attribute of 'Industry' in the politician, you must seek to identify what is his or her personal vision and commitment to industrious activities such as the Performing and Fine Arts, Culture, Junkanoo, Agriculture, Fisheries and Marine life, our abundant Natural Resources, Manufacturing, and the Environment. The laws and legislation which he or she proposes and supports in Parliament should encourage the proliferation of industries that lend to the long-term and sustainable development of the nation.

The distinction between economic activities versus economic development should be clearly distinguishable by the programmes the government encourages or into which they invest the nation's resources. Far too often the government is more interested in the activity of money changing hands, the flurry of what I call 'Day's work' for the purpose of political 'brownie' points, rather than more sustainable long-term projects, like farming, fishing, and natural resources industry projects.

The realization of genuine economic growth will happen when we invest in projects which can provide consistent growth over the medium to long-term. Sometimes, the projects which can provide such sustainability are not always those which are prestigious and appear urbane. Projects such as fruit and vegetable farming, fishing, and agricultural production, are always sustainable and should be encouraged to diversify the economy, bring long-term stability to small island communities, and cut down the import of food supplies into the country.

Additionally, the use of our abundant and inexhaustible Natural Resources like Sand, Aragonite, and Calcium Carbonate, should be nationalized and regulated to provide opportunities for sustained economic development; with manufacturing industries, in various locations throughout The Bahamas to provide sustainable high-paying industrial jobs. These types of industries, where the natural resources are free for residents doing business, will provide the level of funding to the government to eliminate the National Debt. We must place this as a priority if the economy is to be revived from the present level of economic depression.

Long-Term Development & National Development Plan Strategy

The concept of long-term development and nation-building can only be sustained through a National vision. This vision should embody an original set of plans, programmes, policies, and strategies to take the country forward into the next generation and beyond. Without vision or a clear set of goals that span beyond the next five years or the next general election; we, as a nation, will continue to 'mark' time, trying only to improve a situation for the immediate term and an administration's five-year tenure in office.

What we need, in the parameter of national life, is a long-term National Vision embodied in a National Development Plan, possibly with a 25 - 50-year plan. This vision should not be a vision of just a particular political group or class sector, but a consensus of people and divergent groups interested in the development of the entire Bahamas. This should include members of various political parties, private sector interests, and independent persons.

First, we must establish a National Development Plan Commission. They should have both independence and autonomy. Nevertheless, the government should provide key cooperation for the provision of vital data and funding for its work. The Commission could alternate Secretariat and its Chairman several times during the life of the Commission. The Commission should be able to finish its work within the period of three to four years, thus making recommendations to and for approval before a single term of an administration is completed.

Such a plan will be extensive to compile, as contributions should come from each local community, focusing on the vision of that particular community. These visionary ideas can come either from the community's local leadership or the Commission can go to each community and determine its need in conjunction with the local community's leadership. Having canvassed visions and views from these various sectors of the entire country, the National Development Plan Commission should then evaluate and incorporate the information gathered to develop the national vision, with details and strategies as to how and what it will take to accomplish the plan.

This National Development Plan Commission should have a very broad range of the national structure to evaluate and gather information for compiling a national plan. The plan should also include in its Mandate some of the following social building imperatives, namely, but not limited to:

1. Define who we are as a people, and what makes us unique, both culturally and spiritually, encompassing our mission and purpose as a nation.

2. Identify some of the impediments to good governance and recommendation towards the same; while evaluating the governmental system, and recommended changes (like Constitutional, Educational & Public Services Reforms; in addition to recommending mandatory National Service, as an imperative to strengthening the security forces and the defense of the borders.)

3. Identify industries and provide feasibility studies of projects which can be developed and sustained for the long term.

4. Identify strategies to reconstruct existing industries, create new industries, and identify fiscal mechanisms for future developments.

5. Identify and provide educational scholarships to train Bahamians to manage selected new industries.

6. Identify sources of financing for national educational goals of Bahamians relating thereto.

Once these mandates are accomplished, among others, the bi-partisan determination would be that these various projects and industries can be sought out in the future by both the private and public sectors. The objectives must then be, that whatever sector secures the designated industry or project, it takes into consideration the social, financial, environmental, moral, and spiritual implications, on the society and the nation as a whole. Every effort must work and be developed in cooperation and under the regulation of the National Development Commission guiding objectives.

Once the plan has been completed, a mass education process could then be undertaken to educate and encourage the nation and to familiarize them with the plan in detail and provide feedback. After the massive educational process has taken place with the relevant feedback, the National Vision would then go through Parliament for discussion, and then to a National referendum for public approval. This will give the Bahamian people the confidence that what they have planned and sanctioned in the referendum, is truly a bi-partisan plan that will benefit future generations of Bahamians.

Finally, this National Development Plan is not a matter for foreign consultants. Outside consultants or resources can only be utilized if the need for the evaluation and analysis of technical data is beyond the resources of Bahamian companies. While that could be determined at the time, every effort must be made to employ the resources of Bahamians both inside and outside the country. Bahamians should wholly participate and contribute to the gathering and compilation of this information. I believe that there is an abundance of talented and qualified Bahamians available, taking into consideration those who are now living abroad, to contribute to this wholly 'authentic' Bahamian vision. Since this will benefit Bahamians for generations to come, all Bahamians, no matter where they are presently living, should contribute to this Bahamas National Development Plan.

Economic Activity

The encouragement of Industry is also reflected by the government agencies giving quick service and response to Bahamians, or the foreigner who chooses to make investments in the local economy. When a businessperson invests in a business and makes an application for various licenses, the relevant government agency has an obligation to attend with diligence to that application, and subsequently inform that individual or group concerning its approval or non-approval, in a timely and efficient manner.

Moreover, an application for basic utility services such as telephone, electricity, and licenses – whether for business, shop or occupancy, should not be matters that create havoc and financial distress in the process of opening a business. There are many reported stories of licenses taking months, and even years, for approvals. This is somewhat indicative of the fact that because there is no clear-cut policies and national vision, the application for these licenses are most times approved, or not approved based on political considerations.

In many instances, Bahamian businesspersons are frustrated by direct government bureaucracy, resulting in the loss of income and the loss of opportunities. We have seen, in many cases, the frustration of Bahamians involved in industries such as manufacturing, agriculture, fisheries, and crafts, among others. These frustrations have been directly attributed to the government's lack of cooperation, encouragement, and support. When more tax concessions are made available to the foreign investor than to the Bahamian investor, people are prone to wonder whether the government has any commitment towards the development of local industries or businesses actually owned by the ordinary Bahamian and not directly owned by politicians, their political party, and their family, friends or lovers.

While the FNM Ingraham administration, in their last term in office (2007 - 2012), said that they were attempting to correct some of the anomalies orchestrated by the former Christie administration (2002 - 2007); much of their activities were lip service and lacked real 'teeth' when it came to local development and real prosperity for the average Bahamian, not politically connected. Same circus, just different players!

Many Bahamians have been bound to suffer economic persecutions at the hand of the government of the day, both FNM and PLP. It appears that the Bahamian people have to wait until 'their party' gets elected, in order to get something done. And the reverse is also true: whenever 'your government' or 'your party' loses the elections – like the Bahamian vernacular says – in many instances, 'Dog eat your lunch!'

The PLP and FNM administrations have few fundamental differences when it comes to providing opportunities for the ordinary Bahamian, without prejudice. It seems that the philosophy of both political parties has melted down into the same one pot, which materializes in actuality as this: If you are not politically connected, and you need a loan approval or a project approval via the quasi-government agencies, you may, and can encounter an inconceivable long wait or turn around, before any consideration is given.

In many cases, politicians, and sometimes high-ranking officials in some developmental agencies like The Bahamas Development Bank (BDB) and Bahamas Agricultural and Industrial Corporation (BAIC), actually take projects submitted by talented Bahamians, and fund them for their own friends and families, leaving the politically 'unconnected' person, without any economic opportunities, except to go find another job.

And in this regard, persons have little to no recourse against the government's 'malfeasance'. These kinds of activities speak to the need for an Ombudsman office and an Independent Consumer Protection Agency for the ordinary citizen to get recourse or compensation for the defraud of their intellectual property by the government of the day.

Despite a three to four-page statement in Parliament outlining the introduction of a proposed 'Code of Ethics' for Parliamentarians early in the Christie Administration's first term in 2002; the exchange of monies under the table and kickbacks was still the 'order of the day'. As we have observed, some elected officials were running their own schemes for financial gain in many government projects, which went virtually unrestrained by then Prime Minister Perry Christie, even in his last 2012-2017 term; and others are following suit in the present FNM Administration. The actual Code of Conduct never materialized after that initial statement in 2002 – despite activists in the nation calling for the Freedom of Information Act to mitigate against corruption, even up to the present day in 2020. It appears no government, including this Minnis

Administration is prepared to make available the people's business to the people via the Freedom of Information Act.

Prime Minister Hon. Perry Christie & Cabinet Heading to Parliament to present Annual Budget during 2012-2017 Term.

Labour Laws and Trade Unions

Another inference, to the encouragement of Industry, is the promotion and the upkeep of labour laws, as they relate to the protection of workers' Constitutional rights, and the protection of the Trade Union Movement's right to exist. It is necessary for the government to make a commitment to the promotion of excellence and high ethics in the workplace by fostering good relations with the labour industry and recommending that unions and their members maintain a standard of excellence second to none. This can only be encouraged when the laws are the same for all levels of workers in all categories of industries.

It appears that the recognition of unions is encouraged and enforced, such as the Hotel industry and other industries for blue-collar workers, while associations for workers like bankers and other white-collar jobs are at times frustrated. Although Recognition takes place by the Ministry of Labour, there are times that some companies' management are slow to recognize these unions, and the government seems ill-equipped or lack the political will to enforce this Recognition Status upon various company management.

It is recommended that when the management of these institutions flagrantly violate the labour laws of The Bahamas and continue to do so for extended periods, they should be penalized, or sanctions should be levied against them. This is not only in reference to Bahamian institutions, but foreign companies doing business in The Bahamas too. Foreign investors seem to get off 'scot-free' with these abuses, while some Bahamian businesses are penalized.

The government must be fair when enforcing certain recognition of unions while allowing others to be slow in implementation. Whether the employee makes one hundred dollars a week or one thousand dollars a week, each has a right, according to the Constitution of The Bahamas, to the 'freedom of association' of his or her choosing. This fundamental right must be guaranteed and protected by those chosen to be the servants of the people.

Investment in Education

The investment in Education by any administration for its citizens, particularly the young, is also indicative of being Industrious. In addition to the provision of public education, a government must submit a great chunk of its budget to post-high school, tertiary level education, and vocational and technical training; in order to train individuals to maintain the country's industries and provide trained professionals to facilitate the country's workforce.

While it might be considered an additional burden on the government's resources, I wish to suggest that we implement a mandatory one-year post-high school vocational or technical training or some form of academic training in tertiary level education for every high school graduate. So, I am suggesting that the government pay for one-year additional training of high school graduates. The local colleges can design a one-year training, and the students can continue their education beyond this point.

In addition to this option, the BCP agenda to restructure the Public-School curriculum will also remedy this need for tertiary training, by facilitating that children receive career training before they leave high school.

In fact, what I believe is also necessary, is the reconstruction of the government's Scholarship Guaranteed Loan program to a Scholarship Grant program, in which the students are bonded to their area of training for the number of years the government pays their college expenses. The government should be investing more money into Education. Double the Scholarship budget and make the recipients accountable for repayment by a commitment to the National Youth Service program, which will entail investing their time in the development of the country following graduation from Tertiary Education.

This will necessitate that the recipients be committed to returning home and building the country. This may be possible only if we re-consider how we govern the country; so that students obtaining an education abroad can return home to higher-paying jobs in their fields. This investment in Education could revitalize the economy, through training in non-traditional industries for the country's workforce into the future. Even if this matter of free education for all high school graduates is not a continuous investment, we can make this a policy for a number of years, until we have accomplished a higher level of training for the next generation.

The World Bank - World Development Report /1998-99 entitled 'The Power and Reach of Knowledge in Total Factor Productivity (TFP)' gave some enlightening statistics for developing countries about Investments in the Education of its people in its relation to Economic growth.

The Report listed three things essential for Economic growth:

1. Developing unexploited land (e.g. Crown Land)
2. Accumulating physical capital – infrastructure, and
3. Educating the population

While the report lists Education as the third factor in realizing economic growth, it recognizes Education as the key element in what they term 'an investment in human capital'. The report indicates that investing in human capital includes 'Educating people and institutions to enhance capacity and capability to absorb and use knowledge'. It notes that, while physical and human capital accounts for economic growth, 'knowledge increases the part of growth that cannot be explained'.

In response to this World Bank Report, the question was posed as to 'whether our limited ability to fully account for knowledge in growth diminishes its importance for future development?'

As British Economist Alfred Marshall emphasized in the next statement, that it will certainly not.

> 'While nature shows a tendency to diminish returns, man shows a tendency to increase returns. Knowledge is our most powerful engine of productivity; it enables us to subdue nature and satisfies our wants.'

This is corroborated in Nelson Mandela's famous statement that says, 'Education is the most powerful tool we can use to change the World.'

The report supports the action that successful development thus entails more than investment in physical capital, which is infrastructure. It also entails acquiring and using knowledge and closing the gap in knowledge. Developing countries have to position themselves to take advantage of opportunities that minimize risks by adopting effective strategies for acquiring and using knowledge.

These three main strategies include:

1. Acquiring and adapting global knowledge - and creating knowledge locally,
2. Investing in human capital to increase the ability to absorb and use knowledge,
3. Investing in technology to facilitate both the acquisition and the absorption of knowledge.

We cannot access new technology unless we invest in education. New technology speeds demand for education and obtaining knowledge. (Information garnered from the World Bank Report 1998-99)

Education and Discipline in Schools

While on the topic of Education, let's discuss the idea of the removal of Corporal punishment in the Educational system in the nation.

What is really going on in our educational institutions? Are the children now 'running' the schools regarding this? At whose feet do I lay the blame for this unrighteous activity?

Primarily the State, through the Educational system by the removal of corporal punishment from the classroom, out of the hands of the Educator who is responsible for teaching. Teaching and discipline should go hand in hand. Additionally, every single one of us is to blame and should be held accountable at some level of responsibility. I will articulate this later in the chapter.

Based on the Preamble commitment, the children of The Bahamas belongs to God. So, while parents have been given the privilege of bearing and rearing them, they are actually part of the covenant made by our founding fathers of the nation.

Contrary to what you might think, God has our children's best interest at heart and is more interested in the development of them than any other kind of national development. As we have observed, God had no problem giving us Majority Rule and Independence in return for the children of the nation. If he could influence the children, He would have given us anything. Quite like the story of Abraham, God trusted Abraham and kept no secrets from Abraham because He believed that Abraham would tell his children and command them to serve God, to keep the way of the Lord (See Genesis 18:19). This was and is important to God as to how we pass down our values to the next generation.

If you look at most major world religions, even so-called Cults, it is always about the children. Children are about the future. The children determine whether there will be a future.

In concurrence, the Muslim Prophet Khalil Gibran said in one of his writings:

> "Your children are not your children, they are the sons and daughters of life longing for itself. They come through you, but not from you. And though they are with you, they do not belong to you. You may give them your love, but not your thoughts, for they have their own thoughts. You may house their bodies, but not their souls; for their souls dwell in the house of Tomorrow."

In furtherance to the earlier suggestion, God does not take and has not taken lightly, our promise to give Him the children of The

Bahamas, and the generations that follow, in exchange for Majority Rule and Statehood, so that we could determine our own destiny for perpetuity. Many of those persons who prayed those prayers have all but died out and cannot articulate to us what they promised. But I have been given the responsibility to articulate the essence of that promise and the responsibility of that promise on their behalf.

The basic thrust of this message is that God wants the children back. His ability to influence the lives of our children by righteous public policy in Education. Our national behaviour and deportment, whether we are parents, teachers, school or educational administrators, the government, the church, and national leaders, must speak to the responsibility of that agenda, which is to secure the children of this nation and the future of this nation for the glory of God. There is a chosen destiny of this great nation, and it is wrapped up in the children. And if we fail to secure that destiny by our recklessness, we place both our children and our future in jeopardy.

According to what I am aware, we have a problem in the country because we have not properly articulated to our children who they are. We have left them to figure it out for themselves. What is happening in the nation among the youth is because we have refused to give the nation's children back to God over the years; and now we are losing them to evil things such as criminal activity, drugs, gang violence, and even suicide and premature death. Your children are not your children if they are not under your control and influence. And may I bring some news home to some of you, just look at the news, we are losing them daily. We must do something urgently if we are going to secure the next generation of Bahamian children. I am not saying that all is lost, but, as a nation, we must make a concerted effort to facilitate this promise, and save the children, the next generation.

The State does not bear children, it is the Parents who bear them, and they must be the first to take responsibility regarding discipling their children; as this is the plan of God, for parents to transfer good values and proper instructions to the next generation. However, secondly, the school system and in particular, teachers and administrators responsible for Corporal Punishment must carefully and concisely articulate to children what must be done, when they err; and it must be administered by authority figures in a most effective and responsible way. Adversely, it is to be considered that just like any other crimes against a person, parents, or person/s in authority in the school system, who commit crimes against children should be subjected to the penalty or penalties related to the crime. Cruelty to children cannot be tolerated, whether at home or at school.

However, God's word admonishes that we are not to spare the rod or spoil the child. Moreover, Proverbs 22:15 says; 'Foolishness is bound in the heart of a child, but the rod of correction shall drive it far from him.' We should not be selective about what part of God's word we will adhere to when it is convenient for us regarding this matter.

Should We Blame the Government?

As an example, one child dies less than an hour after he was disciplined by a teacher in a public school. The child had Sudden Death Syndrome, even though his condition was not known by the teacher. Another child is caned in a private school, and the mother brings the matter to the attention of the nation that the child was brutalized. In the latter case, the disciplinarian might have been somewhat harsh, but if the child was disciplined at home, maybe he might not have needed to be disciplined at school. These and other circumstances gave way to one of the most foolish responses by our government in the turn of the 21st Century in the early 2000s.

In the first case, after the Attorney General initiated proceedings to put the teacher on trial for criminal negligence in the death of the first child, the Ministry of Education sent down a memo mandating teachers not to discipline, or touch 'other people's children.' Following up on that, the school children seemed to have gotten the impression that they could not be disciplined, reprimanded, or punished by the teachers. Some children have and are still now taking control of the classroom by their many disruptions, and are wreaking havoc on the entire educational system, not only in the government schools but in some instances, in some private and church-operated schools.

As I considered the Ministry of Education course of action in the matter of the removal of Corporal Punishment – at the onset of these decisions – I contacted the Ministry to ascertain what their official position was regarding these unfortunate incidences. An official at the Ministry of Education informed me at the time, that the government had made a determination to suspend discipline by all teachers, except by administrative personnel, specifically assigned to administer discipline and corporal punishment. The Ministry in turn drafted two manuals, one for Teachers and Administrators, and another one for students called Rule /Procedures for Creating Safe Schools. These two manuals were given to me for my information and perusal.

These manuals were distributed to all public-school administrators, as well as private and church-operated schools, as rules for discipline. This mandate by the Ministry of Education covered all public schools and encouraged private schools to either create and submit a manual of their school's disciplinary process to the Ministry of Education or implement the ministry's procedures.

I was somewhat disturbed that some church-operated schools have followed suit and have tailored their own manual to suit the Ministry of Education procedures. Although the Ministry of Education manuals provide some recommendations that are commendable, the spirit of the letter does not go far enough to empower teachers to maintain authority and order in their classroom in all situations. This decision gave cause for several concerns.

My first concern is that the government of The Bahamas has taken away the right of the teacher to discipline in their classroom, and then asks the teacher to control a classroom of thirty or more students and produce adequate grades. How do you enforce learning in an environment where you do not have full control? I cry shame on the FNM government for enforcing this debacle, and I cry shame on the PLP administration for not changing it back then.

It was reported to me around 2011, that the FNM government was likely to sign on to a resolution advocating the total abolition of corporal punishment in the country in all settings, encouraged by a United Nations Convention that was due to be signed at the UN Office in Geneva Switzerland later that month. This was brought to my attention by a very concerned primary school Principal, who was very much aware that without corporal punishment in the school setting, they may not be able to properly manage the school, due to the daily havoc wreaked by disruptive students.

As a nation, we must be cautious not to comply with every recommendation brought forth by 'Liberal, Secular, New-Age Agnostics'. Their recommendations will not assist us to produce godly children. Their recommendations seem to be more suited for fostering disorderly, undisciplined children, who defy order and authority. The Bible admonishes that we should not withhold correction from a child:

Withhold not correction from the child: for if thou beat him with the rod, he shall not die. Thou shalt beat him with the rod, and shalt deliver his soul from hell. Proverbs 23:13-14

My second concern is for the church-operated and charter schools which have complied with this unrighteous plot. Those who have done so should be ashamed of themselves too. I wish to admonish Church-school administrators, to do what you have to do to produce good, productive, and God-fearing children. God is holding you accountable and is depending on you now. Don't worry or concern yourself about what the government is doing or not doing. As a Christian educator, you must push your responsibility even further, with the standards of the Christian church being your primary focus and resolve.

Solomon further offers instructions in Proverbs 22 verse 6 that encourage parents and teachers to, 'Train up a child in the way he should go, because when he becomes older, he will not depart from his training'. And further confirms this in verse 15 when it says that 'Although foolishness abounds in the heart of a child, the rod of correction will soon drive it away'.

The rod or the cane, not academic 'Demerits' will keep a child out of trouble and out of prison. We must endeavour to prepare our children for Heaven and keep them out of Hell. That should be the responsibility of parents, teachers, and administrators towards Bahamian children. The Fox Hill Prison is crowded with 'children' who were too 'good' to get a caning. If we don't discipline (CANE) them now as children, we will have to (CAGE) them later, as adults. We will have to make a decision as to which one we will do.

Another admonition to Church schools, if parents want to take their children out of your school, let them take them out, and keep their trouble. At some point, we must stand up and be Christian educators. We must stand for something or we will fall for anything... And that's what we are doing now, falling for anything! And the state of young people in the country, and the havoc that is being reeked, is evident.

Are the Teachers to Blame?

I must place some responsibility on teachers too. While it seems that their hands are being tied, teachers must push their responsibility to the very limit. Based on the manuals given to the administrators and teachers, teachers must do everything possible to maintain control in their classes. Teachers do have some authority in their classrooms, little though it may be and frustrating though it is. Teachers must take the little responsibility given them in the manual and push it to the very limit.

All teachers, including those belonging to The Bahamas Union of Teachers (BUT), must also band together and make Public School Administrators and Ministry of Education officials accountable to them too if they are to produce good grades and students who are socially and academically prepared. Sometimes, I am convinced that the actions of the executives of the BUT are simply about securing benefits, like raises and insurances for teachers, versus standards that give them more autonomy in their classroom. I believe if the BUT would take a stronger stand in this regard, the people of the country would stand with them.

Many teachers are frustrated, and the children are having a field day in both government and private schools because they know the 'limits' of the teacher's authority. No wonder so many teachers are leaving the profession for other careers. I have taken the opportunity in recent times to assist friends of mine who are teachers to mark test papers. I am appalled at the level to which some children are responding on these tests. Their level of concentration is totally unacceptable. What is happening in the classrooms?

The government must immediately rescind this ridiculous action of removing corporal punishment and discipline from the classroom environment. If not, we may lose an entire generation. All teachers must be given the authority to discipline students under their authority and in their classrooms. I do not advocate violence against any student, but I simply advocate that children must be forced to respect those who must lead and teach them. And if they are disorderly in the classroom, the teacher should have the right to discipline them in the classroom.

A famous quote from African American Frederick Douglas suggests that we must do something now, as it stated:

'It is easier to build strong children, than to mend broken men.'

Strong Instructions to Parents

I must place much responsibility on parents who have left their children to be brought up by the television and the extremely distracting technology of the day. Everybody has become so busy trying to make a living, that they have forgotten whose futures they are working to secure. Does it make any sense, if they leave the valuable item to be destroyed by the vices, while they are trying to provide for it? We need to return to traditional values first and make certain that someone is at home when the children return from school, to assist in whatever is necessary. Or the community must provide more after-school programs, in communities close to home, for availability to parents.

Regarding media and television, entertainment, music, and violence emanating from American television have brought more negative vibes into our culture and have proven very destructive to the children and teenagers in our country. As a former member of one of the Civilian / Police Consultative Committees in Nassau, I was told that the gang culture is a learned behaviour from American television. Young boys are being preoccupied with violence and gang activities, and some parents are unaware that their children are involved in drinking alcohol, and smoking marijuana and cigarettes, sometimes right in their homes.

Many of our young girls and indeed some adult women are walking around practically naked on the streets. Parents are purchasing, and in many cases, allowing their young teenage girls to purchase and dress in highly provocative outfits. Some of our young children are being clothed in items that will turn a grown man's head, with the parents giving the children the impression that they look 'pretty and sexy'.

Meanwhile, we comfort ourselves because everybody else is wearing it, it must be okay. But children should not be sexy, it is an adult theme. No wonder the children cannot keep their minds on their school lessons: they are being influenced by adult themes far too early. This is wrong, and it is against what God has determined for us and our children.

Several things have to be done in regard to television and entertainment in the country.

Firstly, parents need to teach acceptable standards to their children regarding what to watch and to take the responsibility for removing despicable entertainment from their homes. They need to begin to pay more attention to their children. The children are internalizing the values they see on television and producing their own standards as they grow. There has to be some parental figure responsible to supervise: the children's homework, what they are watching, who their friends are, and where they are going after school. Is this not important for parents?

Secondly, the government's Films and Plays Control Board needs to be more vigilant and actually 'get to work' to remove some of these negative television stations off the local cable networks and make those stations 'pay per view' channels. But with the proliferation of smartphones, being available to children as young as ten years old, parents are perplexed as to how to manage what their children watch.

Thirdly, the proliferation of 'reality television' has heightened the exposure to negative stereotyping and adulterous behavior. It is now available for all to admire and for young people to emulate.

- The ratings for movies have to be enforced

- Programming has to be properly screened before they are actually shown in public theatres

- The standard for the level of ratings must be lifted to accommodate what children and young people are allowed to see.

- Many of these adult themes are often included in Family and General Audience movies. Hollywood's rating standards are not considering our Bahamian children, so we must do it ourselves.

In closing this chapter on Industry, the encouragement and protection of industrious activity amongst the citizenry must be part and parcel of the thinking of the individuals who lead, as they are responsible to regulate and exercise stewardship over the nation's resources. This position of responsibility requires faithfulness in stewardship, which is an important attribute of moral leadership.

CHAPTER NINE

The Value Of Loyalty

The third core value is Loyalty. Why was it necessary to include this as relevant to good governance? Webster's Dictionary defines loyalty simply as 'Faithfulness'.

Loyalty implies a 'faithful adherence to one's promise, to one's oath or to one's word of honour'. Roger's 21st Century Thesaurus gives such additional words for loyalty as 'obedience, observance, compliance, respect, duty, honour, submission, subservience, allegiance, homage and devotion'.

Let us examine the word Loyalty in reference to governance and patriotism. The word patriotism simply suggests the 'love and support of one's own country'. The thesaurus in giving alternatives to the word patriotism gives such words as 'philanthropic, humanitarian, benevolence, altruistic, public-spirited, civic-minded and nationalism'. If these words suggest loyalty, then love for the nation should take precedence over many things including partisan political agendas. It means Country first – before Party politics. So, to be loyal, and to adhere to this core value means to be a Nationalist.

With the insertion of this core value, the founders intended to create a community of Nationalists.

Patriotism & Foreign Sovereignty

When you are loyal or exhibit loyalty to a country, this means that your 'support for the country is based on your love for the country, and the desire to see the further growth, development, prosperity, and longevity of the nation'.

The commitment to Loyalty is deeply embedded in a concern for the country that surpasses selfish, personal goals, ambitions, and agendas. So, the reverse is also true, that expression of disloyalty towards the nation will create instability, unrest, or the lack of prosperity for the country. These sometimes can also be considered acts of Treason.

Such acts of Treason to be considered may be related to the following:

- The exchange of confidential and privileged information of the government of The Bahamas, to the agents of another government without lawful and proper authority of the Cabinet of The Bahamas

- Providing information and assistance to another country to subvert any legitimate undertaking of the Bahamian government. These acts can only be rendered by Cabinet members, former Cabinet members, and/or high-ranking civil servants, based on the sensitivity of information to which they have access.

- Acting on behalf of a foreign sovereignty, and attempting to interfere with or subvert the legitimate processes of a General Election

- Lending of assistance to any other foreign government in an effort to add its undue influence, against the legitimate operations of the government of The Bahamas

This does not imply that Bahamians cannot enlist the assistance of professionals of other countries to assist their work or their plight in campaigning for general elections. However, persons offering for national leadership should be vigilant and mindful, not to overstep their bounds, in seeking resources or inviting interference of other foreign sovereignties within the internal operations of our Sovereignty.

It is my opinion, that the only justification for the possible enlistment of another government or Sovereignty would be if good governance within The Bahamas has deteriorated to such a degree, that it is clear that the will of the Bahamian people is being subverted, and the re-establishment of the 'true will' of the Bahamian people is necessary.

Therefore, appropriate measures should be taken by the appropriate citizens or operatives of opposition political parties, to enlist the assistance of another sovereignty to provide resources and expertise, in order to assist the successful campaign for the removal of such an administration from office via legitimate general elections.

In my opinion, there is never an appropriate measure for the unlawful 'Overthrow', 'Coup' or the 'Deposing' of any administration, as these measures do more harm, than good towards the future security of the nation. In my best estimation, while corruption is deplorable, the avenues of legitimate elections are always the best methods to render feasible results.

I am always minded regarding The Bahamas' ongoing relationship with the United States of America, and the role they play, and the influence they may have exerted in General Elections in The Bahamas. While during each administration, the United States Embassy provides tremendous cooperation and involvement in the local affairs of The Bahamas, we also observe their gentle diplomacy during General Elections. While they admit that they do not interfere, it is clear that they make it a matter of urgency to connect or speak with leaders of all political parties vying for elections; although, their regard seems to be more favourable towards the Free National Movement, and it sometimes would appear that they provide logistical and assistance to ensure the FNM advantage.

However, while we appreciate their friendship, and at times expect their assistance, the lines of our Sovereignty as a nation must not be blurred. The Bahamas is not a state or a territory of the United States and should not be considered as such by either the U.S. government or the people of The Bahamas. As the United States is our closest neighbor to the north, we should maintain cordial relations, as our borders provide mutual grounds for continued cooperation, as we have done in the past.

However, the bigger concern for further infringement on The Bahamas' sovereignty is our rapidly growing ties with the communist People's Republic of China, as evidenced by multiple economic investments by China state agencies like China EXIM Bank, and the China State Construction Corporation. My greater concern is what appears to be their cozy relationship with the successive FNM and PLP Administrations; and how far they seem prepared to go to create deeper influence in the nation, and their direct interference in General Elections.

I share this concern with thousands of Bahamians who believe that if this rate of aggressive relations with the People Republic of China is not abated soon, the Bahamian State is headed for a complete annexation by China. This concern can result in a major confrontation between the United States and China over who gets the biggest control over The Bahamas and its territory and the borders we share with the United States.

Over the past twenty to twenty-five years, I am convinced that Bahamian politicians on both sides of the political divide have been short-sighted by providing the level of direct influence into The Bahamas by the People's Republic of China; and have lost view of the determination of the founding fathers for each government to maintain control of the Sovereignty of The Bahamas at all cost.

The greed of Bahamian politicians has ensured the high level of the Chinese government's involvement. The Chinese hefty economic infiltration, their aggressive stance for control, along with their bullying tactics; have now placed the Bahamian economy and the government in dire straits, with pressure being continually exerted by their grave demands. This is a far cry to the Americans' gentler diplomacy, and whose expertise at lobbying, provide a far softer stance for their determination for a share of the economic opportunities in The Bahamas.

Economic Loyalty

As we consider the matter of economic loyalty, I believe that the transfer of the wealth of the country by public officials and private businesses to another country infers a level of disloyalty. This clearly can be applied when the motives for transferring the money are for the sole benefit of securing the economic future for oneself and one's family; perhaps for an escape to that country, should The Bahamas become economically unstable or suffer a dramatic economic slowdown.

While I am not speaking specifically to stealing and corruption by politicians, I am considering the general practice of stockpiling Bahamian currency in another place, without intentions of returning it. This alone ultimately results in economic slowdown and instability in Foreign reserves, and the economy in general. However, this action by public officials, when due to corruption, must be considered treasonous, as they betray the public trust, and use public office for personal gain, in addition to placing the economy at risk.

One of our country's leading economists estimated that as of November 2001, more than one billion dollars of Bahamian currency were in banks in the United States, United Kingdom, and Canada. This sum represented the entire budget allocation of The Bahamas government for the year 2001. Since that time, the figures may have increased significantly, due to a 2015 Report by the International Consortium of Investigative Journalists, that billions of dollars are present in European banks, and in particular Switzerland; with one bank reporting that at least fifty-five Bahamian passport holders have billions of dollars stocked in its bank in Europe.

The present dilemma with the contraction of the Bahamian economy makes it imperative for the return of revenues belonging to Bahamian citizens in other banks across the world, particularly those illegally acquired through corruption from elected public officials or high-ranking civil servants. The return or repatriation of such funds would do well to help rejuvenate and revive the Bahamian economy and increase the Gross Domestic Product.

This concern that we have is the identical concern of the United States administration, the government of Britain, and the G-20 countries, who are seeking to outlaw and disband tax shelters and havens like The Bahamas (which now houses hundreds of billions of American dollars and Euros, owned by Americans citizens and other citizens attempting to evade and avoid taxation by their prospective governments).

Tax Haven Status and Blacklisting

However, I believe that the time has come to discuss The Bahamas' status as a Tax Haven, and how we should go forward as a nation. Presently, the discussion of complying with the OECD requirements, and providing more regulations, has presented the government of the day with a dilemma. We have been here before, and yet the government is still attempting to deal with the problem the way it has always been done. What is the purpose of more regulations in an industry that actually needs to be restructured entirely? Are we not tired of sitting like a frog in a boiling pot, in regards to this matter?

I am of the opinion that The Bahamas need not wait for the G-20 nations' toolbox of 'counter-measures' against tax regimes like The Bahamas, to take effect and suffer the consequences. The political directorate must be proactive, and begin immediately the process of restructuring, and investigating other models of financial frameworks, that will provide us with an industry that is workable and admirable.

The Bahamas, as a Tax-haven and Tax-shelter, was constructed long before our time in modern Bahamian politics, and I believe that the time has come to dismantle the machinery that supports 'Tax Evasion and Tax Avoidance' in our Christian nation. Paying taxes is a part of life, as it was in Jesus' day when He admonished His own disciples to 'Render to Caesar' the things that are Caesar's. He was referring to taxes. It is clear though, that within the framework of running a government, taxes are important to sustaining the government's operation.

I think it is unconscionable though, for us to allow persons who have sometimes stolen monies or cheated poor people in their own countries, to run to The Bahamas to receive protection from the law or evade taxes from their home countries. While I am no expert in these matters, the banking industry that produces fifteen (15%) percent of the nation's Gross Domestic Product (GDP) should warrant the 'putting together of all heads', to come up with a plausible framework for the re-making of our banking sector.

The Bahamas is in a most strategic location to provide opportunities for off-shore banking activities from the United States with multi-national companies to do business considered legal, within the framework of the OECD and the G-20 countries' Global Forum on Transparency and Exchange of Information on Tax Purposes. While The Bahamas has signed almost thirty (30) Tax Information Exchange Agreement (TIEA) for compliance, since the Global Forum restructured in 2009, the restructuring of the banking sector still requires 'modification' to match the core values that should be inherent in the new style of righteous governance slated for a 'restructured' environment in The Bahamas.

In addition to a money management platform, the exploration of other kinds of commerce may provide the possibility of other meaningful streams of income for the nation. This would allow The Bahamas to restructure the whole industry and change the discussion of our offshore 'Bank Secrecy' and 'Tax Haven' sector. New types of legal businesses would allow the government of The Bahamas to continue to maintain its Sovereignty while doing business in a globalized environment in a manner that is more advantageous for Bahamians too. It may be that this present dilemma may force us to reconsider the real diversification of our economy, and the empowerment of the majority of Bahamians. The latter has been suggested and forecasted for many years but never delivered.

Notwithstanding the need to continue with some level of offshore banking, I am of the opinion, that if The Bahamas is going to be hosting, storing, and hiding millions, possibly billions, of dollars of 'other people's money', we should be able to get more substantial benefits, than just a few 'Bank' jobs. The fact that there is no Capital Gains Tax or Income tax for foreign persons doing business in The Bahamas, poses a problem for any meaningful resolution in this discussion for the empowerment of Bahamians. The fact that the investor is not paying taxes where they came from and is not providing a significant contribution to more substantial economic development to The Bahamas, provides a fundamental concern in my mind. There must be some level of fiduciary accountability and responsibility, in regards to the person or multi-national corporation benefiting from the management of their funds by this jurisdiction.

Therefore, if the sector is to remain in its present framework, I believe the time has come that we bring the money that is considered 'Under the Table' to the 'Top of the Table'. I would like to see this off-shore financial sector, with its funds stored away, opened up to accommodate more local investments and loans to Bahamian businesses. This will increase the Gross Domestic Product and empower many more Bahamian businesses at the same time.

I am certain as we go forward, that political will and moral leadership is necessary if development into the future comes packaged with the level of transparency and accountability promised, and yet denied to the Bahamian populace, by both the FNM and PLP administrations. The next generation of Bahamian leadership must require that the sustainable development of our country in the future is based on honesty and goodwill – reflected to all the people of the World – as we continue to invite, attract and motivate people to come to The Bahamas to enjoy the bounties of our Tourism industry and Banking sector.

Personal Loyalty

Individuals who seek national leadership should be persons of character who keep their promises. An old proverb says, 'Your word is your bond'. It simply means that when a person says that he or she will do something, he or she will do their best to live up to that promise or oath. A person who aspires for national leadership cannot be a person who promises and refuses to honour their word when it is within their power to do so.

There are too many elected persons who dishonour their campaign promises. It becomes clear once they are elected, that they have intentionally lied to the electorate, and have no intention of fulfilling their campaign promises. We must lift up a standard in the country where politicians are held accountable for what they promise to do. The concept of recalling Members of Parliament on the grounds of 'lying' or 'failing to keep their promises' must be taken under immediate advisement by the Bahamian people.

Many times, politicians are elected based on promises that are totally deceptive and false; promises they know they cannot and will not be able to fulfill. It means that they were elected under false pretenses. This is considered in the business world to be 'fraud'. It does a disservice to the opposing candidate and the electorate. Legislation must be placed before the Parliament for the recall of politicians who break their promises.

We must seek to examine a person's life outside the realm of politics to ascertain whether he or she is qualified to lead. When seeking to determine who is a suitable candidate, we must ascertain if the person has been faithful on their job or faithful in their vocation. We must know whether he or she is a person committed to completing the task he has been paid to do; or whether his or her business dealings are exemplary or questionable. It does not mean that there will not be any complaint about the person, but it should be that the majority of their dealings have been above reproach. I believe that a person's intention must be to do the right thing and is a key principle of their actions in all situations.

When the biblical writer spoke of persons desiring the office of leadership, he was unyielding in his wish that they should be of good reputation with God and man. While the Apostle Paul spoke about Church leadership, the Preamble encourages us as Bahamians to identify that same core value as relevant, for persons aspiring for leadership within the nation. While we should not subscribe to gossip and witch hunts, if evidence is presented concerning a person aspiring for leadership, it is our duty to at least question and examines the allegations, before proceeding with the confirmation of such a candidate. This is why I believe that institutions like an Electoral Commission should be enacted by law to examine candidates before a nomination is agreed upon. The media should also take a greater role in helping to examine and put under scrutiny, persons coming forward for national leadership.

Family Faithfulness

The area of Marriage and family is a very important aspect of exemplary leadership. There are two key areas of faithfulness, within the context of marriage and family, which are essential when examining qualifications for leadership and which are supported by biblical principles. The two areas are the love and support of the family financially, and fidelity to one's spouse. The Bible calls a man an infidel if he does not support his children and family. Who are we to say less?

A man who wants to be a leader must support his children, whether they live in his house or not. Fathering children, whether by your wife or some other woman, obligates a man to care for those children until they become of age. Too often in Bahamian society national leaders have fathered children by more than one woman and then refused to support the children because they do not live in their household. There should be no excuse for not providing adequate sustenance to children born to responsible adults in The Bahamas.

I do not agree with, nor condone the practice of children being born outside of marriage. Nevertheless, the children are not responsible for being born, so they must be supported by their parents no matter the circumstances of their parents' relationship. The children must be fed. The government must enforce, where necessary, a suitable standard of maintenance for the children of The Bahamas. It will ensure that if 'men and women' are made fully accountable for their actions, they will seek to be more responsible.

Further to that, persons who aspire to national leadership should not be persons who have children with many different partners. If we are seeking to hold a standard that is acceptable for the country to emulate, we must seek to uphold the ideal.

What is the ideal in this situation, you may ask? God's ideal is marriage, and children in the same home. However, since we have perverted the ideal standard in this 'supposed to be' Christian nation, then we must now set a standard which at least represents decency and an acceptable level of moral leadership. The basic foundation of the family structure is Marriage. God's ideal for Marriage is not marriage as an end unto itself, but a loving, Christian relationship where the wife is loved and the husband is respected. The ideal family life for persons aspiring to leadership should be a person whose family life is loving and produces an environment for good emulation by others in the country.

An example of what should not be acceptable for genuine leadership is a couple living in the same house, but who are in an open marriage; something we know is very real here in The Bahamas. This activity that permits each spouse to wander into the life and bed of other people, which happens in both heterosexual and bi-sexual relationships and is inconsistent with faithfulness to the Marriage vow.

These types of relationships and arrangements show that persons are not loyal or committed to the Christian ideals of Marriage and family. In such cases, it would be more appropriate to consider a divorced person or a single person, rather than a person whose marriage is visibly destructive and divisive. It is my view that such persons should not be considered for national leadership until they have gotten their personal and family life in order. Loyalty is therefore an acceptable criterion for leadership in the nation.

CHAPTER TEN

The Value Of Unity

This fourth core value Unity is very essential. The Psalmist declared in Psalms 133:

'Oh how good and how pleasant it is for brethren to dwell together in unity!'

The Oxford Dictionary gives several definitions to the word Unity, but the two meanings I find to be most appropriate are, 'The quality or condition of being one in mind, feelings, opinion, purpose or action: and the harmonious combination together of the various parties or sections in one body'.

The Webster's Dictionary defines Unity as 'the state of being united; in oneness; in agreement. It gives further clarification with the abundance of referral words such as 'identity, agreement, harmony, understanding, cooperation, whole, integrate, indivisible, altogether, unimpaired, completeness, wholeness and solidarity'. The thing that I find enlightening is the reference of 'Identity' as it relates to 'Unity'.

The word Identity brings to mind that aspect of national harmony, which shows who we are as a people, based on our 'oneness and togetherness' in things national or Bahamian. When we consider what makes a nation great, we look for the things that make it 'One and Unified'. Any nation cannot survive with no visible solitary culture, which is why it is important for The Bahamas, an incredibly small nation to pay greater attention to the 'semblance of virtues' which contributes to national identity and national unity. When a State is as small as The Bahamas, each aspect of national life must foster and project both a national posture and national unity, if it is to survive in a multicultural, multi-faceted, burgeoning, melting-pot society, that we are fast becoming. This is why the issue and question of Sovereignty is strongly argued, whenever the idea of its compromise arises.

Politics and Vote Buying

During General Election campaigns, we see more chaos, disputes, and disunity, than at any other time in Bahamian society. During these times, each individual political party seeks to wrestle control of the government, attempting to gain the affections and favour of the Bahamian people. It should be noted that both the PLP and FNM have an almost gang-like mentality when considering the rivalry created between supporters of the two major political parties. While this concept, I am told, is not as strong as in Jamaican politics, the process of general elections is considered an almost cult-like practice of 'a religion' for Bahamians.

It is disturbing to me that the process is always so strongly marred by cheating and unfair play. I am told that the Bahamas is no different from most Caribbean countries, and indeed other third world countries, where the unfair advantage of the 'rich' politician smothers the efforts of the 'poor' politician and delivers the government on every occasion to its special interests. This element continues the perversion of the true wishes of the people. This perversion lies specifically in the purchase of the individual's vote by corrupt politicians for mere pittance. The purchase of votes is reported in exchange for items like refrigerators, stoves, washers, and most times money.

When compared to the 1930s-1960s, there is no difference to what happens today from the iniquitous situations that existed when the white politicians brought bags of flour and rice to black people's houses during General Election time. Only now the gifts are bigger because the stakes are higher. When a poor man is tempted to cast his ballot on behalf of a candidate for money, he is deprived of his God-given right to vote his conscience and to make the right decision. This is why successive governments have not done much to develop over-the-hill communities, like Bain & Grants Town, Centreville, Englerston, Kemp Road, and other urban areas: They want to keep the poor man indebted to the rich powerful politicians.

If a politician has to purchase a vote, then he wants to obtain it for an illegal purpose. It is more probable than not that he doesn't really qualify to lead, and by extending money or political favours, the voter will overlook his deficiencies. This vote buying manipulates the poor to facilitate the rich. It has been a perpetual practice, on many levels, in The Bahamas for decades: Rich families donate considerable funds to both major political parties, to ensure that their businesses and interests are protected, no matter what happens politically in the country. In fact, this 'sector' first buys the politician, and then the politician buys the electorate; a continuous vicious cycle of buying and selling votes in The Bahamas. I often tell people on the campaign trail, 'If a man wants to buy your vote, be sure he will sell you out.'

The majority of our political leaders are not interested in unity, they are simply interested in partisan division, to the detriment of the country and the Bahamian people. The opportunity for a person to democratically elect their government in a general election is a fundamental right, and part of an unalienable liberty provided by a loving God and guaranteed in the Bahamian Constitution. This right must not be manipulated for the benefit of any political party or any special interest group.

This practice of 'Divide and conquer' by political leaders, is responsible for the high level of disunity in the country, and the persistent focus of the people on partisan 'petty' politics, to the detriment of good governance. Whenever an Election is called, it is important that the party that wins the government, places 'politics' aside, after the Election victory, and focuses the minds of the people on the governance of all the people of the nation. This is specifically the reason why the need is real for a new kind of structure of governance. Constitutional Democracy or a Republic system of governance is necessary to ensure more accountability in the process.

The Media & National Unity

The media is referred to as the Fourth Estate under a democracy like ours. This is simply because, other than the three arms of government, the media also enjoys the right and the privilege of unlimited access to both information and the masses. This protection of privilege comes with utmost responsibility. It is the responsibility of the media to encourage and foster National unity.

The media can make or break an individual candidate or political party attempting to enter front-line politics; as evidenced by the 2008, Presidential campaign of Barack Obama in the United States. The mainstream media in America played a major role in protecting the interest of the candidate, facilitating his upward mobility to the Presidency of the United States. Everybody depends on the media for exposure and unbiased reporting of the news, but many times the economic interest of the media undermines objective news reporting and does injustice to the process in regards to fairness and national unity.

Likewise, in The Bahamas, the mainstream media should not be biased, bringing its own journalistic integrity into question, by refusing to disseminate news and knowledge regarding all political questions and parties involved in the Election discussions. This is important in order to give the electorate the opportunity to make well-informed choices and foster national unity in the process.

When General Elections are over, we must be about the business of governance, not just partisan politics. It is amazing how, we, as a people, cannot seem to separate the two issues. The people deserve more than five years of opposition rhetoric just because the government recommended it. The people deserve more than just the blame game from the government, regarding what they consider to be the former government's failed policies. The people deserve to be governed properly. The political party that is given the Election mandate must carry forth the task of unifying and governing all the people of The Bahamas. National unity must be a focus and a priority above partisan politics following General Elections.

National Symbols Dictate Unity

Bahamas Flag

Bahamas Coat of Arms

As we conclude this chapter, let us examine the issue of Unity brought forward in the National symbols, as a means to motivate the people to action. Here are the words of the National Pledge, Anthem and Motto, and the Flag.

The Pledge

'I pledge my allegiance to the Flag and to the Commonwealth of The Bahamas for which it stands, one people United in Love and Service.'

These words specifically augment all the core values of the Constitution, by speaking to the goal of our founding fathers, that the people must be unified if they will serve each other and the world in love. These words were important at the outset to unify the people, particularly since we needed to further develop our own country and our people for the future.

Motto

'Forward, Upward, Onward, Together.'

The National Anthem - 'March On Bahamaland!'

Lift up your head to the rising sun, Bahamaland;
March on to glory, your bright banners waving high.
See how the world marks the manner of your bearing!
Pledge to excel through love and unity.
Pressing onward, march together
To a common loftier goal;
Steady sunward, tho' the weather
hide the wide and treacherous shoal.
Lift up your head to the rising sun, Bahamaland,
Till the road you've trod lead unto your God,
MARCH ON, BAHAMALAND

The National Anthem was written by Timothy Gibson, a native of Eleuthera. As a teacher, he wanted to impress the next generation of Bahamians, that they could be all they wanted to be if they placed values before them as the foundation of their journey. He wanted to show the need for Love and Unity if they were going to achieve anything great and exceptional for the world to see. The words were meant to establish in the minds of the Bahamian people the need to go after great things and excel, despite the rough and treacherous journey that it would take to get them there.

In this Anthem, he sought to impress into the minds of the people, to be proud of who they are; their recognition of which would show the world what the beauty of a united people can achieve, when they are focused on God's purpose for their lives. It was important for the world to know, that we knew our goals were lofty, but we would accomplish them anyway; and that our Christian heritage as a nation, would bring us the kind of strength and commitment to follow through. It was meant to declare to all, that because God was on our side, we would make it to glory as a nation; a journey that ultimately would lead us in service to our God. Accordingly, the four words of the nation's motto brought home succinctly the desire of the founding fathers. They wanted the people to concentrate on achieving the goals of the nation by marching forward and pressing together.

In this regard, the Pledge, the Motto, and the National Anthem speak specifically to Unity as a means to promote the physical, spiritual, and intellectual development of the Bahamian people. In these National symbols, we have observed all the core values enunciated in the Preamble, to help keep us focused as a unified people. Only national unity will take the country forward, fostering longevity and the further development of a Sovereign Bahamian State.

In closing, the U.S. National Endowment for the Humanities (NEH) often addresses the issues of national unity by addressing the importance of culture, noting that the Knowledge of the ideas that have molded us and the ideals that have mattered to us, function as a kind of civic glue. By failing to transmit these ideas and ideals from one generation to the next, we risk dissolution of the bonds that unite us as a nation and as free people. They recently indicated in an article in the online version of *The Hill News*, www.thehill.com:

> 'If we defend our culture, we are defending our country. If we keep our arts and humanities strong, we are showing an example for the world to see. If we celebrate our heritage and our cultural diversity, we will help our people stand together.'

—— CHAPTER ELEVEN ——

An Abiding Respect For Christian Values

When the founding fathers of the modern Bahamas included the statement, 'an abiding respect for Christian values' in the Preamble, they were expressing the underlying sentiment of the community. It was meant to acknowledge that 'things' that had sacred and religious value should be given prominence, reverence, and admiration by all Bahamians. This statement alone gives the implication that the founding fathers wanted to build the new nation on Christian principles.

Over the years, we have always heard the statement that the Bahamas is a Christian nation. While many have the opinion that because the Bahamas is a Church-going, God-loving people, the nation was considered Christian; but the reality is, many things contributed to the founding fathers collectively agreeing in principle, that the people of The Bahamas should be governed by a high standard of biblical morality, with an inspirational influence from the Christian church as part of the creation of public policy. It simply meant that the founding fathers of the nation of the modern Bahamas chose Christianity as its national state religion; just as Muslim countries choose Islam as their national state religion. Additionally, as part of a former colony of Great Britain, still, under the Executive Management of Her Majesty Queen Elizabeth II, head of the Commonwealth and the Church of England – Westminster Abbey; the Bahamas inherited the Anglican Church as its State religion.

While that term has been used unguardedly by some religious leaders, its full implication concerning national leadership and governance has never been fully articulated; thus, many persons have misinterpreted the overall implication.

In light of all of that, let me ask the question, what does it mean when it is said that a nation is a Christian state?

Firstly, let us look at what Christian means and what Webster-Miriam Online Dictionary has to say about it. The Online dictionary states that 'to be a Christian means to be a 'believer in Christ, which is consistent with the teaching of Jesus Christ.'

In practicality, for a government or a State to classify itself as Christian, simply implies that it intends to be a 'good, just and righteous' government, that will rule and govern in the fear of God, using biblical morality and spiritual values to carry forth its political agenda, holding up that standard by law, for the establishment of fair play and equal access to justice.

The United States of America was first established as a Christian nation in 1776. The founding fathers who framed that great nation had a particular goal in mind. Their goal was to build a free society of responsible and morally upright men and women. They wanted to build a symbolic 'city on a hill', a light to the nations', and a 'godly legacy'. They were willing to sacrifice, often giving their lives and livelihood to achieve those goals.

As a result, America became a great nation. It became great because the nation's character was rooted in Christian morality. It is the primary reason America had been established as being the leader of the free world since its inception.

This was also the reason why French Nobleman Alexis de Tocqueville stated during a tour of America in 1832, which was quoted in the book *Democracy in America* by Sherwood Eddy, The Kingdom of God and the American Dream, (1941), chapter 1:

> 'I sought for the greatness and genius of America in her commodious harbors and her ample rivers—and it was not there ... in her fertile fields and boundless forests— and it was not there ... in her rich mines and her vast world commerce—and it was not there ... in her democratic Congress and her matchless Constitution—and it was not there. Not until I went into the churches of America and heard her pulpits aflame with righteousness did I understand the secret of her genius and power. America is great because she is good, and if America ever ceases to be good, America will cease to be great.'

What does that mean similarly for the government and people of The Bahamas?

Is it only the responsibility of the government to maintain the country's status as a Christian nation, or is it the responsibility of all the people of the country?

In response to these questions, both Sir Lynden Pindling and Sir Arthur Foulkes, in their interviews with me, agreed, that while the people do have a firm responsibility, the government should take the lead in maintaining the founding fathers' pledge to this agenda. Both men similarly believed that it is the collective responsibility of both the people and the government to work in cooperation, to uphold the principles upon which the people have agreed to govern themselves by and to live by. This means that the government of the day must always create, encourage, and maintain an environment in the country to foster Christianity and to give high priority to Christian principles when creating public policies.

In addition to what has already been inferred, maintaining an abiding respect for Christian values within the society can also be equated to having respect for spiritual and sacred things, which include values like:

- The protection of a person's fundamental and Constitutional rights, freedoms and property,
- Respect for Church, religious and charitable organizations,
- The sanctity of Marriage and family life,
- The protection of and provision for, children, the elderly, and the underprivileged

All of the above are a confirmation of biblical morality and the indication of what is considered Pure religion which is quoted below.

> 'Pure religion and undefiled before God and the Father is this, To visit the fatherless and widows in their affliction, and to keep himself unspotted from the world.' James 1:27

Over the past two decades, we have seen the increasing reports in the news of the desecration of churches, the break-ins, and robbery of charitable institutions, the abuse of both the elderly and young children, the abandonment, abuse, and even murder of infants and children; among much unholy happenings in the country. These things represent a 'weaning' of respect for sacred things, as the society moves further away from Christian Values to a more secular and liberal stance.

At most times, these types of ungodly activities in society are directly symbiotic of national leadership's lack of respect for spiritual and sacred things. When a government begins to embrace 'secularism' in the governance of the nation and makes decisions that are non-Christian, the society will, in most cases follow suit. The society becomes a reflection of the government and the government is reflective of the society.

Many immoral activities such as sodomy and homosexuality, sweet-hearting, and the preponderance of children being born out of wedlock are very prominent in Bahamian society today, even among national and religious leaders. The level of teenage pregnancy and children born to single parents have now surpassed the level of children born in the confines of marriage. The statistics show that children born outside of marriage in The Bahamas are estimated at sixty-two (62%) percent of live births each year, according to the Commonwealth of The Bahamas Vital Statistics Report 2013. Regrettably, the nation officials presently report that close to seventy (70%) percent of homes are headed by single parents, predominantly women.

The predominance of single parenting by both Bahamians and foreign nationals, are wreaking havoc on society and has been the beginning of many ills we face today. While we appreciate the many parents doing it alone and holding up the responsibility for the rearing of children; the majority of lost and disillusioned young people involved in the enormous gang activities are primarily children from single-parent families, created as a result of illicit and adulterous relationships. I refer to a recent commentary I read from a religious writer in the *Nassau Tribune* which states that:

'There is too much fornication going on in the nation.'

It is imperative that personal integrity and moral discretion be exercised by religious and political leadership in order to discourage young people from mimicking this iniquitous behaviour. Many times, when young people see the flaunting of extra-marital relationships and other immoral improprieties by their leaders, it leads them to follow their own way and set their own standards as to what is right and wrong.

CHAPTER TWELVE

Respect For The Rule Of Law

This final core value articulated by the founding fathers was formulated as a governmental or State responsibility, more so, than that of the people. You may want to know why would the founding fathers consider it necessary to include and emphasize the term, 'an abiding respect' for something that is supposed to be inherent or established already?

The founding fathers knew that the respect for the Rule of Law would be a great challenge for future governments, as the reality of absolute power in their hands, based on the Westminster system, became 'overwhelming'. I believe that additional recognition of the commitment to the Rule of Law was necessary for the government, in order to give confidence to the people that it intends to abide by the law in each and every case.

What is the Rule of Law?

Legal interpretation and definition by modern Academia implies that,

'The Rule of Law is a powerful symbol in legal discourse and carries no single or one-dimensional definition. Rather, it embodies a number of interrelated ideas which combine to express a commitment to government, by and through legal authority, and provides a basis or rationale for the citizen's obligation to obey the law.'

More adequately articulated, the theory for the Rule of Law expresses, that it is...

'A commitment to procedural regularity, which is, due process of law; and also, a commitment to the universality of legal jurisdiction: that all, including both rulers and the ruled, are subject to law, to the same rules of law, and to the same legal institutions. Thus, not only is a citizen subject to law, but there is also a notion of 'a check of or limitations upon' the activity of rulers'.

However, the greatest implication of the Rule of Law is, that the government itself would abide by it, and be obedient to the law of the land; and also, that it would not interfere politically with the Judiciary, regarding the application of its duties to provide equal and fair justice for all, based on legislated policies. The further inference is, that 'the government of the day' has a grave obligation and responsibility, to protect the tenants of the Constitution, thus preserving the State from abuse by the powers of the government itself.

For the ordinary person, this concept may be somewhat puzzling, but the notion is dependent on the Doctrine and Ethics of the Separation of Powers of the three main branches of government. This notion gives the Judiciary full operational autonomy, from the Executive and Legislative branches of Government. Even while the Judiciary must have autonomy, it must also be clear, that its responsibility is to adjudicate the law, and not make its own laws; and or set standards and precedents that have not been duly legislated. Even though, the doctrines of Judicial Restraint versus Judicial Activism is gaining popularity in some jurisdictions, as more High Court's decisions are being decided based on popular political views such as Conservative versus Liberal positions, according to Thomas E Patterson Sixth Edition, 'We The People - A Concise Introduction to American Politics'.

According to Chapter 1, Article 2, of the Bahamian Constitution, this is the Rule of Law:

> 'The Constitution is the supreme law of the Commonwealth of The Bahamas, and subject to the provisions of this Constitution, if any other law is inconsistent with this Constitution, this Constitution shall prevail, and the other law, to the extent of the inconsistency, shall be void.'

Consequently, when the Government makes decisions or Parliament enacts laws for political mileage, which may be against the citizens' fundamental and constitutional rights and privileges afforded under the Constitution, based on the concept of the Rule of law; the citizens have the protection of the law against the government's abuse. This is a key component of the accountability of government, under the concept of the Rule of Law.

This component was confirmed by Sir William Ivor Jennings QC, Litt D (Cantab) LLD (Lond), an expert in Constitutional studies in the early century, regarding the powers of public authorities. Having taught law and political studies in universities in the United Kingdom, the United States, and Canada during the first half of the

20th century, he had earned an academic reputation as a constitutional expert regarding the British Commonwealth and advised Prime Ministers and public officials on the ways forward in the 1930s, by using British Law and precedents to build foundation for the Rule of Law in new territories. His proposition was that elected officials ought not to have large powers.

In a wrap up to these references, there are two fundamental characteristics of the British Constitution from which The Bahamas' Constitution is derived, namely the system of Self-governance and the concept of the Rule of Law. This is exemplified and articulated in S. A. DeSmith's 1971 book, *Constitutional and Administrative Law*, where he wrote the following,

> 'The concept of the Rule of Law is usually intended to imply:

- That the powers exercised by politicians and officials must have a legitimate foundation. The powers must be authority conferred by law
- That the law should conform to certain minimum standards of justice, both substantive and procedural, and must be certain and predictable
- Where the laws confer wide discretionary powers, there should be adequate safeguards against their abuse
- Like should be treated alike, and unfair discrimination must not be sanctioned by law
- A person must not be deprived of his liberty, status or property unless he is given the opportunity of a fair hearing before an impartial and independent tribunal'

Therefore, having respect for the Rule of Law obligates both the leaders and those being led, to a law that is equal in justice for all. It also gives citizens a right and obligation to check daily the activities and behaviour of their leaders and public officials.

There can be no true democracy where the Executive does not observe the Rule of Law. There can be no respect for the Rule of Law by the Executive if the 'transgressors' are not able to be restrained by an independent Judiciary. And there will not be the appearance of an independent Judiciary in the Bahamas, as long as the appointment of Justices, Magistrates, and members of the Judicial Service Commission remains solely in the hands of the Executive branch, mainly the office of the Prime Minister.

Therefore, the sentiments of Aristotle, the inventor of modern politics is correct, regarding the supremacy of the Rule of Law, when he stated that,

> 'The Rule of Law then, is preferable to the rule of an individual citizen'.

(NB. For more information and views on the Rule of Law, please check out the Section on Fundamental Rights in the Chapter – In Defence of Marriage.)

CHAPTER THIRTEEN

Is There A Case For Higher Ethics And Morality In Public Life?

The need for a higher standard of Ethical behavior and Morality in public life remains a crucial issue. As I seek to build a case for more accountable governance, this becomes a critical issue because many persons vying for national leadership in The Bahamas seem to conduct themselves in contradiction of the values that are listed in the Preamble of the Constitution.

Persons who are in public office, primarily Parliamentarians both elected and appointed and those vying for other public offices, should be required to present themselves as suitable candidates who uphold a reasonable moral standard.

You may want to ask, what is a reasonable moral standard? In response, it is the standard of ethical and moral behavior that is decent and acceptable.

Whenever the discussion of a higher standard of morality comes up, people are quick to argue that we are seeking to 'legislate morality'. However, the late teacher, Dr. D. James Kennedy, a

Constitutional preacher of South Florida, consistently noted in his broadcasted sermons and writings that,

'Morality is the only thing you can legislate. That is what Legislation is. It is the codification in law of some particular moral concern; generally, so, that the immorality of a few is not forcibly inflicted on the rest of us.'

The important question is not 'Should we legislate morality?' But rather, 'Whose moral standard should we legislate?' But the reality is, that all laws and legislation have some moral or ethical tenant commended for enforceability in the civic arena.

What is 'Morality' you may ask? The Online Version of the Oxford Dictionary defines Morality simply as 'Ethical Wisdom'.

Based on that meaning, let us first look at the word Ethical, which is derived from the root word Ethics. Ethics is defined as 'the study of right and wrong' in actions, and the 'personal standard or the standard of conduct' adopted by professionals.

Furthermore, let us look at the word Moral, which is the root word of Morality. There are several definitions of the word Moral that help to clarify its meaning in all contexts. Moral is defined as, 'pertaining to character or disposition; or pertaining to the distinction between right and wrong, or good and evil, as it relates to action and the character of responsible beings'; and 'expressing or teaching a concept of right behaviour'; and 'conforming to a standard of right behaviour.'

These definitions imply that to be 'Moral' means 'to be good'. Although many people hold the view that there are 'varying' standards of Morals or Morality, there is no such thing. You are either 'Moral' or you are not. The definition of the word MORAL clearly indicates that it is the standard of behavior of 'Good, Right, and Responsible' human beings. So then the words, Ethics, and Morality are somewhat entwined in characteristics.

Different Authors Concur

In my research, I have discovered some ancient quotes and references to the use of the words Moral and Ethics, which you may find useful to give further clarification to the original connotations of the term. The following statements are simply quotes by the authors stated from a third-party source.

Paley in 1785 said, 'Moral philosophy, Morality, Ethics, Casuistry and Natural Law, mean all the same thing.'

Bentham in 1789 said, 'Ethics at large may be defined, as the art of directing men's action to the production of the greatest possible quantity of happiness.'

Mackintosh in 1830 introduced the thought that 'The purpose of the Moral Sciences is to answer the question, what ought to be?'

Emerson in 1836 said 'Ethics and religion differ herein; that the one is the system of human duties commencing from man; the other from God.'

E. R. Conder in 1877 described the words, 'Justice, truth, love, duty, virtue as the same as morality'.

R.W. Dale in 1878 wrote, 'There may be Morality where there is no religion, but there should not be religion where there is no morality, it is impossible'.

Tennyson in 1887 noted, 'Evil must come upon us headlong if morality tries to get on without religion.'

Boyd Carpenter in 1889 concurred that 'Religion without ethics seems little else than irreligious Religion.'

Concurring with the other quotes, author George Grant in his book entitled *The Family Under Siege* wrote that the Honourable Justice John Jay, the first Chief Justice of the United States of America, re-affirmed the necessity of virtue, for the maintenance of civil society, when he asserted, that:

'No human society has ever been able to maintain both order and freedom, both cohesiveness and liberty, apart from the moral precepts of the Christian religion applied and accepted by all the classes. Should our Republic ere forget this fundamental precept of governance, men are certain to shed responsibilities for licentiousness, and this great experiment will then surely be doomed.'

George Grant maintained that:

'It is interesting, yet ironic, that John Jay intimated at the inception of the establishment of America as a Republic, that the success of the experiment of governance was directly related to the application of the fundamental precepts of the Christian religion. In fact, every major document, every major consultation, and every major institution that the founding fathers of America forged from the fires of freedom, to create and guide the remarkable legal system in America, was a conscious affirmation and imitation of biblical ideals, values, standards, ethics and morals.'

Another writer Robert Goguet, in his paper *The Authoritative History of the Development of Judicial Philosophy of America,* argued that:

'the founding fathers' legislation of biblical morality was more than simply a reflection of their personal faith or cultural inheritance; it was a matter of sober-headed practicality.' From *The Family Under Siege* by George Grant

In this same regard, James Madison, the fourth President of the United States, echoed the sentiment that:

'We have staked the future of all our political institutions upon the capacity of each and all of us to govern ourselves, to control ourselves, and to sustain ourselves according to the Ten Commandments of God.' From *The Family Under Siege* by George Grant

And finally, Charles Murray, in his book, *In the Pursuit of Happiness and Good Governance*, wrote this:

'The practice of virtue has the characteristic of a habit or a skill. People may be born with the habit or capacity of being generous, but become generous by practicing generosity. People may have the capacity of being honest, but become honest by practicing honesty.' From *The Family Under Siege* by George Grant

Bahamas Constitution Inferences to Morality

Therefore, as we consider further the case for Morality, Ethics, and Integrity in public life, we can turn our thoughts to the Bahamian Constitution and see what the Supreme law of The Bahamas has to say about the concept of morality in governance. In Chapter three (3) of The Bahamas Constitution, which deals with the Protection of Fundamental Rights and Freedoms of the Individual, Articles 20, 21, 22, 23, 24, 25, 27, mentions the phrase, 'In the interest of Public Morality'.

What is the Public Morality, according to the Bahamian Constitution? And what does it confer by law?

In my earlier research of the word Morality, one of the definitions of the root word Moral refers to 'the system or doctrine concerned with conduct, duty or behaviour'.

This means then, that based on Bahamian law, mainly concerning constitutional rights and privileges, there is an established standard or a code of conduct that must be upheld by the individual citizen, in regards to their behaviour and actions in the public domain. This also means that this established standard is what the public can expect to be available in society, enforced by Law, and the government, towards the citizens, residents, or visitors.

Prime Minister Hon. Hubert Ingraham Cabinet Heading to Parliament to present Annual Budget in 2007-2012 Term

Here is an example in my estimation of the infringement of the Public Morality.

In 1998, the FNM government gave permission for gay ships to enter the port of New Providence and other ports in The Bahamas. By their agreement for the Gay Cruises, the government consented for gay men and women to come ashore holding hands and kissing in the street. The FNM Ingraham administration defended the rights of the LGBT people under Article 26 subsection 3 of the

Constitution, stating their right not to be discriminated against based on sexual orientation. However, Article 26 does not speak to sexual orientation, but to sex, in regard to 'preferential treatment' of any of the other fundamental rights'.

This same FNM administration, in turn, attempted to squash the demonstrations by the Church, trampling on the constitutional rights of the protestors guaranteed under Article 22, 23 & 24, of Freedom of Conscience, Freedom of Expression, and Freedom of Assembly, respectively. The Protestors had an additional right to protest under Article 23, 24, subsection (1,2), subsection (2a); citing their right to expect the level of morality in the society permissible by law; which infers that their actions were 'in the interest of the Public morality', against behaviour that violated 'the Public morality'.

The public display of homosexual activities was in violation of the Bahamian people's right to expect a high standard of moral behaviour on the streets of the capital. It was the responsibility of the government to indicate to the cruise lines and their passengers, that such lewd behaviour should not be displayed or would not be tolerated while visiting our public spaces.

If there is an acceptable standard to Public morality, should there not be a standard of morality for those holding the 'trust of the public' in high political office?

- Should the personal moral stance of a public official be of importance to the general public?
- Should it matter if he or she cheats on their spouse?
- Should it matter if he or she has a love child with his or her sweetheart?
- Should it matter if he or she drinks alcohol or smokes cigarettes, snorts crack cocaine, or smokes marijuana?

- Does it really matter if he beats his wife, or steals from his job?
- Should it matter if he or she is a homosexual or lesbian?
- Should the personal morality of national leaders concern the general public?

These are just some general questions I wish to pose. However, it is my summation that the leader or public official's personal integrity or moral standard becomes the foundation for his or her actions in leadership and public office.

Therefore, the public has a right to demand both personal integrity and moral uprightness in the individuals they choose to govern them. If the citizenry is expected to uphold a certain code of conduct and behaviour, then leaders should be required and accountable to do the same, or to uphold an even greater standard of ethics and moral conduct in public office. Only persons who are prepared to live and uphold all that they wish their followers to live by and uphold, have the Moral Authority to lead the people. It goes back to the instruction of the biblical writer, 'Follow me, as I follow Christ.' 1 Corinthians 11:1.

The quote by an early 5th Century Chinese Thinker and Philosopher, whose writings are found in the *Analects of Confucius*, give an adage that offers enduring guidance for all who would seek the more ethical practice of governance:

> 'He who exercises government by means of his virtue may be compared to the North polar star, which keeps its place, and all the stars turn towards it.'

CHAPTER FOURTEEN

Legitimacy And Moral Authority

P olitical thinkers as far back as Plato and Aristotle have always had the subject of Legitimacy as a part of their mindset regarding governance and politics. As we introduce this idea, the basic issue of Legitimacy centers on the question of judicial powers, that is, 'the proper legal authority' in a political system based in part on the principle of the majority rule. However, for contemporary political systems in which participation of the people is a criterion of political worth, Legitimacy is a fundamental concept, and no discussion on democratic governance will be complete without reference to it.

It is said, however, that the best-known definition of Legitimacy was formulated by Max Weber (1978), who distinguished that there are three types of legitimacy: the Traditional, the Charismatic, and the Legal Rational. In that regard, no matter what type it is, all systems of power and privilege attempting to lead in any modern environment will seek to establish themselves as legitimate.

According to Mattei Dogan, a renowned Sociologist and Political Scientist in the published essay, *The Concept of Legitimacy*, wrote that:

> 'Legitimacy is particularly important in democracies since a democracy's survival is ultimately dependent on the support of at least a majority of its citizens; it holds that at least a majority must deem the democracy as legitimate. Hence, without the granting of legitimacy by the people, a democracy would lose its authority. On the other hand, legitimacy in this sense of public belief and support is considerably less important in non-democratic regimes. In a dictatorship, while the granting of support or legitimacy by the people may be an asset, it is not of ultimate importance since authority is based on force.'

Mattei Dogan was a Romanian-born French political sociologist and senior research officer emeritus of the French National Center for Scientific Research (CNRS) and Professor Emeritus of political science of the University of California, Los Angeles. He chaired the Research Committee on Political Elites of the International Political Science Association (IPSA) and the Research Committee on Comparative Sociology of the International Sociological Association (ISA). He was also the founder of the Foundation Mattei Dogan. His main research domains include elite studies, international comparative analysis, and interdisciplinary approaches. His publications have dealt with the relationship between political behavior and religious behavior, political legitimacy, and the ruling class. Beyond the age of eighty, he was still writing and providing enlightening commentary on Paradigms in Social Sciences.

Mattei Dogan argues further from the essay, *The Concept of Legitimacy*, that:

> 'Legitimating ideas does not only reinforce, but sets limits to, systems of power; which means that power holders cannot do just as they please. Furthermore, most justification for power incorporates claims to promote the well-being of the subordinate. If these claims repeatedly fail to be realized, a progressive loss of legitimacy will result; although in the absence of an alternative source of legitimacy, power structures can survive for a long time. There comes a point however, when they can only be preserved by the widespread use of coercion.'

Mattei Dogan believes that, while many scholars have the innate tendency to adopt the dichotomy, as to whether something is 'legitimate or illegitimate', the reality is more varied, as it presumes that legitimacy must come in degrees of legitimacy, ranking on an imaginary axis from minimum to a maximum degree of legitimacy.

He further states:

> 'In that regard, legitimacy runs on a scale from complete acclaim to complete rejection; ranging all the way through from support, consent, compliance through decline, to erosion and loss. In the case of a conscious rejection, we may want to term it as 'illegitimate'. The point then can be made, that in theory, the lower the degree of legitimacy there is, then the higher would be the amount of coercion that is used'.

Therefore, 'Legitimate beliefs secure the subordinates or people's consent to the exercise of power and help to promote stability and minimize the costs of coercion'.

These indicators of coercion in society, according to Dogan, can be evaluated based on the level of certain political rights and liberties available in society, such as:

a. freedom of expression
b. freedom of association
c. freedom of demonstration
d. the degree of military or police intervention in the political arena
e. fair elections
f. freedom of religious institutions
g. independent judiciary
h. free competition among parties
i. the absence of government manipulation
j. an unfettered media

Legitimacy and Trust Compared

The whole idea of 'Legitimacy and Trust' is always a very grave concern for the citizens and any elected government. While the concept of legitimacy refers to the whole political system and its permanent nature, i.e., the State; the concept of Trust is limited to the rulers who occupy the power in a transitory way, i.e., a government administration. Sometimes this is difficult for people to differentiate: the difference between the Legitimacy of the State versus the illegitimacy of a government administration.

Accordingly, I wish to concur with Mattei Dogan's illustration to clarify the distinction between Legitimacy and Trust, based on the possible reply to a very simple question he posed:

'Should a police officer be obeyed in any and all circumstances?'

In the first instance, a reply that, 'The officer should be obeyed because his/her order is right' implies 'Legitimacy and Trust.' In the second instance, if the officer should be obeyed because he or she simply represents Authority, it indicates 'Legitimacy without Trust.' Therefore, if the particular officer is wrong, an appeal to a higher authority should be made.

However, the analogy raises the question of whether the Police Force as an institution can be perceived as legitimate, even if a particular police officer or officers may not be trusted. This further raises the supposition, that if too many police officers are corrupt or unnecessarily brutal, the legitimacy of the Police Force as an institution is contested or called into question. The mistrust of police officers can be argued, as well as the loss of confidence in the entire Police Force as an institution.

This argument carries forward to the entire society, that if many institutions are mistrusted, that is, the government, the civil service, the Armed Forces, the Judiciary, political parties, or the media, then the entire regime or State itself could be considered illegitimate.

The Judiciary often represents a regime's or government's last fortress against corruption. So, if the Judiciary is ever fully contaminated, then there is no hope for the ordinary citizen, and you can predict a crisis of 'Legitimacy' in the entire nation.'

'Political trust can be thought of as a basic evolving or affective orientation toward the government. The dimension of trust runs from high trust, to high distrust or political cynicism. Cynicism refers to the degree of negative affect toward government, and is a statement of the belief that the government is not functioning and producing outputs in accord with individual expectations.' (Miller, 1974)

As the above statement clarifies, the level of trust people has that the government is doing what is right for them in the long term is very important to continued peace and stability in the nation. Thus, I support the notion that 'People lose faith in leaders more easily than they lose confidence in the system.' This is evident in the last four General Elections, where the Bahamian people change administration every five years, the perception of the loss of faith in the politicians they trusted.

What is Moral Authority

Is there a connection between Legitimacy and Moral Authority? And if so, what is it that gives a regime or an administration Moral Authority?

Moral Authority is an 'earned' by-product of leadership that is both accountable and exhibits integrity. It is not automatic because of the position of those in leadership. Moral Authority is respect earned by the virtuous action and ethical conduct of leaders. By this I mean, the genuine actions of a leader have the ability, just by virtue of their example, to cause their followers to cooperate because he or she leads by example rather than by mere instructions.

The leader who gets out front, making themselves available to the task, does not need to command people to do what they say, because they provide encouragement just by leading. Their claim to Moral Authority comes from the adage, 'Do as I do' not 'Do as I say!'

Therefore, Moral authority produces legitimacy because the ethical actions of politicians meet the expectations of its citizens and constituents. Thus, Moral Authority must be an expectation of any leadership.

The overall implication is that the leader or the administration exhibits the moral and ethical behaviour that is demanded from followers, constituents, or the citizenry. This consistent behaviour, on the part of the government, gives the public the necessary confidence to expect fair and equitable treatment, because the individuals in government have established, by their own actions, that they are actually 'walking the walk, they talk'. In modern politics today, there sometimes seems to be a difficulty collectively determining what is an acceptable standard of right actions and behavior. We see that in many different aspects because many leaders have varied views on what is acceptable.

While the law is our guideline for keeping order and rule in society, the law is still a minimalist approach to governing people. However, while the use of the law claims to serve the cause of justice, it is oftentimes merely an instrument of coercion in the hand of governments. Consequently, as an alternative to this kind of possible abuse of power by the state or those elected to govern, democracies such as ours, extol and regard the concept of the Rule of Law as a secondary safety net.

The law is like the provision of a 'floor' for both government action and human behaviour. It is like the lines in the middle of the road, and the marking in the parking lot. However, I believe that only morality, integrity, and ethics in its widest sense, can provide the 'ceiling' for government action, and provide the basis for true moral authority in political and national leadership. This means that we must use a higher law than only the law of the land to govern people.

According to Dr. Gregory D. Foster, Professor of Political Science at the Industrial College of the Armed Forces, National Defense

University, in Washington, D.C., in an essay entitled 'Ethics, Government and Security – The Democratic Imperative', he noted that,

> 'The necessary precondition for the effectiveness of government - is a reflection of public trust and confidence. Such trust and confidence is derived from respect, and is best assured by the leadership that comes from setting a consistent example of principled action.'

This first assertion reinforces my supposition, that this primary aspect of 'principled action' is essential to keep the moral virtue of the government consistent in the eyes of the populace and gives the people what they need to be encouraged towards joyful obedience to the law of the land.

In my attempt to build my argument on the concept of Legitimacy and Moral Authority, I am seeking to draw from Gregory D. Foster's abundant expertise, as a Professor of National Security Studies at the Industrial College of the Armed Forces, National Defense University, Washington, D.C. During his tenure at the Industrial College, he has served as Director of the Environment Industry Study; the China Regional Security Study; the Elements of National Power course; the Values, Ethics, and Leadership program; and the New Faculty Development program. Dr. Foster also holds a Doctorate in Public Administration from The George Washington University. He has held adjunct faculty appointments at The Johns Hopkins University and The American University. He has published widely in the areas of national security affairs, civil-military relations, ethics, public management, and futures research. His publications include The Strategic Dimension of Military Manpower (Ballinger, 1987) and Paradoxes of Power: The Military Establishment in the Eighties (Indiana University Press, 1983).

In this published online essay, in The Humanist – Buffalo – Volume 61 – May/June 2001 entitled "Ethics, Government and Security – The Democratic Imperative", Dr. Gregory Foster asserted, regarding Legitimacy that:

> 'All Governments are a social contract between those who govern and the governed - a tacit ethical compact involving mutual rights, obligations and expectations. These are imperatives for public accountability, which is transparency, and popular consent, which is the public's natural right to know. These are symbiotic prerequisites of democracy that require both open government for effective popular rule, and popular rule for effective open governments.'

Dr. Foster referred further to the degree of ethical propriety of the government, which is based on two very important things:

1. The government's use of, and influence upon the military or armed forces of the State, in exercising its self-interested expediency of partisan politics.

2. The public's perception of the government's use of public office for personal gain.

In the first illustration, Foster equates the military-civilian contact as one of the single most important arrangements in the continued viability of the government. He cites the public expectation of the fairness of the military, and the confidence in the armed forces to be an imperative of a democratic government.

This suggestion brings us closer to understanding that the way successive administrations have used the Royal Bahamas Police

Force (RBPF), the Royal Bahamas Defence Force (RBDF), Bahamas Customs, Bahamas Immigration, and the Her Majesty's Prison Service personnel for their own agenda, is indicative of their ethical propriety, or lack thereof.

For example, if the Prime Minister asks the Commissioner of Police to investigate civilians in order to use the results by his political party to gain a certain advantage, this speaks to the direct abuse of power by the Prime Minister. Any such investigation must be initiated by the Commissioner of Police because of suspicion of criminal behavior, not the other way around.

In a more personal reference: in 1998 when I first declared my intention to start The Bahamas Constitution Party, I was investigated. This would possibly be standard when it comes to the intelligence-gathering required by the Security Intelligence Branch (SIB). However, over the following few years leading up to the 2002 election, I was investigated over and over again, and every possible unpaid bill or matter was unearthed, scrutinized, and used to frustrate me.

Do you think that the police investigated me because they thought I was a subversive person or a threat to society? If I was considered unruly or a troublemaker, surely the police would have known. However, a high-ranking member in the government ordered that I be investigated to ascertain any information in an attempt to discredit me and to distract me from going forward with the political agenda. While the Official Opposition (PLP) used private investigators, the (FNM) government used State institutions to pursue their persecutions against me.

The search yielded information that resulted in me being dragged before the Magistrate Court on a two-year Judgement Summons in a civil case that the plaintiff had already dismissed. The authorities in the Police Prosecutions Department allegedly called the plaintiff and asked him if he wished to reinstate the case and re-activate the two-year-old Judgement summons. In that case, I was threatened by a Magistrate that she would send me to Fox Hill Prison, if I did not return to court several days later with the fourteen hundred ($1,400.00) dollars that the Judgement Summons required.

However, when I returned to court several days later with an Attorney; the judge vilified me for showing up to court with an Attorney, despite her Judgment Sentence against me. It was the intention of my 'pursuers' to have me placed in jail, without due process. Having exerted my legal right to due process by getting an attorney, I was able to foil their plans. The matter was resolved within a few days.

What I am trying to establish here is, that elected officials must not abuse their powers by commanding the use of the State's machinery for partisan political reasons. The exercise of power by politicians in this fashion is also symptomatic of questionable moral character.

As an aid to understanding the second item discussed by Dr. Foster, it was noted that where corruption exists, something more fundamental and disturbing is at play than just the use of public office for personal gain. It is a complete breakdown of character of those involved, and the loss of the internal compass we call the conscience.

So then, the question is posed, how do we institutionalize ethical propriety and discourage corruption in public office? Dr. Foster suggests that only a comprehensive response will do.

In this regards, Dr. Foster argued that:

'Individual ethical conduct can only be guided in a positive direction within an institutional climate that recognizes and rewards such ethical behaviour. That institutional climate, in turn, can be sustained only when the larger society demands and supports high standards of human conduct. And if we extend our thinking, to accommodate the forces of globalization, we may even be forced to concede that societies can be held accountable.'

Dr. Foster's suggestions can help formulate creative measures for nurturing ethical propriety within the public service, the armed forces, and national leadership in The Bahamas. He suggested the following in order for ethical propriety to strive:

a. There clearly must be enforceable laws and regulations that denounce impropriety and provide for appropriate penalties.

b. There must be organizational mechanisms available for an Independent Ombudsman office,

c. Ethics officers within the public service and the armed forces, and the like, who highlight the importance of the issues, and provide avenues for monitoring, investigating, reporting abuses, and enforcing standards.

d. There must be sound personnel management programmes designed for screening, recruiting, developing, and promoting personnel with the attributes, aptitudes, and attitudes that are amenable to ethical thinking and behaviour.

e. There must also be adequate systems for remuneration, and recognition that removes the temptation which leads to corruption, provides incentives for propriety, and demonstrates the value society and the institution of government place on moral excellence.

I wish to suggest the following additional Legislations, and legislative changes to accommodate those needs and recommended Policies:

a. The Freedom of Information Act
b. An Independent Ombudsman Office
c. Mandatory Reporting of Public Expenditures
d. Campaign Funding Reform for reporting of all political contributions
e. An independent Judiciary
f. A free Press, and non-governmental Watchdog and Advocacy groups

I wish to concur with Dr. Foster's suggestion that these measures must be in place if ethical propriety is to take root and be sustained within all levels of society. He noted that these measures are meaningless if they are not guided by and undergirded with fundamental preconditions for ethical propriety. The first and most basic measure is Transparency, which is the opening of government to public scrutiny through the various mechanisms that experience has shown are necessary for that purpose.

Dr. Foster argued that even more important than transparency in gendering true self-discipline and self-control in society, is Leadership: the consistent practice by those in authority of exemplary behaviour of walking the talk of virtue, and thus demonstrating one's worthiness for emulation by others. He identified Transparency as the most basic, Leadership as the most important, and Education and Training as the most lasting of the preconditions of ethical propriety. Dr. Foster noted:

> 'Ethical conduct is not something that can be imposed. Nor is it something that can be acquired or adopted as a result

of infrequent mass lectures on standards of conduct. It is a conditioned mode of critical thinking that has to be regularly and consistently instilled, exercised, and tested through rigorous inquiry, reflection, and dialogue. Only individuals thus prepared can reasonably expect to wear the badge of virtue, and only institutions that invest in such preparations can reasonably expect to harvest the fruit of such virtue.'

The restructuring of governmental institutions must become a priority in The Bahamas. The strategic planning that is necessary must include enforceable ethical codes of conduct, in order to preserve and guard these institutions for future generations against further abuses and the ultimate erosion of their status of Legitimacy.

This exercise, over the next few years, of institutionalizing ethical propriety for political and national leadership, will give the next generation of Bahamians confidence and trust in the institutions of leadership within the nation. These measures and set standards will mandate national leadership accountability for upholding a certain basic standard of moral virtue within the governance of the nation.

As one Greek philosopher, Heraclitus once quoted, that 'Character is destiny.' This quote implies that destiny, or fate, is not a predetermined outside force, but that one's future, or destiny, can be determined by his own inner strength of character.

PART THREE

The Components of
Accountable Governance

CHAPTER FIFTEEN

The Role And Purpose Of Government

A s we look at the role and purpose of government, I wish to first
share the admonition of the Apostle Peter as he wrote in his
letters to Christians throughout the ages, admonishing them to
respect the role of the government.

> 'Submit yourselves to every institution of man for the
> Lord's sake: whether it be to the king, as supreme; or unto
> governors, as unto them that are sent by him, for the
> punishment of evildoers, and for the praise of them that
> do well. For so is the will of God, that with well doing you
> may put to silence the ignorance of foolish men. Honour
> all men. Love the brethren. Fear God. Honour the king.'
>
> 1 Peter 2:13-17

This scripture is also in congruence with the Apostle Paul's admonition in his 13th Epistle to the Romans, encouraging people
everywhere to support, and be subject to governments, as they
are ordained by God to do well for society. These admonitions set

a proper tone and precedence as to how Christians and non-Christians everywhere should respond to their government – a divinely ordained institution of leadership in the society.

Constitutional Validity

There is government in all organizational groups at all levels in civil society. Most dictionaries define the term government as 'the agency which administers leadership for a group of people and expresses their conduct'.

As we seek to establish the practicality of governments, some may wish to know whether there is a difference between the Government and the State? And what is the difference?

Yes, there is a difference. Although to some, it seems only technical. Firstly, let us establish in layman's terms, what exactly is the State.

When a group of people, living in the same geographical area, decide that they wish to govern themselves, as The Bahamas desired in the 1960s, it begins the process of the formation or the adoption of a Constitution or the rules as to how they will self-govern. Once the Constitution is recognized and brought into force, it creates Sovereignty for that geographical area, and that declaration of Sovereignty establishes the State or the nation.

The State provides the organizational structure or the legal jurisdiction of the people and their nation. It is the permanent, perpetual machinery with responsibility for the protection of the nation's sovereignty and the safeguard of the fundamental rights and freedom of each individual member or citizen of that State. The overall objectives do not change, despite changes in political administrations.

The Constitution itself maintains the status of the State: which is why, there are set parameters, outlined in the Constitution, that limit the powers of governments from making constitutional amendment without widespread consultation, both from the political parties involved in the Parliament and by a mandated Referendum with consent by the majority of the people.

Regarding Organizational structure, the State consists of the three (3) Arms of Government, namely, the Executive, the Legislature, and the Judiciary. As we discussed in the matter of the Rule of Law, these three Arms of Government require their own Doctrine of the Ethics of its Separation. In most democracies, the Press or the media represents the people, and is considered the fourth (4th) arm of the State, sometimes referred to as the Fourth Estate. The State includes both the government and the people.

The agency which provides leadership for the State is the government or an administration, which is referred to interchangeably. This aspect provides a transitory role, because of the changes in Administrations, through different political parties winning General Elections. Therefore, the purpose of each Administration is to lead the agenda of the State and to protect and preserve the State from abuses, both from foreign and internal forces, during their tenure of administration.

To elaborate and understand more about these ideas, let us discuss further the role and purpose of government. One of the first American Presidents, Abraham Lincoln, made this famous statement:

> 'The role of government is to do for the people what they can't or don't want to do for themselves.'

In this regard, the American Declaration of Independence genuinely reflected the view, by the founding fathers of the United States, that a government is instituted among a people for the very purpose of securing the unalienable rights that all human beings deserve to enjoy. Some of these rights stated below entail:

> 'the right to live and be free, to the right to assemble and speak their minds, to the right to know what their government is doing both for them and to them'.

In his published paper called *The Second Treatise on Civil Government*, John Locke, a 17th-Century English Philosopher, describing the role of civil government, says that

> 'Government is a public trust with duties to the people, whose retained inextinguishable rights, are obtained only through mutual consent; like a tacit form of social contract, in which the people give up a measure of their independence, entrusting a part of their natural power to the government.'

> 'Political power, then, I take to be a right of making laws with penalties of death, and consequently all less penalties, for the regulating and preserving of property, and of employing the force of the community, in the execution of such laws, and in the defence of the common-wealth from foreign injury; and all this only for the public good.'

This notion and concept of John Locke's are succinctly affirmed in the latter portion of the opening refrain of the United States Declaration of Independence:

> 'To secure these rights, governments are instituted among men, deriving their just powers from the consent of the governed. And whenever any form of government becomes destructive of these ends, it is the right of the

people to alter or to abolish it, and to institute new government, laying its foundation on such principles and organizing its powers in such form, as to them shall seem most likely to affect their safety and happiness.'

John Locke believed, contrary to claims at that time that God had 'made all people naturally subject to a Monarch'; that people are 'by nature free.' (Tuckness). This belief was the foundation of his philosophy on Government. To John Locke, a Government existed, among other things, to promote public good, and to protect the life, liberty, and property of its people. For this reason, those who govern must be elected by the society, and the society must hold the power to institute a new Government when necessary.

National Leadership in the Bahamian Context

There are three branches of government under the Bahamian Parliamentary Westminster system.

The Governor-General is Head of State and vested with the Executive Authority on behalf of Her Majesty Queen Elizabeth II.

The Executive - This includes the Prime Minister, who is the Leader of the political party which has won the majority of seats in the House of Assembly. He is officially appointed by the Governor-General in accordance with the law and invited to form a Government. The members of the Cabinet, including Ministers of State and Parliamentary Secretaries, are appointed by the Governor-General, and serve at the discretion of the Prime Minister. The Prime Minister has the prerogative to appoint at least three members of his Cabinet from the Senate.

The Legislature - This includes the Members of Parliament – the Lower House – and the members of the Senate, the Upper

House. The Senate is a politically appointed body, constitutionally, in numbers, proportionate to the elected members in the House of Assembly, of the Governing Party and the Official Opposition. These two houses of Legislature are responsible for introducing and passing legislation for the country. The Legislation also includes Her Majesty's Loyal Opposition, which consists of those elected to Parliament, who are not members of the governing party. From these opposition members, the Leader of the Official Opposition is chosen. The Official Opposition is obligated and mandated to participate in the decisions of the government by constitutional right, with advice and consultation needed from the Leader of the Opposition, by the government for certain appointments.

The Judiciary - This branch includes all levels of the legal profession, ranging from the Chief Justice, the Court of Appeal, the Supreme and Magistrate Courts, all Justices of the Peace, including The Judicial and Legal Service Commission. In The Bahamas, the appointment of all high Judicial offices requires the approval of the office of the Prime Minister, in consultation with the Leader of the Opposition. And where the recruitment and appointment are recommended by the Judicial and Legal Service Commission, it also requires approval by the office of the Prime Minister.

The Fourth Branch - Not always recognized as such, is the Media or the Press. The purpose of the Media is to represent the views and voice of the People, no matter how varied and divergent. The Media/Press have an awesome responsibility to be Free and Unfettered, so that between General Elections, the people's voices can be heard, regardless of who sits in the chair of government.

In democratic countries like The Bahamas, based on the Rule of Law, the Judiciary must be independent and not be politically interfered with, by either the Executive or the Legislature, except for the appointment of such positions. The security of tenure for high judicial office provided for in the Constitution, in most cases, is supposed to provide restraint from political interference by the government of the day.

NASSAU, The Bahamas -- An Official Photo of the new Free National Movement Government Cabinet Ministers was taken with Governor General, Her Excellency Dame Marguerite Pindling (centre) at Government House immediately after the Official Opening of Parliament on May 24, 2017; Prime Minister the Hon. Dr. Hubert Minnis is at centre left, and Deputy Prime Minister and Minister of Finance the Hon. Peter Turnquest is at centre right. Also pictured l-r: Commissioner of Police Ellison Greenslade (second left), Desmond Edwards, Brent Symonette, Carl Bethel, QC, Secretary to the Cabinet Camille Johnson, Defence Force Commodore Captain Tellis Bethel. In middle row, l-r: Marvin Dames, Dionisio D'Aguilar, Jeffrey Lloyd, Lanisha Rolle, Dr. Dwayne Sands, Renward Wells, and Frankie Campbell. Third row, l-r: Darren Henfield, Romauld Ferreira, Michael Pintard, Dion Foulkes, Brensil Rolle, and Ellsworth Johnson. (BIS Photo/Kemuel Stubbs) (Photography by Bahamas Information Services (BIS) Nassau, Bahamas)

The secondary level of national leadership in The Bahamas include agencies of the State, and high-ranking government officials and quasi-government institutions, such as but not necessarily in the following order:

1. The Commissioner of Police & the Deputy Commissioner (The Provost Marshal)

2. The Commodore of the Defence Force & the Deputy Commodore

3. The Comptroller of Customs, Director of Immigration, and Superintendent of Prisons

4. Diplomatic Appointments, such as Ambassadors, Consular General, and Permanent Representatives of Overseas Missions & International Organizations, such as the Organization of American States (OAS), the United Nation (UN), and the United Nations Educational, Scientific and Cultural Organization (UNESCO), etc.

5. The Governor of the Central Bank & the Deputy Governor.

6. The Auditor General & the Deputy Auditor General

7. Island Administrators or Commissioners

8. Chairman and Members of Government Boards and Corporations

9. Chairman / Head of Local Government Councils

Except for the election of Local government officials, the majority of these positions listed above are appointed by elected political leadership, either from the private sector or the existing Civil or Public Service. The positions listed in numbers 1, 5, and 6, presently constitutionally enjoy 'Security of Tenure', in order to minimize political interference in the execution of their duties. While some of the above are political appointments, others are constitutional positions in the Civil Service and should be allowed to execute their duties without being frustrated and manipulated by the transitory political leadership.

(N.B. Although, contrary to the Constitution, the Ingraham Administration during the 2007-2012 term had amended the Police Act to make the Commissioner of Police serve by Contract. Since returning to office in May 2012, the Christie administration has since repealed that amendment. Nevertheless, both administrations have insisted on attempting to 'bully' the Commissioner of Police and interfering with the Office of the Commissioner, in order to carry out their own political agendas.)

Additional positions of authority that can be classified as national in scope, would be other high-ranking members of the public service including:

Permanent Secretaries, Deputy Permanent Secretaries, Under Secretaries, Directors and Assistant Directors, High ranking officers of the Armed Forces, both Police Force and Defence Forces, the Customs, the Immigration, and the Prison Service, including posts varying in levels from Assistant Commissioners of Police to Super-intendents and Officers in Charge (O/C) and their Deputies. There-fore, persons appointed to these high offices must be persons of strong moral character.

National Church Leaders and The Bahamas Christian Council

Although I will not deal in detail with this aspect now, I wish to also list the Church as an aspect of National leadership. This level of spiritual authority warrants our consideration for national leader-ship, because the office of the President of The Bahamas Christian

Council, the leader of the Christian Church in The Bahamas, is ranked ninth (9th) in the nation, in the Order of the National Precedence, and the other denominations are listed regarding their order in the List of Precedence.

President of Bahamas Christian Council

a. The Lord Bishop of the Anglican Church of the Province of Nassau and The Bahamas, including the Turks and Caicos Islands

b. The Roman Catholic Archbishop of The Bahamas

c. The President of The Bahamas Baptist Missionary & Educational Convention

d. The President of The Bahamas Conference of the Methodist Church

e. The President of the Methodist Church of the Caribbean and the Americas

f. The President of the Seventh Day Adventists Church

g. The Bishop of the Church of God of Prophecy

h. The Bishop of the Church of God Incorporated

i. The Leader of the Assemblies of Brethren

j. The Leader of the Assemblies of God

Church leaders and their national organizations, which provide moral and spiritual directions to public policies, are classified in my estimation as national leadership, in the same light as political and governmental officials. They have a moral responsibility to the nation.

Official Table of Precedence

- Governor-General
- Prime Minister

- Chief Justice
- Deputy Prime Minister and Members of the Cabinet
- Leader of the Opposition
- President of the Court of Appeal
- President of the Senate
- Speaker of the House of Assembly
- Former Governors-General
- Former Prime Ministers
- Former Chief Justices
- Justices of the Court of Appeal and Justices of the Supreme Court
- President of The Bahamas Christian Council & other Church Heads
- Parliamentary Secretaries
- Vice-President of the Senate
- Deputy Speaker of the House of Assembly
- Members of the Senate
- Members of the House of Assembly
- Secretary to the Cabinet
- Ambassadors, High Commissioners, Heads of International Organizations, Special Envoys
- Financial Secretary and Governor of the Central Bank
- Commissioner of the Royal Bahamas Police Force
- Commodore of the Royal Bahamas Defence Force
- Spouses of former Governors-General and of former Prime Ministers (if not accompanying the principal)
- Chairman of Commissions established under the Constitution
- Permanent Secretaries, Director of Legal Affairs, Director of Public Prosecutions, Auditor General, Treasurer, Comptroller of Customs
- President of the College of The Bahamas

- Head of the University of the West Indies Bahamas Campus
- Other Heads of Church Denominations and Members of The Bahamas Christian Council
- Senior Government Officials and Heads of Department
- Senior Officers of the Royal Bahamas Police Force
- Senior Officers of the Royal Bahamas Defence Force
- Senior Quasi-Government Officials
- Chief Councilors of Local Government Authorities & Chairman of Statutory Boards and Committees
- Chairmen and Secretaries of Political Parties having representation in Parliament
- Consuls General and Other Members of the Diplomatic Corps/Consular Missions
- Heads of Bank and Banking Institutions, Captains of Industry and Presidents of Trade Union
- Holders of Decorations
- Principals of Schools
- Councilors of Local Government & Heads of Community & Youth Organizations

In establishing these positions of national leadership within the society, we must seek to develop a criterion for the appointment of persons to leadership; and consideration should be for every level of the civil service.

Customer Service in the Public Service

The perpetual government document referred to as 'General Orders,' are the body of rules and policies that were designed to govern the activities and behavior of the Public/Civil service in The Bahamas. Although the rules are determined by some to be antiquated or inadequate, I believe that they should be consistently followed throughout the entire Civil service. It is like the Constitution. While some believe that some of its high moral elements need to be altered or abolished to reflect changing times; I am of the opinion that the high ethical and moral code set as a bar by the founding fathers, for those serving in the Public Service should remain intact.

As we consider Customer Care in the Public service, these things must be re-evaluated and considered for better productivity. If a person goes to a particular government office, and the person at the front desk speaks to them in a derogatory manner or gives them bad service, they refer to it as the 'government' giving them bad service, not just the individual employee. Therefore, since this is the consideration, it behooves top-level national leadership to impose higher standards online staff within all government ministries, to improve the level of customer service that is offered to the public.

I don't think people fully grasp why the people who offer for national leadership are called 'Public Servants' and the system of government employees is called the 'Public Service'. These terms were given because those who offer themselves to serve the public are being paid for their labour from out of the 'Public Purse'. This obligation makes governmental employees accountable to the people, similarly as politicians are accountable, even though their roles are inherently different.

In The Bahamas, it seems many persons only seek to obtain a government job to financially secure themselves, regardless of their interest to work or not to work. It has become abundantly clear to members of the public, and even more obvious to the government employee, that there is still a lack of accountability for effective on-the-job performance. And despite what has been considered in recent times - the periodic reforms in the public sector, with some real improvements – there is still much wastage in the public service of both manpower hours (time) and resources.

Considerably drastic is the problem of employees showing up to work, and having relatively nothing to do all day, except to be on the property. In many departments, some supervisors are experiencing the same apathy, so no one gets blamed. There has to be something fundamentally wrong with that. I am not saying that this applies in all cases, but it is abundant in too many cases. I have been in several government agencies over the years and have observed a tremendous amount of people playing games on their computers during the most productive hours of the day.

I have heard many stories over the years of such comfort of non-productivity in some government departments, that subordinates were chastised by senior staff because they attempt to be creative and make 'work' for themselves. The superiors on the job do not want to be exposed for inertia. So, persons attempting to outshine them, or 'make waves' in a situation, were instead chastised. Persons taking home a paycheck for inertia - where is the accountability in that?

There are many things that are taking place in the sphere of 'government' or 'the public service' that are inherently wrong, that must be changed. While the government has ordered a trimming of the budget for cost savings, a full evaluation of the civil service and the human resources of the government, for the purpose of fostering greater productivity of man-power hours, must be considered. I know that the 'cutting' of government jobs is not politically expedient, but a complete Environmental scan and a SWOT analysis of the entire Public Service (with the reduction of staff if necessary); in order to increase the overall efficiency, productivity, and cost-effectiveness of the people's resources. This is a reasonable undertaking.

In some cases, many politicians are allowed to secure jobs for their constituents, only on the basis of political support and favour. And while many of these persons are on the job, and are not being productive, and are sometimes accused of misbehaviour or malfeasance, their jobs are continually being protected because of their political connections. I have no problem with people being given a job because they qualify and they are willing to work; but when they are not qualified, and they are not willing to work, and there is nothing for them to do, they should not be paid from the 'Public Purse'.

We, the people, must demand that the money that we pay as taxes into the Public Treasury and the Consolidated Fund, are utilized for the good of all citizens and should not be spent on mediocrity, laziness, and what I consider as 'paid' loitering. We cannot encourage the government to use our tax dollars to subsidize this destructive national activity, which has been perpetuated for many years even by the highest office in the land.

Both politicians and the government employees who perpetrate these activities of the plumage of the Public Purse have no concern for the future security of the nation. Thus, the need to make persons in the government, who are both elected and employed, accountable by an acceptable code of conduct.

This kind of behaviour - of facilitating slackness on the job - perpetrated by politicians, is what has raised the National Debt to nearly nine billion ($9B) dollars, due largely to the cost of emoluments to public employees, and unproductive manpower hours and wastage.

For information, the Employee Emoluments of The Bahamas government is now just over fifty (50%) percent of the Recurrent Expenditure of the government's budget. Emoluments are approximately seventy-five ($75) million dollars per month; sixty-five

($65) million for actual salaries, and ten ($10) million for retirement pensions. This amount is basically said to be borrowed monthly.

Therefore, conclusively, a good government exists solely and entirely to provide safeguards for the future security of the nation. A good government is a just, fair, and equitable government, demanding 'Productivity for Pay', of both its employees and its elected officials. And if a government does not represent these values, or does not seek to demand accountability, then that government is not a good government.

'Government is a trust, and the officers of the government are trustees, and both were created for the benefit of the people.'

Which is why 19th Century Attorney, U.S. Statesman and Congressman, Henry Clay, Sr. uttered the above quote. As an aspirant for the Office of the President during his tenure, Clay was a lead negotiator to help steer the fledgling new United States of America; and lead a delegation to broker a peace treaty with Britain.

CHAPTER SIXTEEN

The Definition and Purpose of Leadership

T he word Leadership is all too often described as a position, a status, a title, or the rank of an individual. In reality, these have little to do with it. However, Leadership is the ability to obtain followers. Author and leadership expert John Maxwell quoted in August 2012,

> 'He that thinks he leads and hath no one following is simply taking a walk.'

The Oxford Online Dictionary best describes Leadership as 'the position of a group of people leading or influencing others within a given context'. Additional definitions include the 'action or influence necessary for the direction of an organization', or 'the function of a designated position, and the exercise of the responsibility involved in that position'.

However, I am of the opinion that, to be a true leader infers, that you have 'the capacity and ability to influence, inspire, rally, direct, encourage, motivate and mobilize resources, and activate people towards a designated goal and a common purpose'; while maintaining a level of 'commitment, momentum, confidence, relationships and moral fortitude'.

While many interchange the idea of management and leadership as one, the definition of leadership adds additional concepts of virtues than do the theories of management.

Leaders and managers are two different functions. All managers are not leaders, although all leaders must be managers. Management as a role simply maintains institutions and procedures, but it takes leaders to influence people to follow, or to move a company or an organization in a new direction or chart a new course.

While some ascribe to the adage that 'knowledge is power', it is not always the person with the most knowledge or education who is the obvious one to lead. However, the person who has the greatest ability to get out front, and get people intentionally coming behind them, following their lead, and acting on the vision would most likely accumulate the influence needed to be the leader.

Leadership is simply defined by some experts as influence. Therefore, true influence cannot be designated or assigned; it comes through experience and skill and is most times, just the innate or natural ability to lead. So, if you don't have influence, you will never be able to lead people.

For this reason, author Harry A. Overstreet, an American writer, and lecturer, and a popular author on modern psychology and sociology, whose 1949 book, *The Mature Mind* was a best-selling more than half a million books by 1952, wrote:

> 'The very essence of influence lies in getting the other person to participate.'

Purpose of Leadership

According to noted Bahamian author and preacher, the late Dr. Myles Munroe in one of his original books *Becoming a Leader*, the ultimate goal of leadership is not just followers, but the production of more leaders. He suggested:

> 'The success and effectiveness of a person's leadership is measured by his ability to inspire every follower to become a leader and fulfill his true potential'.

The master teacher, Jesus Christ (Yahshua) showed His desire to produce more leaders when He empowered His disciples and sent them out two by two. In turn, they would produce in their followers what they were becoming. He was empowering them, encouraging them, and inspiring them toward greater effectiveness in their own personal ministries, when he stated:

> 'He that believeth on me, the works that I do shall he do also; and greater works than these shall he do; because I go unto my Father.'

Therefore, the ultimate purpose of leadership is to recognize the potential in followers, and to express faith in them as potential leaders; to affirm that they have the innate ability to achieve as much, and even more than the leader has accomplished. Leadership has to produce more leaders if it is to be rendered effective or successful. It must produce more fruit of what it is if the law of succession is to be authenticated and realized.

Correct Reaction to Leadership

Noted leadership specialist John Maxwell quoted in his book, *The 21 Indispensable Qualities of a Leader*:

'Everything rises and falls on leadership.'

If leadership is meant to influence society, whatever we see in our societies today is an inevitable reflection of societal leadership. Therefore, I wish to intimate that the crisis that society is in is reflective of the crisis in leadership! Nobody else is to blame. We teach what we know, but we reproduce who we are.

In society today, far too often, leaders focus more on image rather than real integrity. Image is what others think we are, but integrity is what we really are. More often than not, the followers are also caught up in the hype of the image and charisma of the person leading, rather than whether or not that person has good character and integrity.

There has been a subtle myth in our local society, and societies across the globe, that stress that political leaders are not saints, and therefore they are not supposed to be the moral advocates of the nation. This concept is wrong but is slowly beginning to change in the minds of people around the world. Many people are coming to realize that political leaders, as well as other national leaders, have a constitutional responsibility to be the watchdogs of the level of morality in the nation. Otherwise, why would they be given the powers to pass legislation?

As legislators, they are responsible for enacting the laws of the land. And most civil laws have their basis and foundation in biblical protocols and morality. Thus, if consideration ought to be made, then legislators should also be responsible for guarding

Christian principles and moral values within the society, not just Church leaders.

In an article published in *The New Spectator*, August 2000, Pastor Mario Moxey of Bahamas Harvest Church, noted:

> 'We as a society live in a Bahamas that is morally bankrupt. The religious, political and civic leadership all share in our moral deficiency. It is called social undermining. It is the opposite of moral guardianship. Social undermining is exhibited when leadership publicly advocates one set of standards, but behind closed doors, engages in the same behaviour that was publicly ostracized. It is subtly practiced by both political and spiritual leadership. This theory of the concept of Social-undermining is also seen when leaders who are supposed to represent everything that is decent and good, in contradiction, engages in private demoralizing activities such as lying, stealing, conspiracy, unforgiveness, hatred, envy, profanity, prejudice, jealousy, drug and alcohol abuse, homosexuality and adultery, just to name a few.'

The exposure of such activities by the media and other public avenues, like social media, in many cases, provokes rebellious behaviour and vigilante activities, when the general public perceives that it cannot receive justice, but persons in leadership can 'get away' with anything.

My belief and advocacy have always been that children and young people mimic what they see reflected in leadership in society. Sometimes followers and citizens are like children: they do what they see leadership doing. It confirms the age-old English adage, 'What is good for the goose is good for the gander'. I believe that, if we have more morally sound and consistent national leadership, we would have a better society; simply because people 'react' to how they see leadership 'act'.

Therefore, the quality of inspiration in true leadership is the capacity to cause others to internalize a quality decision. People can be inspired to follow leadership that is good, just as they are inspired to follow leadership that is bad or corrupt. I believe that true leadership is like parenting. Parents operate in a manner to cause their children to follow them. If they do wrong, their children will most likely do wrong; but if they do right, their children will most likely do right. It is very rare for children of parents who have been good examples - who have educated their children in the wisdom of godly principles - to still go astray. I say it is rare. Sometimes it happens, but it is not the norm.

I believe that every man and woman who is called to national leadership, whether it is appointed or elected, are 'parents' to the nation. Therefore, their behaviour ought to be reflective of good parenting. Good leadership is essential to effective governance; therefore we must strive to have leadership that is exemplary in both its public demeanor and its private behaviour, in order to see the highest level of good and moral behaviour in the society.

Vision – How It Relates To Leadership

'Leadership is the transference of vision,' quotes Hal Reed, American actor, and writer. If this is correct, then leaders cannot be leaders if they have no authentic vision. The articulation of that vision must be a very integral part of why and how leaders lead. And certainly, that is what differentiates them from ordinary people.

What is Vision? According to the Oxford English Living Online Dictionary definition of Vision is 'The ability to think about or plan the future with imagination or wisdom; A vivid mental image, especially a fanciful one of the future.'

The ancient King Solomon, well-known for his Wisdom, states in Proverbs 29:18 that,

'Where there is no vision, the people perish.'

Therefore, let us reflect on what it means to Perish. In this instance, the online Bible Hub defines Perish as to 'cast off all restraints or have no boundaries.' So, we can then understand why people without 'boundaries or restraint' would become in that most precarious position of Perishing.

Just consider a scenario of a small boy who is without any type of restraint on his eating or behaviour. The child would be able to eat at his leisure or act as he wishes. The child's unrestrained eating can result in detriment to his health with lifestyle diseases, or even death. Meanwhile, his uncontrolled behaviour could possibly land him in trouble or in jail. As a result, that child will eventually be 'worst off' because it had no restraint, versus if boundaries were made to curtail his actions.

I submit that 'boundaries and restraints' are not meant to limit us but rather designed to channel our efforts and fine-tune our focus so that we could develop more effectively. So without vision, people have no 'restraining forces' to make them focus. Remember, whatever we focus on, we will develop.

Therefore, the primary prerequisite responsibility of leadership in a society is the acquisition and dissemination of vision. Vision becomes the driving force and the magnet to gain the Commitment, the Cooperation, and the Confidence of people.

Vision gives value, passion, and deep conviction to any leadership. When leaders do not possess vision, they will find themselves abusing and misusing their resources to gratify some short-term desire, while the big picture escapes them repeatedly.

Vision resolves these issues and becomes the point of galvanizing people and resources to accomplish an effective end-goal. Without vision, people and resources are separated and forced to 'cut their own way' through the chaos that may exist.

My friend and colleague Pastor Mario Moxey argued in that article in *The New Spectator*:

> 'Show me a society that has no vision and I will show you a society in chaos. Show me a society with vision, and I will show you good leaders. The leader finds the vision, then the people. The people find the leader, then the vision.'

CHAPTER SEVENTEEN

A Call For Righteous Governance

T he first call for Righteous Governance in The Bahamas came long before my time. While I do not take the credit for the origin of this term, it became the focus of my work and the primary topic of discussion, once we formed the Bahamas Constitution Party back in 1998. This was necessary as we sought to lead the discussion of the return of the nation to the original objectives of an Independent Bahamas, built on Christian Values and the Supremacy of God, articulated in the Preamble of the Constitution.

It is a little-known fact, though, that in 1956, a letter was released and circulated to constituents, by the two young candidates for the Southern District of New Providence, Attorneys Randol Fawkes and Lynden Pindling, which indicated that should they be elected, they would seek to implement Righteous Governance. Subsequently, they were elected during the General Elections in 1956, and went on to continue their pursuit of the righteous agenda in the fight for 'Equal Rights, Equity, Labour Relations, Majority Rule and Independence'.

Nassau, N. P.,
Bahamas,
24th February, 1956.

DEAR FRIEND,

The time is nigh at hand when you shall have to choose whether you want progress or whether you want stagnation!

As candidates of The Progressive Liberal Party we stand four square behind the dreams, hopes and aspirations of our people; for we realize that only by working together as a team can we overcome the numerous obstacles that have in the past bound us hands and feet.

WE ARE DETERMINED TO BREAK THESE CHAINS!

The cause for which we strive is the cause of Righteous Government. This crusade is too big for anyone of us to win alone. We are therefore asking you to join hands with us in order that together we, as a people, may take our rightful place in our native land.

IT IS TIME FOR A CHANGE! !

Yours very sincerely,

PLP CANDIDATES FOR THE SOUTHERN DISTRICT.

A Letter circulated by the Campaign team of Attorneys Randol Fawkes and Lynden Pindling, candidates for the Southern district of New Providence in the 1956 General Elections. (Provided Courtesy of The Sir Randol Fawkes Family Foundation – wwwsirrandolfawkes.com)*

Good Governance Defined

If you were to google the term 'Righteous Governance', on most occasions the term 'Good Governance' comes up. However, Good Governance is a term that has become a part of the vernacular of a large range of developmental institutions and other actors within the international arena. What it means exactly, however, has not been so well established. Almost all major developmental institutions today say that promoting good governance is an important part of their agendas.

Conversely, UNU.edu provides a comprehensive yet complex definition of Good Governance as a concept.

In general, work by the World Bank and other multilateral development banks on good governance addresses economic institutions and public sector management, including transparency and accountability, regulatory reform, and public sector skills and leadership. Other organizations, like the United Nations, European Commission, and OECD, are more likely to highlight democratic governance and human rights, aspects of political governance avoided by the Bank.

Some of the many issues that are treated under the governance programmes of various donors include election monitoring, political party support, combating corruption, building independent judiciaries, security sector reform, improved service delivery, transparency of government accounts, decentralization, civil and political rights, government responsiveness and forward vision, and the stability of the regulatory environment for private sector activities (including price systems, exchange regimes, and banking systems).

In short, working uses of the term good governance include a variety of generally good things. But these good things do not necessarily fit together in any meaningful way. Indeed, good governance would be a great example of a poorly specified concept for an introductory course in social science methodology.

What makes a concept good? In a 1999 article, political scientist John Gerring spelled out eight criteria of conceptual goodness that provide a useful framework.

Four of these criteria are especially relevant here:

1. First, good governance lacks parsimony. Unlike good concepts, good governance has endless definitions, and we always need the details of each to understand if we are talking about the same thing.

2. Second, good governance lacks differentiation. Well-governed countries often sound a lot like functioning liberal democracies, for instance, and it is not clear how they differ.

3. Third, good governance lacks coherence. Its many possible characteristics — from respect for human rights to efficient banking regulations — do not clearly belong together.

4. Fourth, and most important, good governance lacks theoretical utility. It confuses, rather than aids, in the formulation of theory and the related project of hypothesis testing, not least because the concept is so fluid that analysts can easily define it in the way that best fits their data.

Methodological discussions are often esoteric and best kept within scholarly circles, but this one has real-world relevance to development policy. Donor agencies regularly measure and assess the quality of governance and may condition assistance on these measurements.' (Source - unu.edu/publications)

The three top reasons for the problems we have in governments across the globe are based mostly on a lack of proper understanding of Leadership, Corruption, and sometimes on the political system itself. However, good or bad governance is often linked to the character of the leader or leaders in question. And so, for good governance to strive in any environment, it is important that the 'policymakers' are vigilant, transparent, and exercise good stewardship.

Righteous Governance - What the Local Call Means

My concept and definition of Righteous Governance are predicated and based on the core values enunciated in the Preamble of the Bahamian Constitution.

The call for Righteous Governance has been the primary call to the nation by the founding fathers, when they placed in the Preamble, that the 'preservation of our freedom is guaranteed by a national commitment' to 'Self-discipline, Industry, Loyalty, Unity and 'an abiding respect for Christian Values and the Rule of Law.' These six strong core values promote within themselves the ideals of a righteous agenda.

Additionally, the Preamble's secondary commitment to protect the 'fundamental rights and freedoms of the individual' citizen, established the founder's intent to govern in 'a proper and upright way' for and on behalf of all Bahamians. This protection of human rights is a righteous precept.

And in the third instance, the Preamble's commitment to 'an abiding respect for the Rule of Law' establishes the government's commitment to the concept of 'principled governance and procedural regularity' in the governance of the people. These core principles say to the people, that they can expect the government to be fair, and that all people will be treated alike, no matter what their station in life. It also establishes that the government is committed to Accountability and Integrity and gives the assurance that its actions will be honest and open.

All of these principles outlined here are righteous. And nothing can be wrong by adhering to these core values. Therefore, if we can link righteousness to conforming to these principles and standards, then, it is important that person coming forward to leadership in the nation, and the government itself, must conform to these standards.

Therefore, our call to Righteous Governance is a call for righteous leaders, who are capable of leading the nation, to stand and make themselves available to affect good stewardship in the affairs of the nation. And if a person is to be chosen to be in public office, they should be those who conform to godly principles and standards.

However, in the implementation of Righteous Governance, a biblical perspective as to how righteous leaders should operate is essential. Firstly, the book of Psalms 22:28 indicates that 'The Kingdom is the Lord's, and He is the Governor of the nations'; and Proverbs 8:15 states that, 'By me Kings rule, and Princes decree justice.' These scriptural references and others sanction the Authority of God in the governance of nations; And thus, the delegated authority to govern a nation is within the parameters of God who 'set up one king or one ruler and take down another king or another ruler'. Psalms 75:7

The Gift of Prophecy and Components of Prophetic Leaders

What does the Gift of Prophecy have to do with governance? In essence, it has more to do with the components of the gift that are essential for those attempting to change and reform nations.

In definition, the Gift of Prophecy is 'the ability to place in articulation, the heart, the will, the mind, and the purposes of God. It is the ability to give voice to the word of God, in whatever arena or situation your assignment is, and the ability to herald the direct opinions of God in that regard'. This definition was derived from Matthew Henry's Commentary of the Entire Bible.

As you are now familiar with the definition of leadership from earlier discussions, it speaks to some of those very same abilities. In one open-ended definition, someone defines a leader as 'a person who has a Vision, and the ability to articulate it.' Within the definition and connotation of the Gift of Prophecy, it simply identifies that 'the Gift and the Vision, and the Ability to articulate it, come from God' as a spiritual and divine endowment.

The gift of Prophecy does not necessarily make a person a prophet. However, the gift of Prophecy is a specialized spiritual skill set of the prophetic person, who operates under divine mandate for their particular assignment. However, to operate in the Ministry or the Office of a Prophet is the permanent vocation, incorporated in the five-fold ministry under Apostolic authority, based on the Judeo-Christian Church.

I believe that during my formative years in Church ministry, I was evolving in this prophetic gift, with the dreams and visions given to me even as early as my teenage years; and then later, with the ability to interpret them, or sense the mind of God concerning the revelation given in the particular dreams and visions. I am not certain that I am specifically called to walk in the office of a prophet; however, I do believe that I was given the gift of prophecy and taught how to effectively function in it: so that I would know how to utilize it in other arenas.

Subsequent to that, I am convinced that this endowment of the prophetic gift to me is to facilitate the purposes of God in the nation and for the operation of special wisdom for reform of the nation, 'to establish the Kingdom of God in the governance of the nation of The Commonwealth of The Bahamas'.

Components of the Prophetic Person

As I studied the life and work of Prophet Jeremiah and King Josiah, which we shall examine just a little further on in this Chapter, I examined intently Matthew Henry's Commentary of the Entire Bible. Some of its powerful observations and analysis that I have already shared, and I will share below, articulates God's intent for the work of the prophetic person.

Matthew Henry's Commentary of the Entire Bible cites in his commentary on Jeremiah that,

'The Great Creator knows what he will make of each man before he makes them; and therefore, 'what God designed men for, he calls them to.'

It further states that there are three things about the Creator that are certain. They are that:

1. God's purposes cannot be frustrated,
2. God's purpose is unchangeable,
3. God's knowledge is infallible.

These three emphatic statements about God's sovereignty help to substantiate that, when God calls a Prophet, there is a 'special counsel conversant' about that person's ministry. In that, when God first forms the spirit of that man or woman, they are designed for that work, and in turn, fitted for that work with 'Original Endowment'. This is referred to in Latin as, 'Propheta nascitur, non fit'.

Remember Jeremiah's opening text in Chapter one confirms this concept:

'Before I formed thee in the belly I knew thee, and before thou came forth out of the womb, I sanctified thee and ordained thee a prophet unto the nations.' Jeremiah 1:4

According to Matthew Henry Commentary, it is not Education that fits the man or woman for the work of a Prophet, it is 'Original Endowment' by the Divine Creator. It is the actual mind of God, that completes the educational process and preparation in the person for the work. So, whenever God calls anyone to the prophetic, He adequately equips them for the work.

Matthew Henry's Commentary identifies the following particulars that help you to identify the prophetic gifting:

1. **God confers upon the person, the gift of the Tongue.**

   'You will know the gift of the prophetic, because of the person's phenomenal ability to speak and to articulate the ideas. To speak intellectually and powerfully, as one having authority. If you use to stammer when you speak, you won't stammer when the spirit of the prophet comes upon you. It is the very first evidence. It changes your speech.'

2. **God also gives 'Judgement, Memory and Language'.**

   'The prophetic learning and language enables the prophet to understand what God says to him or her. God not only put knowledge in the head but words in the mouth – words that the Holy Spirit himself teaches – to convey God's message in God's words so that men will know it is not just the word of the person. This is also done, so that God can give instructions and wisdom in the same hour, by access through the gift.'

3. **God gives the ability to speak intelligibly, as being acquainted with him.**

   'God's touch sweetly conveys his words to the mouth of the prophet, to be ready at all occasions, so that the prophet will never 'want' for words. The disciples' speech changed, and it was noted by people, that they had been with Jesus. The prophetic gift speaks to the transferring of the words and wisdom from the mind of God.'

4. **One called to the prophetic must have eyes in their head.**

   'They must be seers, as well as speakers. They must be observant and quick to apprehend. They must be a discerner of everything going on around them. The accompanying gift of discerning of spirits is the ability to detect the motivating factor behind actions. This is the ability to know whether the source of movements or action is angelic, human or demonic. The prophetic persons are the Watchmen.'

5. **One called to the prophetic must apply diligence and all seriousness to their work.**

   'One called to the prophetic will never be a jester or a joker. One call to the prophetic will never be a slacker, a lazy person, or a procrastinator. Time is always at the essence; everything is set in a time frame. There is a completion date for everything.'

6. **One called to the prophetic usually experiences a great deal of trauma, pain, and misunderstanding earlier in their life and ministry.**

   'In order to remove them from self-dependence, Prophets are sometimes victims of a great deal of abuse and neglect and have more than an average season of discomfort. This is why the work of a prophet seeks to restore, amplify, and promote God's original intent. Restoration is a very intricate and delicate operation and is not the work of ordinary leaders.'

7. **The Prophetic person is also authorized to read the Doom of Nations**

God ratifies and fulfills that word. In this, it is God's purpose to show how sure the Word of Prophecy is, in order to put honour upon the prophetic gift, so that people would not despise the Office or the Gift of the Prophet.

The Prophetic Assignment and Commission for Righteous governance to the nation is designed to do the following:

- Destroy Idolatry within the governance of the nation, and to extirpate or terminate vicious habits and customs that have taken root in public policymaking.

- To overthrow the kingdom of sin, so that religion and virtue may be planted and built within the nation.

- To introduce and establish that which is good, so that which is evil can be removed.

- To set before them 'life and death' and 'good and evil' according to God's declaration concerning nations and kingdoms.

- To assure those who persist in wickedness, that they will be 'rooted out and destroyed', and those who repent should be 'built and planted'.

It is within this context of the prophetic assignment, that a great trust is committed to the prophetic person to be God's 'Herald-at-Arms', and to follow the task with specific instructions, which will yield good results. These important instructions listed are given to the prophetic person in the execution of their specific assignment:

- Be quick, be busy, speak in season and out of season, and be bold,

- Speak all that has been charged, because every word is weighty,
- Never conceal anything for fear of offending people,
- Never alter anything to make the message more palatable or more fashionable,
- Declare the whole counsel of God,
- Speak to as many people as possible, make the audience wide and varied,
- Never desert the office, and don't shirk the duty of it.

(Sources cited from Matthew Henry's Commentary of the Entire Bible of Jeremiah)

The Model of Prophet Jeremiah & King Josiah

During my study and research, I was led into reading the Commentary on Old-Testament figures, Prophet Jeremiah and King Josiah. These two figures whose symbiotic relationship can be seen as a model for Church and State collaboration for good governance and public policy reform. I believe this perspective on Jeremiah and Josiah will help leadership put the nation in good standing with righteous leadership and governance.

If I may paint a historical perspective briefly, the young Israeli King Josiah, the grandson of King Hezekiah, was only twenty-three (23) years old, when God called Jeremiah as a Prophet to him. During Josiah's early reign, from the age of eight until then, Jeremiah's father Hilkiah worked as the serving Priest, so Jeremiah was familiar with the work and determination of King Josiah. Subsequently, once Jeremiah came forth, he complimented the work of Josiah. The prophetic gift of Jeremiah provided righteous counsel to the King so that Josiah began the process of Reformation and Revival in the nation.

Based on where former generations of kings had taken the nation of Israel including Josiah's father Manasseh, the young King Josiah had to accept divine 'strength and courage' from his association with the young Prophet Jeremiah, in order to shift and carry the nation in the opposite direction from where it was going. The mandate of Josiah, as King and leader of the nation, was to hear and consider the counsel of Prophet Jeremiah regarding all that God had spoken concerning needed reformation in the governance of the nation. The vocation of the King Josiah and the Prophet Jeremiah mirrored each other. (2 Chronicles Chapters 34 & 35)

The Jeremiah Call To The Prophetic

The story of Jeremiah shows that he was called to the prophetic ministry as a teenager. Since he lived in Anathoth, a city for the Priesthood, he was the child of a Priest and would most likely become a Priest himself. Therefore, his training and socialization were deliberately designed for the raising and socialization of a priest. However, the call on Jeremiah's life to step forward to the Office of a Prophet was extraordinary. It came primarily because the nation had gone so far into the evil and secular practices of other neighboring nations, that many of the people, including the Priests and the Kings, had neglected what God's original intent was for the nation of Israel.

The 'Jeremiah Call' spoke specifically to the 'predestination' of the life of a prophet. The call to Prophetic leadership indicates intently, that the life of one called forward to the special task was selected from the womb and was proposed for the pre-assigned task. In the case of Jeremiah, even though he attempted to resist the call, God met all of his objections with the assurances of His protection and ability to equip him to 'complete the assignment' he was given. It also dictates that the 'assignment' on the person would result in that vocation during their entire lifetime. This was shown in Jeremiah's ministry, as he spent forty years of prophesying and speaking to the nation and the kings of Judah.

The call of Jeremiah came with a Commission to Jeremiah. This commission on his life placed him over the nations, in regards to what God would Show, Speak and Declare to him concerning the nation of Israel and their relationship to other nations. This Jeremiah commission was an 'extraordinary' Spirit of Prophecy; because it would be met with much resistance, because of its high-powered mission to the nation:

> 'See, I have this day set thee over the nations and over the kingdoms, to root out, and to pull down, and to destroy, and to throw down, to build, and to plant'. Jeremiah 1:10

The powerful assignment was to facilitate a completion of the work to reform the nation of Israel, without regard that someone else would have to come behind and finish the task. As Jeremiah's powerful assignment was to the nation; so is my task, in the call for the restoration of Righteous Governance in the nation of The Bahamas. I am a contemporary of Jeremiah's prophetic gift and commission to the Commonwealth of The Bahamas.

And for those specially called to righteous leadership and Righteous Governance in the Bahamas, and the nations of the World; please be assured that God's provision will be made, whenever we must face tremendous opposition. I have faced them, as Jeremiah did; and so will everyone seeking to govern in this righteous manner. This is also true for all those called to restore righteous principles in the various institutions in the marketplace, whether it be Law, Education, Business, Politics, the Civil Service, the Church, or otherwise.

However, when seeking to govern in this righteous manner, the resistance will come from many quarters in the nation, and many times from places and people you do not expect. As the crucible circumstances were evident for Jeremiah, the issues stated below are common circumstances confronting persons stepping out to bring meaningful Public Policy Reform:

i.   The kings or governments of the earth would set upon to destroy you with their power.

ii. They would trouble or frustrate your life from every side.

iii. The priests and religious leaders would seek to censure you in their Churches.

iv. The people will slander, libel, and destroy you with bitter words.

No matter how hard the confrontation and fight against you, it will not prevail. God will stand up for you. God will 'protect you, and bear you up in your trial so that no man would sink your spirit, nor drive him from your work, nor stop your mouth, nor take away your life, until you have finished your testimony' (Summarized from Matthew Henry's Commentary of the Entire Bible).

This covenant is made with the prophetic persons that are prepared to bring reform to a nation that has lost its godly heritage promised at its inception.

This nation, and the people of The Bahamas, were called forth and established from its inception to become 'A royal priesthood, a holy nation, a peculiar people'. This scriptural charge was articulated on July 10, 1973, by the late Rev. Dr. R.E. Cooper, President of The Bahamas Christian Council, for the official Ecumenical Service on Clifford Park in Nassau, marking the nation's Independence.

This initial declaration of our mission as a people was designed to establish us as a 'Beacon of Light' and an 'Insignia of Hope' for Righteous governance in these end times, in this region of the World; to shew forth the divine purpose and glory of God in the earth; to prepare a people for the coming of the Lord.

CHAPTER EIGHTEEN

Servant Leadership - A Concept

The pursuit of Servant leadership is not the most exciting concept for most people going forward for leadership. Although this type of leadership does not seem glamorous, it is the most rewarding, and by far the most important for learning experiences and opportunities. The leader who makes him or herself available to this process will find that Servant leadership provides many more opportunities for self-evaluation and self-discovery.

What is Servant leadership, you may ask? In a first response, Servant leadership is the form and type of leadership taught by the world's greatest leader, Jesus Christ, when He instructed His disciples:

> 'But so shall it not be among you: but whosoever will be great among you, shall be your minister: And whosoever of you will be the chiefest, shall be servant of all.'
>
> Mark 10: 43-44

This type of selfless service, given by the leader to those who follow, offers the leader the most reflective opportunity to discover gifts, talents, and virtue that they did not know they possessed. This process takes the leader on a journey of self-discovery, that enables him or her to produce authenticity for their leadership, which is necessary to serve their generation effectively. This authentic kind of leadership produces moral authority. It clearly identifies the integrity of the leader and demonstrates their ability to inspire confidence to those who follow or desire to follow them.

Servant leadership or having the attitude of a servant with responsibilities; allows the leader to discover what is their divine destiny, and what is the real vocation God has called them to. Having the confidence to walk in that authority, they will serve their generation effectively, while empowering and encouraging others to serve as well.

Let me share with you this revelation and lesson about servant leadership that has really encouraged me over the years. I was a member of the Breath of Life SDA Church since 1993. In the early years, during our many Sabbath afternoon Fellowship luncheons, I have often volunteered to 'wait tables' and distribute the food to the people. During serving lunch, we sometimes ran out of items of food that I wanted to eat with my lunch, like my favorite corn on the cob.

Over the years, I have observed the difference in the behaviour of those who were assigned to 'manage the food' in the kitchen. Some of them would put aside a plate of food for themselves, so that when they were finished serving, what they wanted to eat was already secured. Others would simply wait until we had finished serving the people and share what was left with those who were serving.

However, my friend Whitlean Smith, when she was responsible for cooking and managing the kitchen, did something completely special. In fact, what she did set the precedence for kitchen service following her tenure. She would place a separate pot or pan in the oven so that everyone who was serving would not be left out. We were not made aware of this provision until we were finished, and it was time for us to eat. In most cases, when she served us, it was sometimes a much larger portion than that which was served to the people. That became a powerful life lesson in Servant leadership for me.

When you make a decision to serve the people first, there is a chance that you may be shared out. Subsequently, quite like Whitlean did, God will make provision and secure provision for the servant leader without their knowledge. And contrary to what people want to think most times, the portion is even greater than those portions served to the people. That was a powerful revelation to me on the provision made for servant leaders.

How do you make a decision to take care of people first, with the possibility of not having anything left for you? That is a concept of servant leadership that we must understand and consider and be prepared to follow through if we are going to similarly Lead and Serve.

Another revelation my mother taught her children was something quite similar. Whenever something was to be shared between two persons, she would allow one person to do the sharing or the cutting, and the other person to get first choice. This method always caused us to be fair in our sharing or dealings. This exercise was done to make certain that, if we were not fair, we would be the one who was disadvantaged. That principle has always been a motivating factor in how I have served and operated during my life and ministry.

What God wants are leaders who are sincere enough to serve the people first. God wants selfless leaders, who minister to the needs of the people without consideration as to whether anything will remain. God always provides for leaders who place service above self. It takes faith to be a servant leader – and without Faith, your work will not be a pleasure to God or benefit to mankind.

Robert Greenleaf's Observations

This idea of Servant Leadership is not a new concept as we have noted before. However, the late Robert Greenleaf, modern-day Visionary and Author, passionately argued for it, when he discovered that, it was necessary for leadership in the 21st Century and beyond, to bring about a more equitable society, (in contrast to those that are now distorted by the competitive culture in many arenas).

The author of the book, *The Power of Servant Leadership*, the late Robert Greenleaf, whose work experiences and observations were garnered from a long career in the corporate arena, and as a trustee in many institutions in the United States of America; wrote many commentaries and essays on the subject back in the 1960s and '70s. He said that it was his dream and hope that persons who have taken up the mantle as 'servant leaders' would somehow help to bring together 'communities of seekers' who would add a new building force towards creating an evolving, more caring society.

He envisioned for the future that those 'seeking servants' would bring about 'new kinds of institutions' that are radically different from anything they had back in his day. He fore shadowed that this new emergence of 'servant leadership teaching' will provide a hopeful prospect for everyone, particularly young people, in order to make available 'prophetic visions' to the world for the 21st century. He had hoped that the message would be delivered, not just in words, but by servant leaders themselves saying, 'Here it is, Come and See!'

In a wishful gesture, he invited his readers to speculate on what these new institutions might look like. His insinuations were that by applying some of the ideals of servant leadership, these institutions would provide at least 'receptivity for new vision' in our globalized society.

I have long been impressed and empowered by Mr. Greenleaf's contributions to the intellectual mind concerning this subject. I believe that as we look at 'reconstructing' society and the nation, our focus must turn to this simple, yet transforming method of providing both 'service and leadership' in the same institutions and positions of power.

Therefore, I wish to conclude that based upon his dream for the future, by sheer implication, he has given me his permission to expand on his vision and his theories on this subject, for the sole purpose of raising up the next generation of 'seeking servants' to empower our country and our world.

Servant Leadership in the Marketplace

As we go further, many persons have inarguably drawn negative associations or connotations from the word Servant, due to the stigma of slavery and colonialism, and the past and present oppression of blue-collar workers.

However, it is necessary to re-consider what we could gain by embracing the inherent spiritual nature of the pairing of 'leader' and 'servant' in the same abode. Although the coined term 'servant-leadership' seems paradoxical to some, it serves as a new and interesting way to prompt new insights for a better philosophy of leadership for the 21st Century.

While many believe that there is an abundance of so-called 'feminine characteristics' in service-oriented leadership, Greenleaf noted that it is exactly the 'intrinsic worth' that makes it the best quality for both men and women aspiring for leadership. Probably, it is due to the abundance of these so-called 'feminine characteristics', why many more women leaders are taking the lead in the promotion of servant leadership going forward.

In addition to my own experiences which I have added to this section, Greenleaf helps to provide in the listing below, an abundance of observations and recommendations of what servant leadership looks like in the marketplace, and how we can identify traits of a servant leader.

However, there are two questions to consider when evaluating whether one should pursue servant leadership as a personal philosophy or as the mode of operation for an institution. The questions are: Is the role of servant leadership 'weak or strong'? and Is the role 'passive or proactive'?

In his response to these questions he raised in his essays, Greenleaf wanted one to rather consider the primary concept, 'Will anyone be hurt?' This concept is following upon William Shakespeare's statement in Shakespeare's Sonnets, which says:

'They that have power to hurt, but will do none.'

Therefore, the primary 'aim and intent' of a servant leader should be to ensure that their actions do not result in hurting people, knowingly, or unknowingly. It is the servant leader's role to be more 'aware, patient, gentle, forgiving, and skillful'.

It is also noted that in order to create a more 'just and caring' society, where opportunities are provided and people can grow; everyone, including leaders, must raise their performance as 'servants'. The actions of servant leaders should affect 'those serving' and those 'being served' in a more positive way. The implementation of Servant leadership provides greater benefits for the less privileged in society; however, in the application of it, it is hopeful, that those being served should have an obvious change in their condition and welfare so that they themselves would determine to become what they see, that is, to become servant leaders themselves also'.

Youth & Education in Servant Leadership

This philosophy of Servant Leadership must be taught to and accepted by people when they are young. It must become a lifestyle early in their lives if they are to be effective.

It is recommended that young people must begin to be taught the concept at least by secondary school, or even earlier if they are going to be effective as 'generational changers' later in life. Thus, I recommend and commend the concept of Volunteerism and Community work that has been implemented in our high schools for many years and are now being advocated at the primary school level also. It is important and essential to move forward in this regard:

1. Young people must learn early to stand against culture in two critical areas: 'Power and Competition'.

2. Young people must learn early and become aware of Power and its consequences, on both the 'wielder' and the 'object'.

3. Once the young potential servant leader accepts the vision of 'Power & Competition' and their consequences, they will see that 'striving and competition' are pathological, and not a normal trait for effective leading.

4. The young potential servant leader must shun Absolute power, which encompasses wielding roles without trustees or able colleagues, who are equal in serving with them. It is their best protection against Corruption. It is always seeking to be accountable to someone.

5. Teachers must be servant leaders in order to mentor the young.

6. Teachers are anyone who will 'Inspire young people' to rebuild the entire culture, and to 'serve and leave the world better' – while preparing others to 'lead' also. Just a reminder: all will not lead, but some will. Yet all must be trained to serve.

7. Teachers are anyone who will 'Invest the energy' while taking the risk to inspire the young with a vision.

8. Teachers as Servants – must be 'self-regenerating influences' within institutions of all sorts; not just schools and colleges, but entities such as political, governmental, civil, foundational, cultural, youth groups, and non-profit organizations.

9. Teachers are 'sources of prophetic vision' in organizations, to help supporters to build organizational strength.

10. Mentorship of the next generation is important in cultivating servant leadership. The servant leader must 'alert and inspire' the mentors and the mentees, with a vision of the opportunities available in this new way of Serving and Leading.

Government & Trustees of Society

Despite our inherent nature, 'Persuasion not Coercion' must be the tool that is used in getting people to accept the desired decisions of leaders, in the arena of governance and civil society. While many more people in these arenas, feel the need to 'coerce' people into doing what they want, this art of manipulation must be shunned by those looking for a better form of leadership. Persuasion is the key component to Servant Leadership.

Persuasion stands in sharp contrast to Coercion.

The definition of Coercion according to the Online Cambridge Dictionary is 'the act of coercing; use of force or intimidation to obtain compliance; and force or the power to use force in gaining compliance, as by a government or police force.

Persuasion also stands in sharp contrast to Manipulation.

The simple definition of Manipulation is 'guiding people into beliefs or actions' that they do not fully understand. Additionally, the Cambridge Online Dictionary defines it as, 'the action of influencing or controlling someone or something to your advantage, often without anyone knowing it':

1. Persuasion must be the most critical skill of the Servant leader.

2. Persuasion is arrived at by one's own intuitive sense. The act of persuasion will appeal to logic and intuition. This is why education is important. The one being persuaded must come to a decision alone, without being trampled by coercion or manipulative strategies. Both the servant leader and the follower must respect the integrity and allow the autonomy of the other while encouraging the other to find their own confirmation of the 'righteous' action or decision. Provide the information, and let people make the decision.

3. Servant Leaders must be prepared to take the 'Risk' of going out ahead to show people or their followers the way to go. Servant leaders must be consistent in 'leading' even though it appears sometimes that no one is following. Others will eventually follow voluntarily, when they believe or are

persuaded, that the servant leader's way is the right way and a better way than they would have devised or chosen for themselves.

4. A Servant leader is a 'Gradualist' – and will be an 'advocate' for persuasion, rather than 'authoritative' action. It means that the servant leader is prepared to wait for the decision rather than force a decision from people. However, while waiting on a decision from people, other actions can be taken that further the agenda, including teaching and showing the benefits of such a need for the intended action. People will often come to the conclusion or decision because they see the benefit from the actions of the leader.

5. The Servant leader will reject the rapid accomplishment of the desired goal by coercion, in favour of the slower process of persuasion (even if no one is hurt by the coercion). The process of 'waiting' is a fundamental aspect of the theology of Servant leadership.

6. The process of learning and self-discovering is also an important part of being a servant leader. The servant leader will not sell short the process to get the desired result.

7. Servant Leaders will reject a 'utilitarian' position, which would give justice to a small group while disadvantaging many more. Servant Leaders will seek to make certain that the 'majority of the people' are not severely disadvantaged for the benefit of a few.

Creating Stronger Institutions

The basis of Servant leadership and its philosophy is that of creating 'Stronger Institutions'. These strong institutions are ones in which the largest voluntary action is in support of the goals of the institution.

This goal of creating 'institutional integrity', which I spoke about in an earlier chapter, can only be achieved through maintaining these ideals. While Servant Leadership is one of those curious yet meaningful paradoxes, I agree with Greenleaf, that it is slowly beginning to 'gain adherents and sprout seeds' sown in many institutions over the past three or more decades, because of his teachings.

This initiative of Servant Leadership is expected to provide a framework for many institutions and organizations in society to find better ways to treat and manage the people who work within them. Servant Leadership offers 'hope and guidance' for a new era in human resources and development, for the creation of more caring institutions, workplaces, and communities.

Greenleaf wrote in his essay published in 1998 in the book, *The Power of Servant Leadership*:

> 'Serving and Competing is anti-ethical. The stronger the urge to serve, the less the interest in competing.'

Since ours is a very 'competitive' society, you may want to know, how then does servant leadership function in an overly competitive environment?

While some may describe servant leadership as weak, the primary focus should not be on the servant leader as a person, but rather the institution that they serve. Servant Leaders are far more concerned with the consequences of their actions on the people that they serve, rather than the perception of their personal self. The institution is the focus. Strong institutions build stronger societies. Thus, we must look beyond the leader to the institution, as the bedrock of what we are trying to create. In strong institutions, such as the ones servant leadership will create,

- Staff and members do 'the right thing, at the right time' for total effectiveness.

- Staff and members do 'right things' and perform necessary actions without having to be instructed again and again. Why? Because everyone is committed to the organization's goals.

- Staff and members have 'People first' attitudes – it is 'Service above Self' motto, quite like the motto of Rotary International.

- Staff and members are taught to 'serve' 'lead' and 'persuade', which is a pathway to restoring the 'dignity' of the institution. This dignity would have been lost through high competition in both the organization's external business, such as product Sales and securing clients, as well as in staff and employee's inter-relationships. Dignity restored in an organization adds strength to the institution – providing Strength to Serve, both internal and external clients.

Providing Consensus in Institutions

Servant Leadership is also about Consensus building and providing opportunities for 'liberating vision' within the organization. Liberating visions can come from anywhere and anyone, thus the organization must be open to receive and to act upon what and who brings the vision and inspiration to the table.

When people know that their thoughts and intellect are 'valued' within the organization, they will be liberated to dream. In such organizations, the atmosphere must be created to allow voluntary, plus durable, and sustainable consensus to evolve. The environment must be more accepting of others, in that, any employee or staff member can provide a meaningful contribution to the growth of the organization's goals.

In such organizations, it is not always necessary to 'legislate' the change but to provide leadership and encourage wide discussion. It is also helpful to let new directions come, as individuals find ways to work towards such goals, with the hope of wider consensus among staff and key stakeholders. While this is an important move for more participation, leadership must always monitor these actions, directly and indirectly, to maintain focus on the institution's goals and guide the process in an effective and productive manner.

Servant Leadership is always based on the 'gifting'. While all gifts are equal, all the operations are not the same. Therefore, the attitude and the mode of operations must be, 'If you are not leading, then you are serving. And while you are serving, you are leading.'

As I close this chapter, I was reminded recently of the scripture I was given back in May 1999, when the Bahamas Constitution Party (BCP) was first launched, and the basis of our Keynote message that evening. The reference in II Samuel Chapter 23, outlined David's recommendation to his young son Solomon, who was to assume the throne of Israel after him. His primary instructions were directed basically to Leaders and Magistrates, and to those charged with governing, to 'govern as with equals'. These instructions were to be adhered to if Solomon was to achieve a more caring and equitable society.

These powerful instructions by David, extend to us today, as we seek to empower leaders to govern well, with the best regards for the people they serve:

1. Leaders must be just and use their power for the suppressing of wickedness in society.

2. Leaders must use their powers to 'right' the injuries caused by injustice.

3. It is not simply for leaders to do no wrong, but that they not suffer wrong to be done.

4. Leaders should not only rule in the fear of God but possess the fear of God so that they will be effectively restrained from injustice and oppression themselves.

5. Leaders must promote religious and spiritual activities among those they rule and govern.

6. Leaders and Magistrates must be keepers of God's laws and custodians of Honesty.

7. Leaders must live good lives and have a good conscience before those they must serve and govern.

8. Leaders should also order religious affairs in the nation and be a light in the world.

These instructions were ordered by God, through the wisdom of David for good governance. Although, they were often not achieved, yet they must remain valid to advance the kingdom of God on earth; to bring honour and holiness to the conduct of godly leaders. Therefore, it is important that all in the nation show genuine interest in this agenda for leaders, as it is for the salvation of the soul of the nation.

CHAPTER NINETEEN

Transformational Leadership - A Model

During the summer of 2002, immediately after the General Election, I received an invitation to participate in the Transformational Leadership (TL) Project sponsored by the United Nations Development Fund for Women (UNIFEM) in the Caribbean. The Project was expected to explore elements of Transformational Leadership in selected thematic areas such as Gender Sensitive Policy Analysis, Participation in Formal Politics and Local Government, Economic Empowerment, and Peace Promotion.

The Transformational Leadership Project was chosen for discussion because UNIFEM's programmatic framework is bounded by three themes: Human Rights, Economic Empowerment, Good Governance, and Leadership. Based on the context of the latter, the need for a stronger, sustainable, more accountable, transformative leadership style, was becoming increasingly clear, as the global environment was changing so rapidly, with negative effects on women leadership.

The UNIFEM's Transformational Leadership initiative in the Regional Secretariat had anticipated to illuminate the concept from a Caribbean perspective and to use the new understanding of the term to identify transformational leaders, individuals, and organizations, and to find ways of lending UNIFEM's support to their activities.

The Regional initiative, envisaged as a mobile learning community, was expected to engage its selected partners, in several islands across the Caribbean, through research, public education, and training, so as to ensure the participation of women of all ages as agents of change towards a more equitable and gender sensitive society.

The first discussion held at the United Nations (UN) House in Christ Church, Barbados, in October 2002, began a process, which I believe, with wise guidance and direction, should have accomplished its objectives towards transforming governance and leadership in the region, through the work of governmental and non-governmental sectors. The three-member Bahamian team included the following: the leader of the now-defunct CDR, former leader of PLP business in the House of Assembly, and Member of Parliament for Bains & Grants Town, the late Dr. Bernard Nottage; a Social & Gender Policy Advisor, Mrs. Andrea Roberts; and me. We joined an additional thirty (30) persons in Barbados for an intense two-day informal plenary session on the theme discussion.

UNIFEM's Definition and Theme Statement of Transformational Leadership

The definition of the theme formulated from workshops with gender trainers, researchers, activists, and young people describes the concept of Transformational leadership as:

'A visionary process that starts at the individual level and transcends the personal, to express itself at the group and institutional levels. It leads to the redefinition of gender and power relations, and the strengthening of leadership that is bold and innovative and builds on the skills of women and men in society. It is leadership that depends on people's participation and challenges the beliefs, practices and structures of inequality, including gender inequality, that are detrimental to women's dignity, health, safety and well-being. It is leadership that seeks to ensure the empowerment of women. Transformational leadership is grounded in the principles and values of equity, equality, justice, democracy, caring, non-violence and cooperation.' UNIFEM Handout from the Seminars in 2002.

In keeping with UNIFEM's global initiative, the long-term objectives were expected to meet the following goals, based on UNIFEM Handout from the Seminars in 2002:

1. To assist women in understanding the cultural and other attitudes and factors that keep them from seeing themselves as leaders;

2. To assist women in understanding leadership and the environment in which it is exercised, so as to provide mechanisms through which lessons learned can be channeled into developing an alternative type of leadership;

3. To ensure that project outcomes are sustained through the transferal and sharing of skills to potential youth leaders;

4. To draw on the lessons learned and identify best practices in promoting cross-regional learning for organizations and individuals.

Understanding How Transformational Leadership Is Produced

In an attempt to understand the root of the theme, I researched the word 'Transformation'. Transformation means to 'change or alter completely in nature, form or function'. The thesaurus gives other words such as Alteration, Reformation, Modification, and Metamorphosis. However, the most interesting synonym I found was 'Conversion'. Conversion, which means to 'shift, change, or regenerate' brings strong perspective to the word Transformation.

I believe that the fundamental nature of leadership is supposed to affect transformation in the environment. However, the challenge has been that many aspects of traditional and hierarchical leadership have become corrupted and are therefore dangerous and detrimental to real growth in the society. Thus, I commend the discussion to provide recommendations to transform the whole spectrum of leadership in the governmental arenas, in both form and function.

As we continue to explore understanding this Transformational Leadership concept, we find that there are many different reasons why people select a certain type of individual to be their leader. Some are good reasons and others not so good, but they all represent a rationale. It is my opinion that the two reasons listed below, give a general indication of the contrast:

1. Most people are generally lazy, so they select or vote for a person or a group who will do all the work for them without requiring them to do much.

2. Some people select individuals who best represent their ideals and values, so they can work and collaborate with.

While the latter is most ideal, many persons refuse to demand more of their leadership because they do not want the responsibility of the work themselves. The rationale is if they disturb the status quo they will have to step forward and do more towards sustaining the leadership or changing the society. Therefore, most people are generally reluctant to 'rock' the boat. However, they admit by their own actions or inactions, a refusal to consent to transformational changes in leadership and governance. This kind of action speaks to a shirking of greater responsibility and participation by individual members of society. Therefore, I wish to offer my opinion on how to forward the ideals of transformational leadership in our region.

Firstly, the objective of producing transformational leadership must not be only towards the transformation of leadership, but also the transformation of the people themselves. While we may wish for the transformation of societies to come from 'top-down' which is ideal; the reality is, that we may have to concentrate on seeking transformation from 'bottom-up'.

So, if transformational thinking comes from the people first, and they demand their leaders to more accountable governance, then the leaders may feel obligated to change their style of leadership. However, if the leadership does not seek to change when provoked by the people, then the actions for transformational change have to begin with the people themselves.

The people must undertake the initial changes and force the transformation of leaders to follow. It is what some communities call 'grassroots' leadership, where activists and protestors, promote and demand changes in government action, to ensure changes in society.

This may result in a greater revolution coming from the society itself. Once society rises up and begins to change, the people, in turn, elect leaders who represent the transformational ideals they stand for. This type of change is very sustainable and more lasting.

In The Bahamas, and in many of our Caribbean countries, it is necessary for people to be instructed and guided as to what qualities they should look for when selecting a leader. It is like a Magistrate's instructions to the jury. The judge chooses the evidence that the jury should consider and sets the boundaries on which they should allow their minds to reflect. The Judge would recommend that any evidence outside of those parameters should not be considered. This brings the jury closer to a judgment that is fair and concise. This kind of agenda-setting allows only the best results to be achieved, based on the boundaries that are set. In such circumstances, mistakes are minimized.

There is an adage that says, 'You get what you negotiate'. So, what we have been getting in leadership and governance, is what we have negotiated and settled for. However, the time has come for the people to sharpen their negotiation skills, and to demand what they want, and to eliminate the election of the types of leadership that are compromising and corrupt. Only then will the transformation begin to take place in gigantic proportions.

Identifying Transformational Leaders and Leaderships

In the following segments, I will seek to identify what transformational leaders and leadership look like, and how they can be recognized at first sight. These items are not just characteristics or a combination of core values we can adopt or implement as a leader, but rather they are qualities we must identify as a people, and then promote. These items show the particular 'skill-set' of the leader or the leadership that is transformational. Servant Leaders are transformational because it is who they are: It is what their character dictates, it is what their personalities demand or mandates.

The three lists below were constructed during the two-day workshop and plenary sessions at the United Nations House in

Christ Church, Barbados, in October 2002. The named professionals were all leaders of the three plenary sessions that produced these ideas for discussion from different perspectives. I obtained permission from each of them to use their handwritten notes for my study.

Transformational Leadership ID List Number One – Professor Dr. Neville Duncan, Jamaica

The first list is from Dr. Neville Duncan, who holds a Bachelor of Science and a Master of Science Degrees from the University of the West Indies (UWI), and a Ph.D. from Manchester University, England. He was a Professor in Government at UWI Mona Campus in Jamaica at the time when this list was constructed. He is a renowned Political Scientist in the Caribbean. Professor Duncan's list seeks to identify ten (10) items to recognize as transformational, not only in governmental arenas but also in non-governmental organizational leadership structures:

1. Transformational Leadership is giving birth to the imagined future.

2. Transformational Leadership is a radical project to change all aspects of contemporary life rooted in tradition and hierarchy and to inaugurate new forms of social organizations and personal experiences.

3. Transformational Leadership is about generating 'speeded-up' energies, to make second nature behaviour and attitudes that counter unproductive societal relations.

4. Transformational Leadership in the political realm must seek to achieve transparency in decision-making; to place limits on authority; to achieve leadership accountability

and to promote new forms of 'interest representativeness' and the building of new institutions within the society.

5. It must also enable a government to achieve the governance capacity to 'coordinate the aggregating of divergent interests'; and thus promote policy that can credibly be taken to represent the public interest.

6. The challenge for Transformational Leadership is how to provide a framework of good governance that institutionalizes women's participation, as at least, co-equal to that of men, and achieve strong democracy.

7. The Transformational leader believes that 'the majority of individuals' stand to gain in self-esteem and growth toward a fuller affirmation of their potentialities by participating more actively in meaningful community decisions.

8. The Transformational leader knows that neither ideas nor institutions are self-implementing; they demand a base: A political movement composed of committed democrats intent on establishing strong democracy.

9. The Transformational leader looks to wage a second war for Suffrage; a second campaign to win the substance of citizenship promised but never achieved by the winning of the vote.

10. The Transformational leader believes in...
a) Strong Democratic Talk (deliberating, agenda-setting, listening, and empathy); b) Strong Democratic Decision-making (public decision, political judgment, common policymaking); and c) Strong Democratic Action (common work, community action, and citizen service).

The above are avenues and activities that build trust in community leadership. What I like about Professor Duncan's list, is that he has coined some new innovative phrases that bring excitement to this discussion, and which will give strength and substance to future discussions of how we go forward to achieve strong and productive leadership.

Transformational Leadership ID List Number Two - Grace Talma - Trinidad and Tobago

The second list is from Grace Talma, CEO of Grace Talma & Associates; a Human Resources Consultant whose Leadership Development skills were used to train front-line managers and leaders in the Organization of Eastern Caribbean States. Grace's list also identifies transformational leader's characteristics beyond the sphere of government to include organizational leadership in other environments.

These are characteristic of what Transformational Leaders are and do:

1. An agent of change – a catalyst for change.
2. Has the habit of reflection.
3. Has a compelling vision – a holistic view, which serves as a reference point for all activities.
4. Engenders optimism for the future of the organization.
5. Can align the organization to its future needs.
6. Must be able to communicate that vision both to external and internal constituencies.
7. Able to inspire the members of the organization to aspire and to achieve, more than they thought possible.
8. Has the strength and compelling nature of the vision and empowers the organization members to excel.

9. Raises the organization's level of consciousness.
10. Serves as a model of the new values.
11. Motivates, inspires, and gives value to intentions and actions.
12. Indicates priorities.
13. Shows strong advocacy.
14. Is able to persist through the long term.
15. Must have passion to achieve the goals and vision.
16. Are expected to engage in a cycle of continuous improvement, where everything is constantly being evaluated for its relevance to the vision.
17. Has the authority to build trust, is honest and empathetic.
18. Can share power with others.
19. Knows how to celebrate achievements and acknowledge the accomplishment of others.

Transformational Leadership ID List Number Three – Carol Narcisse - Kingston, Jamaica

This third list comes from Carol Narcisse, a Consultant on Social Policy Analysts for Gender, Social, and Community Development. She was a broadcast Journalist living in Jamaica at the time of this list construction. She is responsible for an NGO called 'Women Working for Transformation'. Carol's list identifies what activities and attributes transformational leadership, and leaders exhibit.

1. Creates change that radically alters existing realities.
2. Involves reflection and evaluation of personal values,
3. And has a habit of reflection and learning from one's actions and is willing to confront one's internal barriers.
4. Challenges and alters conventional definitions of powers.

5. Views Power as relational, i.e., Power within and power without (internal and external).
6. Exercises power in a collaborative/cooperative and non-corrosive way (Separates Authority from Authoritarianism).
7. Values equally each type and expression of Power – for content/knowledge, technical, spiritual/intuitive; and facilitates equity of opportunities for the contribution of these to the transformational process.
8. Is grounded in vision that is holistic and is guided by principles, values, and practices that support that vision.
9. Radically alters both the external environment (home, community, nation, region, and world); as well as the internal (personal) environment and character.
10. Is committed to creating equity - gender, social, etc.
11. Sees everyone as an agent for change and facilitates that agency by raising consciousness and acting to eliminate structural and systemic barriers.
12. Is inspirational.
13. Builds self-confidence, self-esteem among all stakeholders.
14. Is based on values of honesty, responsibility, openness, simplicity of living, determination, integrity, commitment, and stick-to-itiveness.
15. Promotes participation and builds partnerships.
16. Has cultural grounding but is not limited by that grounding.
17. Demonstrates an understanding of linkages between such aspects of development as health, environment, economics, politics, etc.
18. Is centered on love and respect.
19. Is passionate.
20. Creates structures and opportunities for vision to be passed on and enlarged.

Transformational Leadership Revolutionizes:

1. How persons see, understand, and value themselves and others.
2. How persons relate to each other (respect, love, mutuality, community, individual agency)
3. The institutions and structures of society, so that they engender and reinforce equity and generalize the possibility for extraordinary results within the whole society.
4. Human agencies, such that extraordinary results are possible and are achieved.
5. Communication- listening, thinking, speaking, and doing.

The exhibition of these lists is meant to assist persons in evaluating their leaders' character, and to determine whether the leadership has transformational characteristics. It should also assist persons in knowing how to encourage and cultivate these attributes to the further development of their own organization's leadership, as well as their own personal leadership skills.

Both Carol's and Grace's lists were compiled at the end of the first day of intense consensus discussions that took place in Barbados. Neville's list was compiled in a plenary session, specific to political leadership and governance of which I was a participant.

Women's Leadership and Gender Equality

When we talk about the subject of women's leadership, it provokes different feelings and thoughts for both genders. Generally, most men have one concept about women's leadership, while most women have another. While there are some men and women who think women should not lead in any case, there are others who have a completely opposite view.

I believe that the issue regarding whether women can lead or whether women should lead has been positively established, as we see women who have made great strides in the field of business, church, and government, within our region and indeed the world.

Some women who have stood out in governmental leadership in the twentieth century in our region were Dame Doris Johnson, who headed the Women's Suffrage Movement in The Bahamas in the 1960s; Dame Nita Barrow, former Prime Minister of Barbados in the 1980's; the former Prime Minister of Dominica, the late Dame Eugenia Charles; former British Prime Minister, the late Margaret Thatcher, referred to as the 'Iron Lady'; former Prime Minister of Pakistan, the late Benazir Bhutto; and former Israeli Prime Minister, the late Golda Meir, who served her country in the late 1960s and early 1970s.

In more recent times, others who have achieved national leadership in the 21st Century have been Germany's first female Chancellor Angela Merkl; Jamaica's former Prime Minister Portia Simpson-Miller; former U.S. Senator and former Secretary of State, Hillary Rodham Clinton, who was the Democratic Party's nominee in the United States' 2016 Presidential Elections; and former Alaskan Governor Sarah Palin, the Republican selection for Vice Presidential nominee in 2008.

The Bahamas has also gone a long way to challenge the status quo to provide many opportunities by placing women in major roles, both in the private sector and the public arena. The women representing major milestones and making history in various fields include the following: the first female Governor General, Dame Ivy Dumont; the first female Speaker of the House of Assembly, Rome Italia Johnson; the first Deputy Prime Minister, Cynthia 'Mother' Pratt; the first woman to be elected to Parliament and first female in the Bahamian Cabinet, Hon. Janet Bostwick; the first female Chief Justice and former President of Court of Appeal, Dame Joan Sawyer; the present President of the Court of Appeal, Anita Allen; the former Presidents of the Senate, Sharon Wilson and Lynn Holowesko; the first female Director of Public Works, Melanie Roach; and the numerous Permanent Secretaries, Cabinet Ministers, school principals, and other government officials. In addition, myself, who was the first female to organize a political party in May 1999, and to lead the party into the General Election in 2012 and 2017.

Despite these accomplishments, however, the sharing of political power in this nation still poses some challenges for women. It appears that the bestowment of power on women is, at most times, merely token. It seems that a woman cannot assume to take political power, she must be given it by a man. It is a situation where one wonders whether the men will let her pass. For some, this stereotyping is specifically in regard to political situations. It is clear that politics is a man's game, and women's participation is guarded at best. It requires a miracle for the rise of a woman to national political leadership. Whether this concept is myth or reality will have to be determined in future elections going forward, whether the Bahamas is prepared to put a woman in the top office in the land.

Challenges to Women's Leadership

During the discussions in Barbados in 2002, I was convinced that the UNIFEM discussion should not seek to link the concept of Transformational Leadership entirely to gender equality and women's leadership. By this, I meant that Transformational Leadership must be the objective, and gender equality and more women in leadership roles should be one of the expected results. I was concerned that if the UNIFEM project took the approach to demand more women in leadership roles as a primary means to promoting the implementation of transformational leadership, it might create an even greater challenge going forward, and we may make no great progress. I had determined that this cannot be the primary objective. This was my first introduction and discussion of the concept of Feminism in action.

While I was wholeheartedly committed to the advancement of transformational leadership within governance in the region, my point of departure was the fear that a radical 'feminist agenda' would overtake and hijack the agenda. While I had no problem with having more women in leadership roles, my problem was putting forward more women just to make up the numbers, in the name of gender equality. What I wanted to see was an authentic empowerment, and the ascension of women to leadership roles because they qualify and were the best to lead.

I was truly of the opinion that accepting the transformational leadership concept, would have resulted in putting the best-qualified person to lead, whether they were male or female. At the time, I was of the opinion then, and still of the opinion that no one should be denied the opportunity to lead simply because of their gender.

However, over the years, since our 2002 discussion in Barbados, I have come to realize what the real issue is. And to have more women at the table will become the catalysts needed for the transformation of leadership in The Bahamas and the region. The 'feminine' characteristic inherent in women's leadership, breaks the Boys-Club mentality of governance, and allows for new thinking and ideas to emerge in the decision-making process, which will change the male-dominated, traditional style of leadership practiced in politics, to the detriment of the nation as a whole.

Power & Order – The Difference Between the Sexes

Recently, God gave me a revelation of two very important components that differentiate the leadership styles of men and women. The components are 'Power' and 'Order'. Men generally lead by Power, and Women lead by Order. This is why both men and women are needed to be at the leadership table on all levels of society including political leadership and government.

When leadership is dominated only by men, we see more Power wielding than Order being implemented. These power struggles at times become ineffective, and the need for a greater level of coercion is necessary to get things accomplished. Power and Coercion are based on Ego, and Ego does not submit. Therefore, once the power struggle and the competitiveness ensue, corruption in the regime will ultimately be the result.

On the other hand, when women lead, they are more concerned with Protocol and Order. Generally speaking, women are not particularly concerned with the Power issue of leadership, because her view is on the problem that exists, and how she will fix it. She is stronger at that level because it doesn't require that she fight. She uses her brain and not her might, so it gives her the ability to produce more. If you check the statistics, women's leadership in government is rarely corrupted, unless she steps out of the framework of Order, to operate from the framework of Power. Therefore, more women in leadership roles are an imperative for the level of transformation that we are seeking.

With that in view, the mechanism needed to help more women to leadership roles are the following:

- To strengthen or build the capacity of women to lead

- To improve the capacity of women to recognize the skills and talents that they do possess for leadership

- To encourage women to volunteer to use those gifts towards engendering good governance and a more productive society

- And the financing of women going forward for political leadership

Historically, women have had ambivalent views on power. The concern has always been whether they could be or should be stakeholders with men in the equal sharing of power, or whether they should just be the ones over whom power is exerted. On the other hand, the way a woman views Power will determine whether she wishes to lead in any context. Power is inherent in all leadership roles, and in order for more women to accept leadership positions, they must internalize a new concept of power and the use of authority. I believe that a redefining of the concept of power and authority will assist women to see that through their own personal experiences, they can learn to exercise power in leadership roles without being intimidated or intimidating others.

When God made man and woman in the Garden of Eden, he made them both with the capacity and ability to work and cultivate the garden. They were made one. The woman was to be the helpmate of the man in the home and assist him in all his work. She was to operate with his authority, with his permission, in every capacity that they both deemed necessary.

In contrast to this first notion, societies over the centuries have attempted to make void the capacity of women to contribute to societal welfare outside of the home, thus the hierarchical introduction of inequality based on the woman's gender.

However, what I believe concerns most women is whether their use of power will make them seem more masculine and less feminine and diminish the positive perception of their primary role as caregivers. I believe society has dictated to both men and women, that women who are leaders are unruly, and men, who agree to women in leadership roles, are weak. This stereotyping is incorrect and has caused much grief in the world.

Primarily, women have always exercised power and acted in powerful ways in the home. This has been done while exercising authority over their children to the betterment of their families. The control of the family's finances, in many cases, has also allowed women to control the family's affairs and maintain order in that environment. Women, mainly mothers, have exercised advocacy for their children at PTA meetings, and at other school functions, and have accomplished much through their work and the exercise of that authority in community-based programs.

Many women, though, still have not seen that these traditional roles as mothers and wives have actually been ways of exercising power and authority. The idea of exercising that same type of authority outside of the home and family life is what scares most women and poses the greatest challenge to women getting what is considered an equitable share of power with men in governance and politics.

As I envision it, there may always be a greater challenge to getting more women in leadership roles in governance in the foreseeable future, because more women than men are the primary caregivers to their children and families; thus, minimizing and eliminating many younger women as prospects, during their most child-bearing productive years. So, the expectation is for more women to participate during their older years when building the family and educating children are over.

However, women's role in leadership should and must be facilitated based on the talents, knowledge, and wisdom that they bring to the table, whenever they are ready to come forward. If a woman is talented, courageous, and has the desire to be in leadership, she should be given the opportunity to do so. Whether a woman chooses the traditional role as a mother or a wife or remains single, she should be allowed to flourish in leadership. To deny her the privilege of fulfilling her potential in leadership diminishes the positive contribution that she can make to the organization of the country. What I believe will determine any woman's effectiveness as a leader will be her personal submission to God; and her ability to prioritize, and 'juggle' her home and family life with her civic duties.

While all women who aspire to leadership do not exhibit transformational qualities, the role women can play in leadership and governance will enrich and enhance the development of the country. Women's role in public life and governance does assist in providing many positive attributes to the transformational process and brings a new dimension of insight and intuitiveness to the implementation of the organization or the government's agenda.

Furthermore, because women are so intimately involved in caregiving in society, and have a natural knack for observation and details, their involvement will open many avenues for building trust and confidence among the people in the political process.

However, the threat of men being direct challenges to women's leadership is still very real. Many men are still insecure with the idea of a woman exercising authority over them and will use whatever method to curtail a woman's ascension to positions of power and authority. In addition to the fact that many men are not prepared to give up their ambition and their opportunity, for a woman to have the opportunity to go forward. This is a reality.

On the other hand, the reality is 'knowledge is power', and he or she who gains more knowledge, and gains more access to resources, has the opportunity to gain more power. As local and global statistics have shown, more women than men are enrolled in institutions of higher learning. Thus, more women have taken the opportunity to gain more knowledge than men, hence the possible shift in the balance of power to some degree to women's advantage.

Consequently, men who have not adequately prepared themselves, both technologically and educationally, for the challenges and threats of globalization in the local environment, may find themselves being overtaken by women who have prepared themselves. If more women are availing themselves with such resources, they will soon find themselves in a position to catch up and share equal power with men; thus, breaking the barrier, and eliminating the real threat of men maintaining absolute power over them within the workplace, and within the civic and political arenas. The reason I did not include the home in this list is because the male man will always be head of the family, no matter how educated and ambitious women become. It is a God-given role that no amount of education and secularism in society can replace.

And as a last apprehension, men are more often than not still bigger and stronger than women, and the fear of them hurting or overpowering us, will continue to serve to keep women from forcibly trying to take power. The issue of fear for my security continues to keep me cautious, no matter how adequately I have prepared myself.

The Role of the Mass Media

The role of the media is very crucial in facilitating gender equality at all levels of society, including national leadership. The media, which is responsible for the dissemination of relevant news information and entertainment, is basically responsible for displaying both class and gender stereotyping through various types of messages.

The media most often portrays men as ultimate leaders, but rarely portray women in the same powerful roles in business and politics. Many times, the media glamorizes what is the unachievable, and causes women to place limits on what they should expect out of life, and what they should pursue or not pursue.

At times, the media places more emphasis upon and preference towards men's contributions rather than those of women. Rarely do newscasts reflect the views of ordinary women and their contribution to political questions in society. Thus, the need is there for the media to pursue the views of ordinary women, rather than just the views of the more popular women in society, in order to give a correct perception of women's divergent interests, views, and roles.

Whenever the media ignores or minimizes the ordinary women's activities and contributions to public life, they underestimate their impact and contribution to the wider society. Since the media largely determines the types of roles and images that are portrayed to the society, it must be held largely accountable and exercise responsibility to minimize stereotyping, which facilitates inequality based on gender at all levels of society, and particularly leadership.

Strategies for Implementation

As we seek to determine some strategies for the implementation of transformational leadership within the context of governance in the region, we must consider firstly, that transformational leadership cannot and will not just be implemented: it must be identified and promoted. The cultivation of the environment for which such an alternative type of leadership will flourish must begin in a society where national leadership is opening avenues for an honest and accountable society.

If we examine Professor Duncan's contributions early in this chapter, we will see that the theme of his contribution is that transformational leadership is an ideal we must strive for. His idea is that transformational leadership is an 'imagined future' which is attainable, once we are prepared and committed to engage in strong democratic talk, strong democratic decision-making, and as a result, take strong democratic action. A component of strong democracy is the establishment of new political institutions that challenge the hierarchical forms of leadership and governance, and that makes it easier to identify and promote transformational leadership as the 'model' for the future.

Professor Duncan's reference to the rule of law and leaders' accountability, gives a sound foundation for the cultivation of the environment of transition; from where we are now, to where we need to go. This concept, the encouragement of participation by all levels of society, and the inclusion of divergent ideas within the society, is a responsibility of both the leaders and the followers towards Transformational Leadership as a Model to consider.

CHAPTER TWENTY

Political Culture Redefined /
Conservative vs Liberal

The whole discussion of moral standards for leaders is what has brought us to this conversation about Conservative versus Liberal views. It is certainly noted that no matter whether a person has a Conservative or Liberal viewpoint, we all want to achieve some of the same things for the nation, such as freedom, prosperity, opportunities for businesses, healthy children, a crime-free society, and the ability to alleviate the suffering of as many persons as possible. However, the divergence lies in the methods conceived to achieve these goals.

Liberal Thinking is a belief system that 'government action' is required to achieve equal opportunity for all. It is the ideology that obligates the government to alleviate social ills, provide equality, protect civil liberties, and to secure individual and human rights, to guarantee that no one is in need. The concept of Liberal policies generally emphasizes that it is the government's responsibility to solve all the problems of society. It is the belief system that fuels what some call 'big' government.

On the other hand, Conservative Thinking is a belief system that speaks to the personal responsibility of citizens, the concept of limited government, the ideals of a free-market economy, the pursuit of individual liberty, the traditional American and Christian values, and a strong defense of the nation. It is the ideology that believes that the role of government should be to provide the environment necessary for people to pursue their own goals. Conservative policies generally put emphasis on the government's empowerment of the individual to solve their own problems.

While the ideologies of Liberal and Conservative beliefs both have wonderful ideals for good governance, the pursuit of either will determine how the society evolves in the medium to long-term.

Even though I am eager to see us establish a new political divide on the grounds of Liberal thinking versus Conservative beliefs, I am still somewhat concerned that the unconditional segregation of both views may produce a wider gap in society and build an even greater wall in the political discussion; in favour of the concept of political tribalism, which I hope to avoid. This political tribalism is even now more evident today in Bahamian politics, as it has been in many of our neighboring Caribbean countries for some time. Although, in the Bahamas case, it is over personalities rather than ideologies.

In our 2012 General Election campaign, the Bahamas Constitution Party had categorized itself as the first real Conservative political party in the country. That assessment had been based primarily on our rationale regarding Christian values in governance, and the demand for a high moral standard for personal and ethical behaviour of political leaders. On the other hand, in relationship to more complex issues, I believe it may be necessary for us to reconsider how we articulate that view. As we go forward, though, I believe it may be necessary to combine some of the ideals of both sides of the strata, to bring about a more equitable and effective consideration of how we should govern society today.

Further to that, while both of the two political parties in The Bahamas, the Free National Movement (FNM) and the Progressive Liberal Party (PLP), had many empirical ideological differences in the past, it has become obvious to most Bahamians, that they have both degenerated into a microcosm of the same political creature.

As an example of this, while world events and economic depression at the turn of the Century have altered the economies of many countries, both FNM and PLP governments had not shifted their thinking to focus on the re-diversification and redevelopment of the Bahamian society for the long term. Both the FNM Hubert Ingraham and the PLP Perry Christie administrations had done the same thing to reemphasize its pursuit of investments for the Tourism Industry and the Financial services sector.

It would have been more appropriate to refocus its efforts on the real empowerment of Bahamians in the Agricultural, Marine, and Industrial sectors in a sizable way, with the use of the abundant and inexhaustible natural resources like Aragonite and sand. We should also have pursued the urgent task of 'feeding' ourselves. It is a billion-dollar import bill that would have been reduced with an aggressive food growth program. While they had paid lip service to these issues, both administrations had failed to adequately pursue real ownership of industries for Bahamians; and have left our natural resources, including much of our land and sea resources, basically in the hands of foreign interests; and have involved foreign interest in the matter of food security programs for the nation, such as the Chinese involvement in BAMSI.

While smaller investments have been made, I believe that greater emphasis and funding should have been planted in sustainable long-term industries, so that, by the time we came out of the past recessions; the visible growth from an emerging industrial sector would have been able to propel us forward, with new local and international revenue streams for income. It simply shows that the places from which Economic philosophies are derived for both the PLP and the FNM are generally the same – a Liberal ideology of Borrow, Tax, and Spend.

And even though the Bahamas in 2019-2020 has experienced Economic Depression based on devastations brought on by the catastrophic damages of Hurricane Dorian, and World events such as the COVID-19 atrocities, the present FNM administration stands in the same place as former administrations, by delaying it thrust towards diversification of the Bahamian Economy, with sustainable economic growth programs and the empowerment of the masses for the future, particularly an ambitious Food security program; instead the primary focus of both FNM and PLP has been to place the minds of the people on fickle political issues.

The Hon. Dr. Hubert Minnis & Cabinet Heading Heading to Parliament to present Annual Budget (Photography by Bahamas Information Services (BIS) Nassau, Bahamas)

Redefining Political Thought in The Bahamas

After almost fifty years as a nation, the time has come to evaluate who we are and what makes us different, politically. In recent times, we have not differentiated our politics, except with the division of PLP and FNM, and the leadership of Perry Christie versus Hubert Ingraham. As I alluded to earlier, the differences are primarily about personalities rather than ideologies. However, being politically defined helps to clarify the ideologies of political parties for the general public, so that persons can choose to align themselves based on what ideals best represent their own.

The Westminster system of governance in The Bahamas has served to keep smaller political parties from real participation and succeeding in Bahamian politics. Although, it is clear that over the years, it has been the 'Third Parties' that have brought the real ideas to any political discussion during General Elections; the important issue going forward is how to make these 'Third Parties' relevant in the political discussion for inclusion.

In the 1960s, when the Bahamas was in the struggle for Majority Rule, Women Suffrage, and Workers rights, there was a clear delineation in the country between the two political groups. During those days of struggle, the people making up the Progressive Liberal Party and the United Bahamian Party, all knew exactly and in no uncertain terms, what they wanted politically, and were able to effectively articulate that vision. This was because their entire life depended on their politics. It was a matter of whether they were free or not, as relates to the Negro population; or whether they lost or retained power over the Economy, as relates to the white Colonialists.

The children of both groups were indoctrinated on what they stood for because it meant the kind of Bahamas they would grow up in. But since, the black majority had attained the 'status' and the freedom and privileges that came following Majority Rule and Independence, the ideals that distinguished political demarcation does not seem to play that important a role as before. It has become clear that the majority is only concerned with maintaining Majority Rule or black power; thus the matter of governance has become merely about 'personalities' rather than 'ideologies. However, that is a thought to ponder, as to where we will end up in the future.

Issues Facing Bahamian Society

The concept of Conservative versus Liberal thinking has its primary basis in American politics. However, the opinions of many young people are that a more 'Americanizing' of Bahamian politics will bring a more accountable and acceptable form of governance suited for their modern mindset. This idea helps to bring the political student closer to describing or contemplating the way forward.

It is said that when 'the United States of America sneezes, The Bahamas catches the cold.' Although primarily American issues, as you will observe in the next section, many of them are becoming issues now facing Bahamian society today. The issues that now have major moral implications in The Bahamas are Embryonic Stem Cell Research, Same-Sex Marriages, Abortion, and the Death Penalty. These issues have evoked serious concerns and conflicts for the majority of the citizenry, causing me to believe that the Bahamian society is still a far more conservative society than a liberal one.

Although the majority of Bahamians have inherited and maintained our values from our religious forefathers, as a God-fearing, church-going society, this, in some way, is fundamentally, slowly changing. As a society, we are fast becoming more of an imitator and reflector of what we see outside the country, and on American television, versus being the originators or perpetrator of our own ideas and values. The advent of social media is crushing many values inherent in Bahamian society; and in some instances, exposing others' value systems or the lack thereof.

However, I believe that the presence of and the respect and admiration for, their aging parents has provided an enormous restraint for many younger Bahamians, from going headlong behind secularism in an accelerated fashion. And one thing that is certain about most Bahamians, they do not wish to shame their aging parents.

So, while many negative moral elements are beginning to be imposed upon or are surfacing in Bahamian society; the perception of ourselves and how we think others see us, keeps us from fully exposing ourselves individually and as a people, as more liberal, secular thinkers. This is the reason why there are so many more 'closet' homosexuals and lesbians in the Bahamian society, than those openly flaunting their abnormal sexual lifestyle. So, while some engage in immoral behaviour, it is preferable for them to publicly 'demonize and vilify' the immoral act, even though they fully participate in it in private.

Issues Creating the Political Divide in American Politics

These are the American definition and delineation of Conservative and Liberal thinking, which create the political divide. The issues are defined and stated below are provided from www.Student-newsdaily.com but paraphrased in some instances.

Abortion

Liberal View – A woman has the right to decide what happens with her body. A fetus is not a human life, so it does not have separate individual rights. The government should provide taxpayer-funded abortions for women who cannot afford them. The decision to have an abortion is the personal choice of a woman regarding her own body and the government must protect this right. Women have the right to affordable, safe, and legal abortions, including Partial-Birth abortions which are performed during the fifth (5th) month or later of pregnancy.

Conservative View – Human life begins at conception. Abortion is the murder of a human being. An unborn baby, as a living human being, has separate rights from those of the mother. Conservatives oppose taxpayer-funded abortion. Taxpayer dollars should not be used for the government to provide abortions. Conservatives support legislation to prohibit partial-birth abortions.

Affirmative Action

Liberal View – Due to the prevalence of racism in the past, minorities were deprived of the same education and employment opportunities as whites, therefore the government must work to make up for that. America is still a racist society, and due to unequal opportunity, minorities still lag behind whites in all statistical measurements of success. Therefore, a federal Affirmative Action law is necessary.

Conservative View – Individuals should be admitted to schools and hired for jobs based on their ability. It is unfair to use race as a factor in the selection process. Reverse-discrimination is not a solution to racism. Some individuals in society are racist, but American society, as a whole, is not. Preferential treatment of certain races through Affirmative Action is wrong.

Death Penalty

Liberal View – The death penalty should be abolished. It is inhumane and is 'cruel and unusual' punishment. Imprisonment is the appropriate punishment for murder. Every execution risks killing an innocent person.

Conservative View – The death penalty is a punishment that fits the crime of murder; it is neither 'cruel' nor 'unusual' punishment. Executing a murderer is the appropriate punishment for taking an innocent life.

Economy

Liberal View – A market system in which the government regulates the economy is best. Government must protect citizens from the greed of big business. Unlike the private sector, the government is motivated by public interest. Government regulation in all areas of the economy is needed to level the playing field.

Conservative View – The free market system, competitive capitalism, and private enterprise create the greatest opportunity and the highest standard of living for all. Free markets produce more economic growth, more jobs, and higher standards of living than those systems burdened by excessive government regulation.

Education – Vouchers & Charter Schools

Liberal View – Public schools are the best way to educate students. Vouchers (or Subsidies to Private schools) take money away from public schools. Government should focus additional funds on existing public schools, raising teacher salaries, and reducing class size.

Conservative View – School vouchers (Subsidies) create competition and therefore encourage schools to improve performance. Vouchers will give all parents the right to choose good schools for their children, not just those who can afford private schools.

Embryonic Stem Cell Research

Liberal View – Support the use of embryonic stem cells for research. It is necessary and ethical for the government to fund Embryonic stem cell research, which will assist scientists in finding treatments and cures for diseases. An embryo is not a human. The tiny blastocyst (embryos used in embryonic stem cell research) has no human features. Experimenting on embryos/embryonic stem cells is not murder. Embryonic stem cells have the potential to cure chronic and degenerative diseases that current medicine has been unable to effectively treat.

Conservative View – Supports the use of adult and umbilical cord stem cells only for research. It is morally and ethically wrong for the government to fund Embryonic Stem Cell research. Human life begins at conception. The extraction of stem cells from an embryo requires its destruction. In other words, it requires a human life to be killed. Adult stem cells have already been used to treat spinal cord injuries, Leukemia, and even Parkinson's disease. Adult stem cells are derived from umbilical cords, placentas, amniotic fluid, various tissues and organ systems like skin and the liver, and even fat obtained from liposuction. Embryonic stem cells have not been successfully used to help cure disease.

Energy

Liberal View – Oil is a depleting resource. Other sources of energy must be explored. The government must produce a national plan for all energy resources and subsidize (partially pay for) alternative energy research and production. Supports increased exploration of alternative energy sources such as wind and solar power. Supports government control of gas and electrical industries.

Conservative View – Oil, gas, and coal are all good sources of energy and are abundant in the U.S. Oil drilling should be increased both on land and at sea. Increased domestic production creates lower prices and less dependence on other countries for oil. Supports increased production of nuclear energy. Wind and solar sources will never provide plentiful, affordable sources of power. Support private ownership of gas and electric industries.

Euthanasia & Physician-Assisted Suicide

Liberal View – Euthanasia should be legalized. A person has a right to die with dignity, by his own choice. A terminally ill person should have the right to choose to end pain and suffering. It is wrong for the government to take away the means for a terminally ill person to hasten his death. It is wrong to force a person to go through so much pain and suffering. Legalizing Euthanasia would not lead to doctor-assisted suicides of non-critical patients. Permitting euthanasia would reduce health care costs, which would then make funds available for those who could truly benefit from medical care.

Conservative View – Neither Euthanasia nor physician-assisted suicide should be legalized. It is immoral and unethical to deliberately end the life of a terminally ill person (euthanasia) or enable another person to end their life (assisted suicide). The goal should be compassionate care and easing the suffering of terminally ill people. Legalizing euthanasia could lead to doctor-assisted suicides of non-critical patients. If euthanasia were legalized, insurance companies could pressure doctors to withhold life-saving treatment for dying patients. Many religions prohibit suicide and euthanasia. These practices devalue human life.

Global Warming/Climate Change

Liberal View – Global warming is caused by an increased production of carbon dioxide through the burning of fossil fuels (coal, oil, and natural gas). The U.S. is a major contributor to global warming because it produces 25% of the world's carbon dioxide. Proposed laws to reduce carbon emissions in the U.S. are urgently needed and should be enacted immediately to save the planet. Many reputable scientists support this theory.

Conservative View –- Change in global temperature is natural over long periods of time. Science has not shown that humans can affect permanent change to the earth's temperature. Proposed laws to reduce carbon emissions will do nothing to help the environment and will cause significant price increases for all. Many reputable scientists support this theory.

Gun Control

Liberal View – The Second Amendment does not give citizens the right to keep and bear arms, but only allows for the state to keep a militia (National Guard). Individuals do not need guns for protection; it is the role of the local and federal government to protect the people through law enforcement agencies and the military. Additional gun control laws are necessary to stop gun violence and limit the ability of criminals to obtain guns. More guns mean more violence.

Conservative View – The Second Amendment gives citizens the right to keep and bear arms. Individuals have the right to defend themselves. There are too many gun control laws – additional laws will not lower gun crime rates. What is needed is enforcement of current laws. Gun control laws do not prevent criminals from obtaining guns. More guns in the hands of law-abiding citizens mean less crime. Quote of the Second Amendment to the U.S. Constitution:

> 'A well-regulated Militia, being necessary to the security of a free State; the right of the people to keep and bear Arms shall not be infringed.'

Healthcare
Liberal View – Support free or low-cost government-controlled health care. There are millions of Americans who can't afford health care and are deprived of this basic right. Every American has a right to affordable health care. The government should provide equal health care benefits for all, regardless of their ability to pay.

Conservative View – Support competitive, free-market health care systems. All Americans have access to health care. The debate is about who should pay for it. Free and low-cost government-run programs (socialized medicine) result in higher costs and everyone receiving the same poor-quality health care. Health care should remain privatized. The problem of uninsured individuals should be addressed and solved within the free-market healthcare system – the government should not control healthcare.

Homeland Security
Liberal View – Airport Security – Passenger profiling is wrong, period. Selection of passengers for extra security screening should be random. Using other criteria (such as ethnicity) is discriminatory and offensive to Arabs and Muslims, who are generally innocent and law-abiding. Terrorists don't fit a profile. '...Arabs, Muslims, and South Asians are no more likely than whites to be terrorists,' says the American Civil Liberties Union - ACLU.

Conservative View – Airport Security – Choosing passengers randomly for extra security searches is not effective. Rather, profiling and intelligence data should be used to single out passengers for extra screening. Those who do not meet the criteria for suspicion should not be subjected to intense screening. The terrorists currently posing a threat to the U.S. are primarily Islamic/Muslim men between the ages of 18 and 38. Our resources should be focused on this group. Profiling is good logical police work.

Immigration

Liberal View – Supports legal immigration. Supports amnesty for those who enter the U.S. illegally (undocumented immigrants). Also believes that undocumented immigrants have a right to all educational and health benefits that citizens receive (financial aid, welfare, social security, and Medicaid), regardless of legal status; and should have the same rights as American citizens. It is unfair to arrest millions of undocumented immigrants.

Conservative View – Supports legal immigration only. Opposes amnesty for those who enter the U.S. illegally (illegal immigrants). Those who break the law by entering the U.S. illegally do not have the same rights as those who obey the law and enter legally. The borders should be secured before addressing the problem of the illegal immigrants currently in the country. The Federal Government should secure the borders and enforce current immigration laws.

Private Property

Liberal View – Government has the right to use eminent domain (seizure of private property by the government–with compensation to the owner) to accomplish a public end.

Conservative View – Respects ownership and private property rights. Eminent domain (seizure of private property by the government–with compensation to the owner) in most cases is wrong. Eminent domain should not be used for private development.

Religion & Government

Liberal View – Support the separation of Church and State. Believes that the Bill of Rights implies a separation of Church and State. Religious expression has no place in government. The two should be completely separate. Government should not support religious expression in any way. All references to God in public and government spaces should be removed (e.g., the Ten Commandments should not be displayed in Federal buildings).

Conservative View – The phrase 'separation of church and state' is not in the Constitution. The First Amendment to the Constitution states 'Congress shall make no law respecting an establishment of religion, or prohibiting the free exercise thereof...' This prevents the government from establishing a national church/denomination. However, it does not prohibit God from being acknowledged in schools and government buildings. Symbols of Christian heritage should not be removed from public and government spaces (e.g., the Ten Commandments should continue to be displayed in Federal buildings). Government should not interfere with religion and religious freedom.

Same-Sex Marriage

Liberal View – Believes that Marriage is the union of people who love each other. It should be legal for gay, lesbian, bisexual, and transgender individuals, to ensure equal rights for all. Support same-sex marriages. Is opposed to the creation of a constitutional amendment establishing marriage as the union of one man and one woman. All individuals, regardless of their sexual orientation, have the right to marry. Prohibiting same-sex citizens from marrying denies them their civil rights. [Opinions vary on whether this issue is equal to civil rights for African Americans.]

Conservative View – Believes that Marriage is the union of one man and one woman. Opposes same-sex marriages. Supports the Defense of Marriage Act (DOMA) passed in 1996, which affirms the right of states not to recognize same-sex marriages licensed in other states. Believes that requiring citizens to sanction same-sex relationships violates the moral and religious beliefs of millions of Christians, Jews, Muslims, and others, who believe marriage is the union of one man and one woman.

Social Security

Liberal View – The Social Security system should be protected at all costs. Reduction in future benefits is not a reasonable option. [Opinions vary on the extent of the current system's financial stability.] Social Security provides a safety net for the nation's poor and needy. Changing the system would cause a reduction in benefits and many people would suffer as a result.

Conservative View – The Social Security system is in serious financial trouble. Major changes to the current system are urgently needed. In its current state, the Social Security system is not financially sustainable. It will collapse if nothing is done to address the problems. Many will suffer as a result. Social Security must be made more efficient through privatization and/or allowing individuals to manage their own savings.

Welfare

Liberal View – Support welfare, including long-term welfare. Welfare is a safety net that provides for the needs of the poor. Welfare is necessary to bring fairness to American economic life. It is a device for protecting the poor.

Conservative View – Opposes long-term welfare. Opportunities should be provided to make it possible for those in need to become self-reliant. It is far more compassionate and effective to encourage people to become self-reliant, rather than allowing them to remain dependent on the government for provisions.

Taxes

Liberal View – Higher taxes (primarily for the wealthy) and a larger government are necessary to address inequality or injustice in society. Government should help the poor and needy using tax dollars from the rich. Supports a large government to provide for the needs of the people and create equality. Taxes enable the government to create jobs and provide welfare programs for those in need. Government programs are a caring way to provide for the poor and needy in society.

Conservative View – Lower taxes and a smaller government with limited power will improve the standard of living for all. Supports lower taxes and a smaller government. Lower taxes create more incentive for people to work, save, invest, and engage in entre-preneurial endeavours. Money is best spent by those who earn it, not the government. Government programs encourage people to become dependent and lazy, rather than encouraging work and independence.

United Nations (UN)

Liberal View – The UN promotes peace and human rights. The United States has a moral and a legal obligation to support the United Nations (UN). The U.S. should not act as a sovereign nation but as one member of a world community. The U.S. should submit its national interests to the greater good of the global community (as defined by the UN). The U.S. should defer to the UN in military/peacekeeping matters. The United Nations Charter gives the United Nations Security Council the power and responsibility to take collective action to maintain international peace and security. U.S. troops should submit to UN command.

Conservative View – The United Nations has repeatedly failed in its essential mission to promote world peace and human rights. The wars, genocide, and human rights abuses taking place in many Human Rights Council member states (and the UN's failure to stop them), prove this point. History shows that the United States, not the UN, is the global force for spreading freedom, prosperity, tolerance, and peace. The U.S. should never subvert its national interests to those of the UN. The U.S. should never place troops under UN control. U.S. military should always wear the U.S. military uniform, not that of UN peacekeepers. [Opinions vary on whether the U.S. should withdraw from the UN.]

War on Terror/Terrorism

Liberal View – Global warming, not terrorism, poses the greatest threat to the U.S., according to Democrats in Congress. Terrorism is a result of arrogant U.S. foreign policy. Good diplomacy is the best way to deal with terrorism. Relying on military force to defeat terrorism creates hatred that leads to more terrorism. Captured terrorists should be handled by law enforcement and tried in civilian courts.

Conservative View – Terrorism poses one of the greatest threats to the U.S. The world toward which the militant Islamists strive cannot peacefully coexist with the Western world. In the last decade, militant Islamists have repeatedly attacked Americans and American interests here and abroad. Terrorists must be stopped and destroyed. The use of intelligence-gathering and military forces is the best way to defeat terrorism around the world. Captured terrorists should be treated as enemy combatants and tried in military courts.

Expert Analysis on the Differences

According to the experts who study political leanings, Liberals and Conservatives are different. Not just because they see things differently, but even their personalities and their unconscious reactions to the world around them. For example, in an article published online scientific America in 2012, on a UNL study, a team led by psychologist Michael Dodd and political scientist John Hibbing of the University of Nebraska in Lincoln, discovered that when viewing a collage of photographs, Conservatives' eyes unconsciously lingered fifteen (15%) percent longer on repellent images, suggesting that Conservatives are more attuned than Liberals to assessing potential threats.

Meanwhile, examining the contents of the bedrooms of almost one hundred students, as one part of the UNL 2008 Study group, revealed that Conservatives possessed more cleaning and organizational items, such as ironing boards and calendars, confirming that they are more 'orderly and self-disciplined'. Liberals, however, owned more books and travel-related memorabilia, which confirms previous research, suggesting that they are more 'open and novelty-seeking'.

'These are not superficial differences. They are psychologically deep,' says Psychologist John Jost of New York University, a co-author of the Bedroom Study.

Meanwhile, studies by Jost and others suggest that political views reside on a Continuum; that is, mediated in part by universal human emotions such as fear. Under certain circumstances, everyone can shift closer to the middle – or drift further apart. Even with the television series *The Fear Factor*, Psychologists have found that Conservatives are fundamentally more anxious than Liberals, which may be why they typically desire stability, structure, and clear answers, even to complicated questions.

> 'Conservatism apparently helps to protect people against some of the natural difficulties of living. The fact is we don't live in a completely safe world. Things can and do go wrong. But if I can impose this order on it by my world-view, I can keep my anxiety to a manageable level.'

Says Social Psychologist Paul Nail of the University of Central Arkansas noted above. In another of his research, he indicates:

> 'Anxiety is an emotion that waxes and wanes in all of us, and our political views can shift in its wake. Generally, when people feel safe and secure, they become more liberal, and when they feel threatened, they become more conservative'.

Research conducted by Psychologist Paul Nail and his colleagues at the University of Arkansas in the weeks after September 11,

2001, showed that people of all political persuasions became more conservative in the wake of the Terrorist attacks.

According to the *New York Times*, in his 2012 social psychology book, *The Righteous Mind – Why Good People Are Divided by Politics and Religion*, Jonathon Haidt, a social psychologist at the University of Virginia, identifies several areas of morality which values both groups share.

He noted that Liberals tend to value 'caring for people who are vulnerable' and for them 'fairness' tends to mean 'sharing resources equally'. Although Conservatives also care about those things, for them 'fairness' means 'proportionality – that people should get what they deserve based on the amount of effort they have put in'. He noted that Conservatives also emphasize 'loyalty and authority', which they believe are values helpful for maintaining a stable society.

In their 2009 University of Virginia study, Haidt and two of his colleagues presented more than eight thousand (8,000) people with a series of hypothetical actions. Among them, were the following scenarios:

- Would you kick a dog in the head?
- Would you discard a box of ballots to help your candidate win?
- Would you publicly bet against a favourite sports team?
- Would you curse your parents to their faces?
- Would you receive a blood transfusion from a child molester?

Participants had to say whether they would do these deeds for money and, if so, for how much:

a) $10?   b) $1,000?   c) $100,000?   d) More?

Based on the study, Liberals were reluctant to harm a living thing or act unfairly, even for $1 million. However, they were willing to betray group loyalty, disrespect authority, or do something disgusting, such as eating their own dog after it dies, for cash. However, Conservatives said they were less willing to compromise on any of the moral categories.

Subsequently, Professor Haidt has a message for both sides. He wants the Liberals to acknowledge that Conservatives' emphasis on laws, institutions, customs, and religion are valuable; and that Conservatives' recognition that democracy is a huge achievement, and that maintaining the social order requires imposing constraints on people.

On the other hand, Professor Haidt message for Conservatives is, that Liberal values also serve important roles, which are: Ensuring that the rights of weaker members of society are respected; limiting of harmful effects, such as pollution by corporations sometimes passed on to others; and fostering innovation by supporting diverse ideas and ways of life.

Therefore, based on these studies and their findings published recently, the professionals have confirmed what I suspected, that both groups both Liberals and Conservatives have much to offer in contributing to good governance; although there is a clear demarcation of the thought-trend of each group regarding these highly sensitive moral, ethical and economic matters.

CHAPTER TWENTY-ONE

In Defence Of Marriage

Marriage is a religious and civil union between a man and a woman, or a male and a female. In The Bahamas, the law is emphatic: A man can only marry a woman, and a woman can only marry a man: Any other marriage union is illegal.

The Bahamas is governed by Domestic Legislation. In this regard, there is a Marriage Act, which, supported by the Matrimonial Causes Act, defines Marriage as between one man and one woman. Our law provides that any union between parties of the same sex is deemed null and void.

For the sake of this discussion, since the push for Same-Sex marriage is becoming a louder debate worldwide, the need to outline the correct description of Marriage is essential. Therefore, I will do just that.

In a survey put forward by *The Tribune* in Nassau in February 2013, the percentage of those agreeing and disagreeing for Same-Sex marriage was almost fifty-fifty. The small slice of the 'maybes' threw the majority in favour of the NOs. I was profoundly appalled that The Bahamas has sunk to this level of perspective, only forty

(40) years after the establishment of a Christian nation at Independence in 1973.

However, an opinion poll just one year later in February 2014, by a local Survey company found that ninety percent of Bahamians polling voted No to Gay Marriage. This is somewhat more encouraging and comforting for me.

According to the Oxford Online Dictionary in 2013, the definition of Marriage is the formal union of a man and a woman, typically as recognized by law, by which they become husband and wife.

The Merriam-Webster Online Dictionary in 2013 agrees with that perspective, that Marriage is, 'the state of being united to a person of the opposite sex as husband or wife in a consensual and contractual relationship recognized by law'.

Merriam –Webster secondary description of Marriage states that it is:

> 'A legally and socially sanctioned union, usually between a man and a woman, that is regulated by laws, rules, customs, beliefs, and attitudes that prescribe the rights and duties of the partners and accords status to their offspring (if any)'. It further explains that 'The universality of marriage is attributed to the many basic social and personal functions it performs, such as procreation, regulation of sexual behaviour, care of children and their education and socialization, regulation of lines of DESCENT, DIVISION OF LABOUR between the sexes, economic production and consumption, and satisfaction of personal needs for social status, affection, and companionship. Until modern times marriage was rarely a matter of free choice, and it was rarely motivated by romantic love. In most eras and most societies, permissible

marriage partners have been carefully regulated. In societies in which the extended FAMILY remains the basic unit, marriages are usually arranged by the family.'

Spiritual Perspectives on Marriage

In addition to the secular definitions for Marriage, Marriage is a gift from God since the Garden of Eden, designed to give Adam a companion, perfectly suited for him. The true concept of Marriage is only properly understood in the light of the Creation story in Genesis, according to the SDA Commentary. In the backdrop of the task of Adam naming the animals, he recognized that, while there were a male and a female of each species, there was no mate for him. In that vein, the God who created that scenario agreed with Adam's recognition and determined that...

'It is not good for man to be alone.' Genesis 2:18

God was deliberate in his plan to make a 'mate' suitable for Adam; one who would complement his characteristics and allow him and his mate to form a relationship that will symbolize the love relationship between God and his people. Subsequently, God took a rib from Adam's side, to form the woman from the ground, and brought her to Adam.

One 19th Century SDA Theologian, Ellen White noted, that it is intimated in Scripture that Adam was so excited when he saw the woman, that he wrote a poem and sang a song, saying,

'This is now bone of my bone, and flesh of my flesh. She shall be called Woman, because she was taken out of Man.'
Genesis 2:23.

As we consider further the backdrop of Adam naming the animals, perhaps God intended to create in Adam the logic that something was missing in his own existence, which would make him that much more appreciative of the gift that the Lord was going to give him in a wife.

The Seventh-Day Adventists theologian, the late Prophetess Ellen White, quoted:

> 'God celebrated the first Marriage. Thus, the institution has as its originator, the Creator of the Universe. Marriage is honourable, and the bed undefiled according to scripture (Hebrews 13:4). It is one of the first gifts of God to man, and it is one of the two institutions that after the fall, Adam brought with him beyond the gates of Paradise. When the divine principles are recognized and obeyed in this relation, Marriage is a blessing; it guards the purity and happiness of the race; it provides for man's social needs; it elevates the physical, the intellectual and the moral nature.' Ellen White, *Patriarchs and Prophets*, Pg. 46

In accordance with, and as a strong component of this good gift of Marriage, God created Human Sexuality: one of his greatest gifts to humanity. In creating it, he also provided rules to govern human sexual activities: in Marriage, between the man and the woman.

As I further examined the biblical basis in defense of Marriage, I wish to share Mrs. Mary Fairchild's perspective on Marriage from her online commentary www.christian.about.com. She noted that there are three commonly held beliefs about what constitutes a Marriage in the eyes of God. Let us examine her three hypotheses.

- The couple is married in the eyes of God when the physical union is consummated through sexual intercourse

- The couple is married in the eyes of God when the couple is legally married

- The couple is married in the eyes of God after they have participated in a formal religious wedding ceremony

Let's break this down and see what the Bible says about the marriage covenant. According to Malachi 2:14-15, we see that Marriage is a holy covenant before God.

In the Jewish custom, God's people signed a written agreement at the time of the Marriage to seal the covenant. The marriage ceremony, therefore, is meant to be a public demonstration of a couple's commitment to a covenant relationship. It's not the 'ceremony' that's important in a marriage; it's the couple's covenant commitment before God and man. It's interesting to carefully consider the traditional Jewish wedding ceremony and the 'Ketubah' or marriage contract, which is read in the original Aramaic language.

The husband accepts certain marital responsibilities, such as the provision of food, shelter, and clothing for his wife, and promises to care for her emotional needs as well. This contract is so important that the marriage ceremony is not complete until it is signed by the groom and presented to the bride. This demonstrates that both husband and wife see marriage as more than just a physical and emotional union, but also as a moral and legal commitment. The Ketubah is also signed by two witnesses and considered a legally binding agreement. It is forbidden for Jewish couples to live together without this document. For Jews, the Marriage covenant symbolically represents the covenant between God and His people Israel.

For Christians, Marriage goes beyond the earthly covenant also, as a divine picture of the relationship between Christ and

His Bride, the Church. It is a spiritual representation of our relationship with God."

When Jesus spoke to the Samaritan woman at the well in St. John 4, He revealed something very important, something we often miss in this passage. In verses 17-18, Jesus said to the woman:

> 'You have correctly said, 'I have no husband. For you have had five husbands, and the one whom you now have is not your husband; this you have said truly.'

The woman had been hiding the fact that the man she was living with was not her husband. According to the New Bible Commentary notes on this passage of Scripture, Common Law Marriages had no religious support in the Jewish faith. Living with a person in sexual union did not constitute a 'husband and wife' relationship. Jesus made that plain here.

Therefore, Position number 1 (the couple is married in the eyes of God when the physical union is consummated through sexual intercourse) does not have a foundation in Scripture.

Romans 13:1-2 is one of several passages in Scripture that refer to the importance of believers honouring governmental authority in general:

> 'Everyone must submit himself to the governing authorities, for there is no authority except that which God has established. The authorities that exist have been established by God. Consequently, he who rebels against the authority is rebelling against what God has instituted, and those who do so will bring judgment on themselves.' (NIV)

These verses give Position number 2 (the couple is married in the eyes of God when the couple is legally married), a stronger biblical basis of support. The problem with marriage as a legal process only, however, is that some governments require couples to go against the laws of God in order to be legally married, (such as in the case of Same-Sex Marriages). Also, there were many marriages that took place in history before governmental laws were established for marriage. Even today some countries have no legal requirements for marriage. Therefore, a more correct biblical position for a couple, as believers, would be to submit to governmental authority and recognize the laws of the land, as long as that authority does not require them to break one of the laws of God.

Mary Fairchild concluded that:

'As Christians, it is important to focus on the true purpose of Marriage when considering the wedding ceremony. Although the details are ultimately between the couple and God, the scriptural example encourages believers to enter into marriage in a way that honours God's covenant relationship, submits to the laws of God first and then the laws of the land, and gives public demonstration of the holy commitment that is being made. This can be carried out in a simple, private ceremony with only a few witnesses, or a large traditional wedding. The details are not what's important, but rather, the couple's covenant commitment before God and men.'

(Mary Fairchild – www.christian.about.com)

Fundamental Rights & the Protection of the Law

Please allow me to set a foundation regarding my commitment to the Constitution and the Fundamental Rights of all Bahamians, and people in general. As I have always indicated, the primary underpinning philosophy of governance in The Bahamas should always be the Preamble of the Bahamian Constitution.

The two primary tenets in the Preamble, for establishing policies in the nation, must be:

1. The recognition of the Supremacy of God,

2. The belief in the fundamental rights of the individual.

These two tenets bring front and centre, a God-given right for each individual to have fundamental freedoms, and all that the latter entails; and to enjoy these rights unhindered and undisturbed by others. It is placed in Chapter three of the Bahamian Constitution, (specifically Article 15), which states the following,

Whereas every person in The Bahamas is entitled to the fundamental rights and freedoms of the individual, that is to say, has the right, whatever his race, place of origin, political opinion, colour, creed or sex; but subject to the rights and freedoms of others and for the public interest, to each and all of the following, namely:

- Life, liberty, security of the person and the protection of the law:
- Freedom of conscience, of expression and of assembly and association; and
- Protection for the privacy of his home and other property, and from deprivation of property without compensation,

The subsequent provisions of this chapter shall have effect for the purpose of affording protection to the aforesaid rights and freedoms subject to such limitations of the protection as are contained in those provisions, being limitations designed to ensure that the enjoyment of the said rights and freedoms by any individual does not prejudice the rights and freedoms of others or the public interest. (Chapter 3, Article 15, subsection (a, b, c)

While the notion of a fundamental right is general for the sake of Article 15, the categories are specific as are outlined further, as the subsequent Articles identify:

- Article 16 – Protection of the Right to life;
- Article 17 – Protection from Inhumane Treatment or Torture;
- Article 18 – Protection from Slavery and Forced labour;
- Article 19 – Protection from Arbitrary Arrest or Detention;
- Article 20 – Provision to Secure the protection of the law (Fair trial & adequate defense);
- Article 21 – Protection of Privacy of home and other property;
- Article 22 – Protection of Freedom of Conscience (Religions convictions);
- Article 23 – Protection of Freedom of Expression (Speech & published opinions);
- Article 24 – Freedom of Assembly and Association (Free to join unions and other groups);
- Article 25 – Protection of Freedom of Movement;
- Article 26 – Protection from Discrimination on the grounds of race, etc.
- Article 27 – Protection from Deprivation of Property (by Govt without compensation);
- Article 28 – The Right to the Enforcement of Fundamental Rights;

While fundamental rights are paramount, the purpose of defining the terms and parameters of each fundamental right is necessary to cause people to understand the boundaries and limitations of the 'Protection' of the law.

The law is never without limitations. The law always has limited and conditional protection. The law is designed to provide for the protection of everyone's individual rights. However, the law does not carry its protection of one individual, to the prejudice of another individual. The law is meant to give each individual member in the society, and/or the public interest, equal protection and equal access under the law.

As you would surmise from my commentary, there are three compelling interests competing for the protection of the same law.

1. The individual right,
2. The public interest, and,
3. The law itself.

The law has wide flexibility and discretions when there are no other 'Competing interests.' Once the competing interests are introduced and exist, the law must 're-calibrate' to make certain that each individual right is within the boundary of the law.

For instance, if a person has a party and uses loud music, he may be free to do this within his right, because he has obtained the relevant permits. As long as his neighbours do not complain or object, he can play the music as long as he wants to. He is within the confines of his right. However, once the neighbours decide that they are going to bed, and do not want to hear any more loud music, it is now within their right, according to the law, to complain that the music must be turned down or off, because it is disturbing their sleep. The law now requires that the person having the party turn the volume of his music lower; so now he can continue to enjoy his party, but also the neighbour can go to sleep. The law provides protection for both individuals.

Further to that, if the party begins to present a problem for the neighbourhood, in that, the attendees at the party have spilled into the street, with disorderly behaviour and are causing the disruption in the flow of traffic, the other competing interest in this scenario is the 'Public's Interest'. So, it is not just the individual's right any longer, but it is the public interest that is also competing for the protection of the law. If the 'law' does not do what is necessary to protect the public interest, the integrity of the law itself comes into question.

And in the final analysis, if the police come in to stop the disorderly behaviour and the disruption of the flow of traffic, and then begin to arbitrarily arrest persons in the area – without regard that all persons transitioning in the area, may not necessarily be concerned with the matter of the party - it will breach its own boundary, and the integrity of the law, by infringing on the rights of persons by unlawful arrests. The police officers, who are the guardians of the law, must also have a commitment to the 'rule of law'.

I brought this setting forward, to indicate that the law if it is to operate for the protection and defense of all, must have clear-cut boundaries and limitations so that all concerned will receive equal protection within the operations of the law; and that no one individual preference deprives the right of another individual. It then takes on a moral connotation; that of, giving more right to one person over the other – it is inequity and a direct contradiction to the concept of the Rule of Law.

The reason the founding fathers established the nation on spiritual values, was to bring focus on the Rule of Law, in order to provide equal protection to all individual citizens as a high moral imperative. If we give more rights to one person over the other, it defies what we have determined to be a 'moral high ground' which is the commitment to the Rule of Law.

Therefore, the fundamental rights listed in the Constitution were intrinsically placed there to make certain that, 'no man, woman or child' would be infringed upon by another. While the Constitution still has minimal traits of discrimination, which it was not meant by design, however, the 'spirit of the letter' was inherently tempered with good values, in good faith, so that the provision and the protection of the natural, human rights of all citizens would be secured.

The intention of the drafters of the Constitution was geared at maintaining a moral high ground, which is referred to in most of the articles of Chapter Three as 'in the interest of public morality'. The matter of 'public morality' was so enshrined, that the public should always expect to have in society, a high level of public behaviour, that is acceptable to all. It was to be a standard upheld by the law. Therefore, providing rights and freedoms in the context of 'sexual orientation or sexual preference' would not have been afforded equal rights as other natural rights under the law.

Let me explain why. All fundamental rights and freedoms that are contained in the Constitution are actual moral rights and human rights – just check the list above. They are all-natural rights, meaning that they are good and proper civil liberties. It is why the term is used 'fundamental rights' – because they are something that is basic and elementary, and everybody should have access to them. However, nothing inferred from natural 'rights and freedoms' can cause a wrong thing to be done.

Therefore, if we begin to give 'rights' to issues that are immoral or unnatural, we will begin to infringe on the rights of other individuals, because it extends beyond the basic, elementary status of that which everyone should have access to without infringing on others' civil liberties. Think about it, if something is morally wrong, according to Leviticus 18:22; and you make it morally right, you begin to move the 'foundation' of that which is 'just' and 'equal' in society. It is unfair and unwarranted to give the bad in society more 'acceptability' than the good in society.

In a further illustration, when we survey property and land, we establish markers to divide the land. We place 'land-posts or stakes' to delineate one person's property from the other. Ever since ancient times, it was an abomination to move the land-posts. Therefore, if someone moved the stake that gave equal share, it would mean that one person would now have more land than the other, resulting in one person having more rights than the other. Inequity or unfairness would result because one person has stolen some land from the other person. It was a matter of wealth and resources. If you had more land, you could grow more crops resulting in more income. This would create a disadvantage over the other person.

Moreover, this matter of the moving of the land posts in the society was abominable because it brought into 'compromise' the actual foundation on which the 'trust' of the society was built, which is the commitment to the 'Rule of law' – Equal access before the law by every citizen.

Many things in society are dependent on the commitment to the 'Rule of law.' Economic development and growth are critically dependent on the 'Rule of law' in society. Property rights and private ownership are all dependent on the commitment to the Rule of law. If we cannot expect the government to have a commitment to the Rule of law, it throws every other thing in society 'offline' or 'out of sync.' This commitment to the Rule of law preserves the capacity of the government to provide the protection of fundamental rights and freedoms of individuals. If we have no Rule of law, we have no fundamental rights and freedoms!

Let me draw your attention to another very important example; one which the whole world, at one point, had to consider - 'The right of a person to smoke cigarettes, wherever they wanted to'. I remember when I was growing up thirty to forty years ago, and even as far back as the 1950s and 1960s, a person was permitted to smoke wherever they wanted to smoke. There were smoking sections for planes, restaurants, hotels, and in most public places. It was fashionable to smoke. At first, the smoker's rights took precedence over the non-smoker's rights, which resulted in disadvantages to the non-smokers. So, if you were on a plane or a restaurant, whether you liked it or not, you had to endure the smoke of those enjoying their cigarette, because they had a right to smoke.

After a while, a lot of people started developing lung cancer, and they were not persons who were cigarette smokers. People began to question why this was happening. It took them a while, but researchers finally figured out that 'second-hand smoke' gives people lung cancer, just as easy, or even easier, as those who smoked. So, societies had to withdraw the 'right' of smokers to smoke anywhere they wished, because that right to smoke trampled and disadvantaged the rights of non-smokers.

Millions of dollars had to be paid out in class-action lawsuits, just because people who enjoyed smoking had the right to do it wherever and whenever they wanted to. This 'right' of smokers has caused millions of non-smokers their lives. This could only happen when you give an unacceptable thing, the right to have an acceptable existence. That is essentially wrong. Therefore, we cannot grant special rights to one individual to the disadvantage of another individual.

No LGBT Rights Needed

As I noted before, in The Bahamas the law is emphatic. However, the push by some to legalize same-sex marriages cannot be facilitated under our present law, as many factors must come into play in order to even consider this.

I wish to concur with the view of a religious leader in a recent Letter to the Editor in one of the local daily newspapers, The Tribune, which noted that in order to facilitate Same-sex marriages, the entire breakdown of the Bahamian society would have to take place.

Let's look for a brief moment as to how we divide the responsibility.

Personal – If a man or a woman wants to be a homosexual or a lesbian, it is his or her personal right. That is between them, and their God. What they do in their house, on their private time, on their private property, is their right. It is their right and their personal sin. The fact that it is morally wrong, and that it is a sin, is not relevant for the point of my argument at this point. If they decide that they will tell no one, it means we will never know what they are doing. It does not mean that there is no sin going on, it simply means, as a society we do not know. It will not directly affect anyone at that time. It is not a societal problem. It is the person's issue and their personal sin.

Community – Now when they decide that they wish to begin to recruit persons to engage in that activity with them, and begin using their residence or a club, for group activity like mingling and fellowship, it will begin to affect the community: particularly if what they are doing is infringing on any community ordinances, such as illegal parking or loud music during their parties or orgies; or if children are being exposed to this behaviour. Once these activities become a concern for the community, that is the point where his issue leaves his house and has joined us outside in the community. It has become a community concern; it becomes a community problem.

Once the activities of these few individuals begin to affect the lives of other citizens, then the community as a whole has the right to voice their opinion. The community can decide that they do not want these kinds of activities affecting the quality of life in their neighbourhood. Policies and regulations can now be put in place to affect such activities and its location in the community. It now becomes the community's problem and responsibility. Conversely, if the community agrees with the activities and decides to sanction it by law, then it becomes a community transgression. The parameter of the problem and the transgression is growing.

National – Now when we come to the point where the whole nation has a concern about LGBT activities, they can choose to sanction it or regulate against it. If the nation determines, that, by and through legislation, they will give constitutional rights and privileges, in support of persons with diverse sexual orientation and preference, as bestowed upon natural heterosexual relationship, it then becomes a national issue. It means now that the whole nation has determined to sanction someone's personal transgression and bring it to national prominence.

Therefore, the people must understand that personal sins receive personal judgments; but national sins engender national judgment. In this regard, no one is exempted from national judgment, as seen in the biblical account of Sodom & Gomorrah. Everyone gets to be disadvantaged or disaffected by national judgment, even if they had nothing to do with it. This is why when you vote in a Referendum for an issue, even if it is defeated or passed, your vote is counted, for or against the matter, even so in the records of Heaven.

The legislation and adjudication of any matter concerns the nation as a whole. It is because Legislators and Magistrates are chosen from among the people to make their judgment and determination on behalf of the people, and not just for themselves. Leaders and Judges should use their best discretion in their decision-making; however, they must operate only by authority conferred on them by law. And for Magistrates and Judges, they cannot adjudicate what has not been duly Legislated. This is why the idea of Legal Activism is wrong, whenever it is exercised by the Judiciary, who have not been given such authority or power by direct Legislation.

Discrimination Against LGBT Should Not Be Allowed

Every Bahamian citizen has the same rights according to the Constitution to live and work and pursue happiness. Therefore, when a person is a secret homosexual or lesbian, nobody discriminates against them, because nobody knows that they have abnormal sexual proclivities unless they say so. They are allowed like everyone else to get a job, get an education, open their businesses, etc. They were given the right to do these things based on their 'rights' afforded in the Constitution, as a Bahamian, as a person, as a man, or as a woman. Therefore, constitutionally speaking, there is no Discrimination.

So, what is the purpose of requesting additional 'constitutional rights' for an individual based on their sexual preference or sexual orientation, because they are Lesbians, Gays, Bisexual, and Transgender (LGBT) in society? I submit that if the LGBT community in the society wants additional privileges just because they are of that sexual persuasion, then they are attempting to gain more rights above persons who are not Lesbians, Gays, Bisexual and Transgender (LGBT).

Many have argued that the government should not attempt to 'Legislate' morality, because by legislating morality, the government is forcing people to not do what they want to do. But if that argument is true, then what is the government supposed to do regarding regulating behaviour in society? However, the assessment of the late Dr. D. James Kennedy in the statement below regarding setting standards, simply indicates that 'legislating morality' is only putting into law the standard for which people should behave in society.

> 'Morality is the only thing we can legislate. Morality is the codification in law of some particular moral concern; generally, so that the immorality of a few is not forcibly inflicted on the rest of us.'

So, it is what Legislators have done over the centuries: It is their work, to place in law the standard for people to do good, and the best practices for the moral operations of society. Legislation gives right and power for the entire nation to change or alter its mode of operations, in all spheres of society. Legislation actually establishes and maintains what is the 'Rule of law' for that jurisdiction – to maintain Peace, Order, and Good governance.

According to Article 52 (1) of the Bahamian Constitution:

> 'Parliament may make laws for the peace, order and good government of The Bahamas.'

The government through the House of Assembly and the Senate has the power to make laws in order to govern society; and we, the people, make the final call as to what kind of laws we want them to create. Therefore, if we consent for the government to amend the Constitution to give 'legal' rights to people just because of sexual orientation or preferences or abnormal proclivities; Parliament will in fact be 'legislating' immorality. They will be placing into law, the standard for people to operate in an immoral way, just as they have done for people to operate in a moral way. So, the legislating of immorality will directly contradict Article 52 (1) of the Constitution.

Therefore, if people do not think it is acceptable for the government to legislate Morality, how then should it be acceptable for the government to legislate Immorality? If the government does not legislate an acceptable standard for society to operate in, then the government creates Anarchy, which leaves the door open for everyone in society to do as they please. In this regard, the government will have created disorder and set in motion a machinery of lawlessness and mayhem. Legislation is the primary machinery to maintain Order and Peace in society.

Let's look at the Ten Commandments... They are the basis of the law of the land: 'Thou shall not kill (Murder); Thou shall not steal, (Robbery & Armed Robbery); Thou shall not bear false witness, (Perjury), among others. If anyone breaks these laws, there are dire consequences. If we begin giving special rights to murderers, child molesters, rapists, armed-robbers, thieves, and the like, because it is their preference to commit wrong, the society would become a chaotic, lawless, and dangerous system, like the old wild, wild west.

In fact, similar results can now be seen in our society today, with the courts granting Bail to persons with numerous charges for the capital offenses of Murder, and Armed Robbery. These persons are freed into society and continue to commit more crimes. How far will we go and where will it end?

Due to the fact that neither the Constitution nor other domestic laws can provide rights for a person's sexual preference or orientation; then no avenue or door can be opened for same-sex marriages in The Bahamas, without changes to Chapter Three, Article 26, subsection 3 & 5 of the Constitution.

However, a Constitutional Referendum was called in The Bahamas to create changes to the aforementioned Articles, in June 2016. It was resoundingly defeated by the electorate across the entire country because the Bahamian people were adamant that they stood against any changes made to the Article 26, which would result in clearing the way for Same-Sex Marriages.

I submit that Sexual orientation or Homosexual preference is not a human right by the law of the Commonwealth of The Bahamas, and indeed the laws of God; and the voice and vote of the Bahamian people wishes it to stay that way. Therefore, it has no justification for serious consideration in The Bahamas. Therefore, I wish to surmise, and hold firms to the fact, that every person has human rights because they are human, whether they are homosexual or not; and no additional rights are needed by law to augment the rights they already hold and are privileged to.

During the debate leading up to the 2016 Constitutional Referendum, the former Attorney General, Allyson Maynard-Gibson indicated that the law regarding the registration of same-sex marriages in The Bahamas can be challenged, which seemed to invite legal proceedings from same-sex couples, wanting to be legally married in The Bahamas. The follow-up insinuation by a well-known Bahamian Human Rights & LGBT Activist, and self-proclaimed lesbian, that same-sex couples that have been married in so-called churches in The Bahamas, should be made legal, flies in the face of the laws of The Bahamas, and the laws of God.

Consequently, if we wish to engage the wrath of God against this nation, we can seek to remove all the moral safeguards that the founding fathers put in place and move The Bahamas towards Same-sex marriages, and Sexual orientation as a fundamental right.

The Worldwide Homosexual Agenda

The agenda to legislate LGBT rights in The Bahamas and around the world is based on 'inequity'. This worldwide Gay/LGBT agenda has set out to institutionalize that if a person chooses to be gay, those rights should be established by law so that they should not be discriminated against on any basis. I wish for your consideration, to answer the question, 'What does it mean to be 'discriminated' against?' Please pause before you read the next sentence and consider the question I have just posed. Let us look at several scenarios.

Firstly, if a gay person who is sick shows up to a hospital, does he need to say to the attendant or the doctor, 'I am gay!' No, he does not. However, if he is HIV positive, and his exposure to other people will affect them, he simply needs to say, 'I am HIV positive!'.

Secondly, if a person shows up to apply for a scholarship does he or she have to say, 'I am a homosexual or a lesbian!' Or does a person attempting to get a job as a cashier, as a security officer, as a teacher, as a Policeman, or as Defence force officer, have to say, 'I am gay!'

Would the interviewer need to know their sexual preference in order to determine their qualifications for that position? If a person does not say that he or she is a homosexual or lesbian, there is no reason why they should be discriminated against or treated any differently than a heterosexual individual in any of the same situations.

The only reason that the matter of one's sexual preference should come into question when seeking a job, is if that person is seeking a position as a 'sex worker, a prostitute, a pornographic model, a porn star or any other job in the sex industry. Otherwise, it should not come into consideration.

Unless, of course, the person doing the 'hiring' wants to know, so that they may render special favours on the grounds that the person is a LGBT person; or in contrast, to deny privileges on the same grounds. Therefore, I believe that the drive to legislate non-discrimination on the grounds of protecting LGBT rights is not in fact designed to protect against discrimination, but rather to give special privileges to this group, up and above those given to the non-LGBT person. When we sanction this by law and require for 'non-discrimination for LGBT persons', we will also give license for the 'discrimination against non-LGBT' persons.

In most cases, if a person who is openly gay has the authority to hire individuals in an establishment, they will hire more LGBT persons, than they will hire non-LGBT persons. This is my observations from my experiences with many mid-level managers and supervisors involved in homosexual activities. So, while this may not be the case in every single employment scenario, the majority of persons involved in this agenda will always 'recruit' for domination in the workplace. We will therefore authorize for the further recruitment of this lifestyle with the sanction of the law, for some to engage unsuspecting young persons.

Simply put, it is my opinion that the worldwide Gay Agenda is all about Recruitment and Domination. Therefore, as a community, we must not give license for the recruitment and domination of a primarily moral society by immoral proclivities. I have concluded that this is the main objective of the drive for the legislation of privileges for LGBT on the grounds of non-discrimination. And it is an immoral objective at that.

If a man or woman wants to be homosexual or a lesbian, they have a personal right to be so. Nevertheless, they do not have the right to force society to accept their sexual proclivities or to tolerate the flaunting of it publicly. LGBT people do not need us, as a society, to justify their right to be gay by legislating it. They may want us to, but they certainly do not need us to. I do not think it is justifiable for societies to be forced to Legislate more rights to LGBT people, while they openly flaunt that inequity and iniquity in front of us.

Meanwhile, I cannot condone violence against people because they are a homosexual or deny somebody medical attention as HIV/AIDS patients because they are gay. The same would apply to the discrimination against somebody because they are disabled, something we so often do. However, as Bahamians, all must be afforded the same access to care and protection under the law, not just because they are gay, but because they are a human.

I don't believe in discrimination against any person, because we are all people who God loves and wants to save. Many young people are unwillingly pulled into this homosexual lifestyle by evil men and women, whose main objective is to fight against God's ideal for the human race. So, as Christian men and women, we must attempt to pull young people out of this life of sin.

In conclusion, the suggestion that people should have more rights because they prefer to go against the laws of God, to defy the ideals of human sexuality, as God planned and ordained it, must be rejected. It has no basis in law and should not receive special protection under the law. To make such a law, opens the door for even greater societal breakdown, like moral segregations, which may result in even more violent confrontations over this immoral issue. Therefore, societal norms and the laws of decency must prevail. As the codification into law of abnormal sexual preference is not valid, the argument should be nullified and rejected.

The United States in Particular

As we can see, America is going well towards the judgment of God, in this regard, as it appears that they are seeking to protect, exalt and exert constitutional rights for all persons who become involved in an LGBT lifestyle. As I indicated before, God loves all people, but he hates the Sin of Homosexuality, as He does with all sins. It is not the will of God that the Sin of Homosexuality be the foundation of a 'constitutional right' in any nation.

In June 2014, President Barack Obama signed into law unprecedented rights and protection for LGBT activities in America, including a new protocol for LGBT persons serving in the Military.

While America is fundamentally good, only selected states over recent years, have voted to have same-sex marriages made legal, with no-discrimination of any kind for the lifestyle of gay men and women.

In furtherance to this Gay Agenda, in the summer of 2015, the Supreme Court of the United States, returned a decision to make Same-Sex marriages in all fifty (50) States constitutional; in response to a single case placed before them. This unprecedented move was endorsed and celebrated by the administration of the former President Barack Obama. This was certainly Legal Activism at its core, as legislation in all fifty (50) States do not support the Marriage of Same-Sex couples.

However, the statement by former Vice-President Joe Biden, that there will be a strong stance in the United States' Foreign policy against nations who do not support the United States posture on Gay Rights and Same-Sex marriages, took the matter of precedence to another level. It was an explicit attempt to force other nations to comply with America's dubious decision. This would obviously pose a problem in continued cordial relations with The Bahamas, a Christian nation, should the United States insist that The Bahamas comply with this stance.

The former protocol that was usually observed in the United States military of 'Don't Ask, Don't Tell', provided a far better state of affairs for gay persons serving in the military. The new policy for men and women to outwardly declare their abnormal sexual preferences, in an environment of the magnitude of Military service and the Armed Forces, must be most intimidating for the leadership in the United States.

In the U.S. military, Article 134 of the Uniform Code of Military Justice makes criminal the Act of Adultery when certain legal criteria, known as 'Elements,' have all been met, although few have ever been prosecuted by the policy. Therefore, Fornication, a companion sin to Adultery, which is the primary sin of LGBT people should also be considered a crime.

Have you ever wondered why so many people who are leaving for overseas duty, choose to get married before they leave? In addition to other benefits, persons in the military requesting 'leave' from the battlefield, to see their wife rather than a girlfriend, or husband rather than their boyfriend, is more acceptable in the United States Armed Forces.

These laws were created in the Military to not only observe biblical morality that 'Marriage is honourable; but that sexual activities outside of Marriage, particularly involving the spouse of another officer would be categorized as offenses; and to keep the moral code, of those serving as esteemed members of the World's most elite Armed Forces, the United States Military, at a high and reputable standard, particularly if it brings disrepute on the institution.

As a society, why would you want to know that a high percentage of the armed forces have abnormal sexual proclivities, and are involved on the job and off the job, in illicit sexual activities? This must provide a tremendous National Security risk and threat to the United States military in general, and to personnel servicing, particularly overseas.

In order to facilitate the new protocol, there will have to be an entire dismantling of the fundamental concept of decency; an action whose motive is simply to facilitate the declaration and engagement of homosexuals to openly serve in the military, without compromising the morale and confidence of the entire force, on the local level of the Battalion and Squad.

What would be the ultimate purpose for a person to declare him or herself to be 'Gay' in a military environment? Can you imagine that the enemy and the adversaries of the United States of America can determine how to compromise an entire nation because they are aware of the sexual orientation or preferences of the men and women who are serving in the Military? Can you imagine having this information readily available for assessment by the adversaries of the great United States of America? I can only imagine the end result – how tragic! It is my submission that it can only result in the weakening of the entire U.S. Military and Armed Forces, as a whole.

It would appear, however, that the Gay Agenda in America has won the battle to celebrate the immoral proclivities of gay men and women, and give them more rights than non-gay persons, to the detriment and to the compromise of the nation, and the infringement of the rights of the citizenry. This is where the problem lies. They have replaced right with wrong but have hesitated to replace wrong with right.

In conclusion, and in my final acumen in defense of Marriage, how do you tell the 'God' who created Marriage, that you will do it how you want to do it, and He must accept it, and sanction it?

Certainly, you cannot make fried chicken how you like it and call it Kentucky Fried Chicken or KFC. Only Kentucky Fried Chicken or KFC has the franchise for the Colonel's brands of eleven (11) herbs and spices. And only if you pay for the franchise, can you sell

KFC. The same is inferred of the institution of Marriage, except to a greater more solemn degree.

God created and ordained Marriage for His purpose. While every country has recognized Marriage as a civil union also, Marriage is still a Christian institution; and even if the persons are not Christians, once a man and a woman are legally married, that institution and their Marriage is recognized by God as a holy institution.

Therefore, I submit that a civil or sexual union of a man and a man, or a woman and a woman, can never be a Marriage – even if they obtain a license from the State. It is the right of God alone, to recognize only what He wishes as Marriage, the institution He created and ordained.

However, it was good to see that during his early days in office, the former U.S. President, Donald Trump, was bent on over-turning and rescinding some of those dubious policies regarding LGBT rights and Same Sex-Marriage. We will wait to see what is achieved hereafter; now that former Vice-President Joe Biden is now President of the United States. It is my sincerest hope that the United States of America can find its way back to a place of righteous principles, as the founding fathers of the Republic built it upon.

CHAPTER TWENTY-TWO

Bahamas Elections and Parliamentary Procedures, 2012

This chapter is designed to familiarize the citizen or the intended candidate with the process of Elections in the Commonwealth of The Bahamas. This information was gathered from information contained in the Parliamentary Elections Act 1992 (15th January 1992).

This chapter outlines the procedures from a layman's perspective, to help a person to follow the path from the Calling of an Election, Voter's Registration, the Nomination of a candidate, Qualifications for Members of Parliament, and the Swearing in of Members of Parliament.

This information was graciously contributed to by former Parliamentary Commissioners, Mr. Errol Bethel in 2004, and re-confirmed by Mr. Sherlyn Hall in February 2016.

The Calling of a General Election

Several things happen that enable a General Election to be called.

Firstly, the Prime Minister at his discretion, advises the Governor-General to dissolve the Parliament. The Proclamation from the Governor-General is read on the steps of the House of Assembly (Parliament), by the Commissioner of Police, acting in his capacity as the Provost Marshall.

Commissioner of the Royal Bahamas Police Force & Provost Marshall, Mr. Ellison Greenslade reads the Proclamation to Prorogue Parliament in April 2012. He is joined by Attorney General John Delancy & Secretary to the Cabinet Anita Bernard, and other Police Officers.
(Photo by Bahamas Information Services – Derek Smith.)

Subsequent to the dissolution, the Governor-General issues Writs of Election, for the holding of an Election. The Writs of Election are issued to the Returning Officers for each constituency, who may be the Parliamentary Commissioner, or an officer appointed by him, under Section 12 of the Parliamentary Elections Act (PEA). The Writ of Election is a written and legal command from the

Governor-General to the Returning Officer. A Writ is issued to each of the thirty-nine (39) constituencies, presently situated throughout the Commonwealth of The Bahamas.

Once the Returning Officer receives the Writ from the Governor-General, he or she must publish a Notice for the holding of an Election, no later than two days after the proclamation has been read. Subsequently, Notices of Election are published in the daily newspapers; one for each constituency. The Notice would signify a fixed date for the Elections, and a fixed date for the Nomination of candidates, under Section 35 of the Parliamentary Elections Act (PEA). The date and time of the Election Polling shall not be earlier than twenty-one (21) days, or no later than the twenty-sixth (26th) day of the publication of the Writ.

Voter Registration

Somewhere between twelve to eighteen (12-18) months preceding a General Election, the Parliamentary Registration Department, may commence the creation of a new Register of Voters to replace the Current Register of Voters, which would come to an end by a certain date, which is generally five years from the commencement of the previous Register of Voters. The Parliamentary Registration Department will invite citizens to register before the Current Register comes to an end or is closed.

When persons present themselves to register, they must take an oath of eligibility, to become a voter in the constituency in which he or she is seeking to register. This oath puts the responsibility on the voter to give true and accurate information concerning themself.

A person will not be registered unless, he or she is a citizen of The Bahamas, that have attained the age of 18 years, and have been ordinarily resident for at least three months in the constituency. Even though a Voter's Card is prepared upon registration, it will not be issued to the voter, until after the Boundaries Commission has convened and finished its Report, recommending any changes that may be necessary.

A Register of Voters is prepared, with respect to voters in each polling division and each constituency. Each voter will be given a number, which is not used by any other person registered as a voter at the same polling division. The Registers' of Voters are published and are available to the public upon request for a small fee at the Parliamentary Registration Department.

A person can object to the registration of a new voter or the removal of a person from the Register, if the person has proof that a person does not qualify to become a voter in a particular polling division or constituency. Once this information is reported to the Parliamentary Commissioner, appropriate steps are taken to verify the information. Once the information is verified, the person attempting to register is cautioned that a request has been made regarding their ineligibility to register in the constituency.

In this regard, it is at the discretion of the Revising Officer to accept or reject the documents for registration, based on his or her determination of its authenticity, in accordance with Section 19 of The Parliamentary Elections Act. Subsequent to that, if a person makes an oath that is false or misleading, or gives information that is untrue, the person can be liable, or face charges of perjury.

Qualifications To Be Elected To Parliament

The following information is the listed qualifications for persons seeking to be elected to the House of Assembly. This information is contained in The Bahamas Independence Order 1973 (the Constitution), Chapter V, Part 3, Articles 47 & 48, entitled "House of Assembly".

Article 47

A person shall not be qualified to be so elected unless he

    a. is a citizen of The Bahamas, of the age of twenty-one years or upwards; and

    b. has ordinarily resided in The Bahamas for a period of not less than one year immediately before the date of his nomination for election.

Article 48

1. No person shall be qualified to be elected as a member of the House of Assembly who

    a. is a citizen of a country other than The Bahamas having become such a citizen voluntarily;

    b. is, by virtue of his own act, under any acknowledgment of allegiance, obedience or adherence to a foreign power or state;

    c. is disqualified for membership to the House of Assembly by any law enacted in pursuance of paragraph (2) of this article;

    d. has been adjudicated or otherwise declared bankrupt under any law in force in The Bahamas and has not been discharged;

    e. is a person certified to be insane or otherwise adjudicated to be of unsound under any law in force in The Bahamas;

    f. is under sentence of death imposed on him by a court in The Bahamas, or is serving a sentence of imprisonment exceeding twelve months imposed on him by such a court or substituted by competent authority for some other sentence imposed on him by such a court, or is under such a sentence of imprisonment, the execution of which has been suspended;

g. is disqualified by any law in force in The Bahamas by reason of his holding, or acting in, any office the functions of which involve:

    i. any responsibility for, or in connection with, the conduct of any election;

    ii. any responsibility for the compilation or revision of any electoral register;

h. is disqualified by virtue of any law in force in The Bahamas by reason of his having been convicted of any offense relating to elections;

i. is a Senator; or

j. is interested in any government contract and has not disclosed the nature of such contract and of his interest therein by publishing a notice in the Gazette within one month before the day of election.

2. Parliament may by law provide that, subject to such exceptions and limitations (if any) as may prescribed therein, a person shall be disqualified for membership of the House of Assembly by virtue of

a. his holding or acting in any office or appointment specified (either individually or by reference to a class of office or appointment) by such law,

b. his belonging to any armed forces of The Bahamas or to any class of person so specified that is comprised in any such force; or

c. his belonging to any police force or to any class of person that is comprised in any such force.

3. For the purpose of sub-section (1) (f) of this article:
   a. two or more sentences of imprisonment that are required to be served consecutively shall be regarded as separate sentences if none of those sentences exceeds twelve months, but if any one of such sentences exceeds that term they shall be regarded as one sentence; and,
   b. no account shall be taken of a sentence of imprisonment imposed as an alternative to or in default of the payment of a fine.

Nomination of Candidates

In respect to the Nomination of a candidate for General Elections, several forms must be filed with the Returning Officer of the constituency that the candidate is contesting. It is recommended that any person seeking to nominate as a candidate, should go early to the Parliamentary Commissioner and seek the relevant information to complete his or her forms correctly. The staff at the Parliamentary Registration Department is very helpful in providing information without bias to all intended candidates.

There are three forms, which must be filed by the candidate. The first form is the Nomination Form, Form C. This form should be signed by at least five subscribers, who are registered and residents in the constituency for which the candidate is nominating. While there is a required minimum of five, there can be as many people as desire to sign as a subscriber. This form must be accompanied by four hundred dollars ($400), payable to the Treasurer of The Bahamas, and will only be refunded should the candidate receive more than 16.7% of the votes cast.

The second form is Form D, which is a Declaration of Oath of Qualification. This form must be signed by the candidate and a Justice of the Peace. The third form is Form E, which is a Declaration

Form, disclosing the Assets, Liabilities, and Income of the candidate. Form E must also be signed by a Justice of the Peace. This form is necessary to determine the net worth of the intended candidate, and to give proof that they are not insolvent or bankrupt.

Nomination takes place between the hours of 9:00 am to 12:00 pm on Nomination Day. If a person does not present his or her nomination papers by noon on Nomination day, their forms will not be accepted. The Returning Officer has the discretion to reject the Nomination papers, if the forms have not been prepared in the correct manner, or if he or she deems that the information is not authentic. Once the nomination process is over, the forms are then returned to the Parliamentary Registration Department. The Nomination forms are Gazetted; which means that the Nomination papers of all candidates in the General Elections are published in the newspapers for the public's information.

Local Government Elections

In the case of Local Government Elections, the same procedure applies in regards to the Notice of Election and the Nomination process, except for several variations, namely:

- A candidate can only nominate in the polling division in which he resides

- A candidate must be on the register for that constituency

- The candidate does not have to make a financial declaration but must make an oath of qualification, and file a nomination form

- The nominating fee is fifty dollars

Election Day/Counting of Votes

On the day of General Elections, the polls are open for ten hours, from 8:00 am until 6:00 pm. Candidates are allowed to have at least three agents stationed inside the polling stations. The candidate is also allowed to visit periodically during the day. During the opening of the polls, each candidate's agents are allowed to witness the opening of the ballot boxes, to ensure that there are no irregularities taking place.

During the polling day when a person goes to vote, he or she is taken through a procedure to authenticate their registration and their eligibility to vote. When a voter presents him or herself to the polling station, the guard at the door will call the individual's name, allowing agents of all candidates to verify the person's name on the Voter Register. The agent of the Parliamentary Registration Department takes the Voter's Card and checks the name on the Voter Register; and locates the counterfoil made during the Voter's registration process. Once the counterfoil has been located, the number is cross-referenced to the number on the Voter Registration, which is verified by agents of all candidates.

The voter's finger is dipped in indelible ink so that the individual can be identified, should they attempt to vote again during that polling day. The voter is then given a ballot, which is signed on the back by the Presiding Officer. The number on the ballot is also recorded on the copy of the counterfoil of the voter. The voter is sent into a booth to mark their (X) for the candidate of their choice. Once the voter marks their (X), they then fold the ballot, and show the Presiding Officer the signature on the back of the ballot, then deposit it in the locked ballot box. The voting process is completed. Their Voter's card is returned to the voter before they leave the polling station.

At the end of the polling day when the polls close, each candidate is allowed four agents including themself, to supervise the counting of the votes in each polling station. Once all the votes have been tallied, the box is sealed, and taken by armed guards to the Returning Officer at the designated place. The Returning Officer recounts the votes the following day and then makes an official declaration of a winner.

Election Results

Once the official election winner for the Constituency is declared, the Returning Officer then endorses the Writ that was sent to him from the Governor-General, and prints on it, the name of the candidate who won the contest and returns it to the Governor General. In this regard, the thirty-nine (39) Writs of Election must follow that same procedure.

In our system of Parliamentary democracy, the person who commands the support of the majority of those elected is invited by the Governor General to form a Government. In our case, it is the leader of the party that has won the majority of seats in the Parliament. The leader of that party would be sworn in as the Prime Minister by the Governor-General, by the end of the day after the official count, and the winners of the Elections have been declared.

In the days following, upon the advice of the Prime Minister, the Governor General would swear in the Cabinet ministers. The Prime Minister has the discretion to appoint no more than three persons who have not been elected to the House of Assembly to his Cabinet. Those persons would be sworn in and given their Instrument of Appointment as Senators by the Governor General. This will be done during this interim period, prior to the official opening of the Parliament, while the remaining members of the Cabinet are being selected and appointed.

The symbol of Sovereign British Rule as the stature of Queen Victoria still sits in Parliament Square in The Bahamas.

Opening of Parliament/Swearing In Of Members

During the time, which transpires between the date of a General Elections, and the date selected for the opening of Parliament, the Governor General appoints a person to take the results of the General Elections to the House of Assembly. The person usually appointed would be the Parliamentary Commissioner.

At the opening of Parliament, the Parliamentary Commissioner goes to Parliament and delivers the results of the General Elections. He calls the names of all the persons who were elected as members of the House of Assembly. The Clerk of the House of Assembly also calls the names and invites the members to choose a Speaker. The Speaker is first sworn in by the Clerk. Then the Speaker officiates the swearing-in of the other Members of Parliament by the Clerk.

Once all Members of Parliaments have been sworn in, a Committee is appointed to invite the Governor-General to speak to the Parliament. The Committee leaves the House of Assembly and goes to the Government House to invite the Governor-General to come to the Parliament. Upon their return, they inform the Speaker that they have delivered the request to the Governor-General.

Meanwhile, in the Senate, persons who have been chosen to become Senators follow the prescribed procedure to elect a President and swear in all Senators. Following the swearing-in, Senators prepare to receive the Governor General to read the speech from the Throne. As a tradition, the Governor General cannot go to the House of Assembly, the Lower House, but instead goes to the Senate, the Upper House.

(N.B. In 1992, the Ingraham Administration temporarily moved the Senate Chambers to Rawson Square in order to allow more persons to witness this process of governance. It has remained a practice with successive administrations since that time. Therefore, the set-up assembled in Parliament Square on the morning of the opening of a new Parliament represents the Senate Chambers, not the House of Assembly.)

David Forbes, Deputy Clerk (now Chief Clerk) of the House of Assembly carrying the Mace, in front of the Honourable Dr. Kendal Major, Speaker of The House of Assembly during the Opening of Parliament on May 23rd 2012. (Photo by Bahamas Information Services)

Governor-General His Excellency Sir Cornelius A Smith Inspects the Guard Downtown at the Opening of Parliament.

Once the Governor-General arrives at Parliament Square, he or she would be seated in preparation for the Speech from the Throne. It is customary for the Senators to be seated in the Square before the arrival of the Governor General. As a tradition, the Governor General then sends the Clerk of the Senate, which is considered the Black Rod, to the House of Assembly to request the Parliamentarians to come and listen to the Speech from The Throne.

Upon the approach of the Black Rod to the House of Assembly chambers, the door is customarily shut in their face. The Black Rod must then knock loudly on the door. The question would be asked why they came. The Black Rod would give the request from the Governor-General to attend the Senate proceedings, and then return to the Senate with the confirmation that the message has been delivered.

Once that message was delivered to Parliament, the session is dismissed, and Parliamentarians are invited to leave the chambers to go to the Senate to hear the speech from the throne. During their visit to the Senate for the Speech from the Throne, they must stand for the entire process, because no seats are provided for them. During the Speech from the Throne, at every acknowledgement by the Governor General of the Prime Minister and Members of Parliament, they must bow their heads in return acknowledgement.

Following the Speech from the Throne, both the Senate and the House of Assembly separately schedule a Session where they would officially thank the Governor-General for the Speech from the Throne. All members are invited to address the Parliament in response.

His Excellency Sir Cornelius A. Smith, Governor-General of The Commonwealth of The Bahamas (Photography by Bahamas Information Services (BIS))

Overseas Voting

The only changes to the Parliamentary Elections Act (PEA) 1992, has been the amendment to facilitate Overseas Voting, which was made in 2012. The Parliamentary Elections Act was amended to allow for Overseas Voting by Bahamian students and Government Officials stationed overseas in Embassies and Foreign Missions; according to Section 49, A, B C of the Parliamentary Elections Act (PEA) 2012.

The Overseas Voting would ordinarily take place in the office of the Bahamian Embassy, General Consulate Office, or Foreign Mission in that jurisdiction. The polling can only take place after an advance request has been made by each voter wanting to vote overseas, with the submission of Form J by the relevant overseas Mission office, by a specified deadline; so that provisions can be made to have staff designated from the Parliamentary Registration Department to supervise the polling.

Other Observations

There are several observations, about the Parliamentary process, that I wish to articulate that are sometimes misconceived by society, and at times by the Media.

1. The House of Assembly is honourable not the members. It is the Honourable House, not honourable members. Only Cabinet Ministers are Honourable members. After being a Cabinet Minister for ten years, a person can be given the title of Honourable for life. All Senators are Honourable, whether they are Ministers or not.

2. The Prime Minister is not necessarily the Right Honourable Prime Minister. A person becomes the Right Honourable when they have been appointed to Her Majesty's Privy Council. It has long been a misconception. Being elected to the post of Prime Minister does not automatically make a person the 'Right Honourable'. The Prime Minister of Britain, at his discretion, recommends the appointment of a person or in the case of a Prime Minister to the Privy Council. Once that appointment has been designated, then a person can choose to carry the title.

3. I have two concerns regarding the Oaths of office that are taken by Parliamentarians:
   a. At no place in the Oath of allegiance, Oath of qualification and the Oath of office as Cabinet Ministers does it obligate the Parliamentarian to the people of The Bahamas. Allegiance is rendered to Her Majesty, her heirs, and successors, but never to the people.
   b. The oath should not ask persons to swear. Based on the commitment in the Preamble that The Bahamas is a

Christian nation, leaders should not be asked to swear while taking the oath of office. At present, there is a footnote that a person could choose to either Affirm or Promise, rather than Swear.

c. An affirmation or a promise should be the standard pledge of allegiance for public office, rather than it being just a choice. As a nation, which acknowledges 'an Abiding Respect for Christian Values', we must not advocate swearing, which is forbidden according to biblical principles. (James 5:12)

4. Further, the Oath that is taken by persons being sworn in as Naturalized citizens is the very same Oath, as the Oath of allegiance used in the swearing-in of Members of Parliament. The Oath of Allegiance given to people who are becoming citizens should require them to make a promise to obey the law of the land and to do their best to protect the sovereignty of the Commonwealth of The Bahamas. These matters must be seriously considered as we seek to obligate persons to protect and honour the laws of the country, both as leaders and new citizens. These commitments must be a part of the official pledge and promise as persons become new citizens or new leaders of the country.

Bahamas Electoral System

I believe that we as a nation must seriously consider our electoral system. Although all members of the Commonwealth are democratic countries, there are different kinds of electoral systems.

These systems are:

1. First to Pass the Post.
2. Mix-Member Proportional or Proportional Representation.

Our system is like the first, First to Pass the Post – Winner takes all. Within this system, it is possible to have fifty-five (55%) percent of the votes and have 85 percent of the seats. Most times the election results do not reflect the correct representation.

In Proportional Representation, the system is set up to ensure that the support base of any faction in society is represented. There are different concepts that can be put in place to ensure this type of representation. I believe that we as a nation must consider whether we want to make a change, and what should be the change that provides greatest equity in political representation.

Campaign Funding Reform & Media Support

Campaign Funding Reform is something that politicians all around the world are talking about. But who has the political will to actually challenge the status quo, and do something about it when they are elected to office?

Campaign Funding and Reporting on donations is a sore spot in political campaigns. While everybody wants to collect financial support for their campaign, no one wants to declare where it is coming from. Law relating to Campaign Funding reform has long been advocated for, but no Administration has taken the mantle to change the laws.

The recently passed Non-Profit Organization (NPO) Bill 2019 Legislation in the Bahamas, has recommended strict measures to Counterterrorism and Money-Laundering but failed to place political parties under any obligation. While there has been wide-spread consultation by Civil-society and other governance activist groups regarding the Legislation; the FNM Government and the PLP Official Opposition have agreed to make political parties exempt under the Act. This is an affront to the work of good governance, as political activists like myself and others have been calling for this transparency for political funding reform for decades. The conversation is now louder and stronger regarding the matter.

The Olicharghy and other special interest groups benefit from providing funding to both major political organizations based on what political favours they can secure in return. The special interest continues to win, regardless of which party wins the election. The financially supported parties who can provide food and drinks, T-shirts and money, will always be able to gain more support for their party, over the other political groups who have little money to fund such elaborate activities. Although people are not aware, it is illegal to provide free food and drink, or entertainment once an Election has been declared. The law must be enforced in this regard.

The law must be changed or amended as it relates to broadcasting when Elections are declared. The campaign is unbalanced when candidates who have more campaign money can purchase more air-time and media space on the mainstream media than those with a smaller budget. We must consider the limiting of how much commercial campaigning is allowed with personal radio and television commercials and newspaper advertisements. Since the candidate has only their constituents to persuade to vote for them, their publicity should be confined to the constituency. The candidate should only be allowed to print literature and conduct meetings in the local area.

Regarding the National party's campaign machinery, there should be a limit on how many national campaign meetings a party can have under the guise of Mass Rallies. Mass rallies are only designed to eliminate the candidate working in the local community by throwing a big party to attract all and sundry. We must mandate that the local candidate get to know the local constituents and allow only the National leaders of the political parties to be featured on newscasts and press conferences as a rule.

While we may insinuate that it is already the rule, then the rules must be enforced. The Media must be fair in reporting the messages of all political organizations in the political discussion, to provide some degree of fairness, equity, and balance regarding the reporting of the General Election prospects and participants.

What has now become a salvation for many political campaigns is the advent of social media. While the mainstream media continues to be funded by Special Interests, with the agenda to keep different voices from the national General Election discussions; social media and online presentations will be major influencers in Elections going forward. The smaller parties have now been given a level playing field to compete with larger organizations for their share of the electorate's attention. As it was for Barack Obama in the U.S 2008 Presidential Campaign, so it will be for the inclusion of smaller parties to advance their bid to become the government.

I believe our biggest problem as a society, is that we are duplicitous and hypocritical in this regard. We cry for reforms when we are being disenfranchised, but once we get money into our campaign, or are elected to office; the Campaign Funding Reform discussion and the issue of Media unfair practices are no longer necessary issues. The society as a whole has little political will; and unless people with strong, moral convictions step up to the plate, the whole idea will continue to be only talked about when it is politically convenient.

CHAPTER TWENTY-THREE

A Project For Reform

There can be no meaningful discussion on the reconstruction of a nation without Constitutional Reform. In the case of the Commonwealth of The Bahamas, we fought for our first Constitution from Britain in 1962 for Internal Self-governance. Prior to that, the white Colonialists called 'The Bay Street Boys', governed the country, controlling both the Legislative and Economic agenda.

The 1973 Constitution was enacted as a Statutory Instrument of the British Parliament, (Bill No. 1080) of the Caribbean and North Atlantic Territories. It is entitled The Bahamas Independence Order 1973. The Statutory Instrument has listed on its cover:

- Made - 19th February 1973
- Laid before the British Parliament - 26th June 1973
- Coming into Operations - 10th July 1973
- Printed by Her Majesty Stationery Office in London.

This makes it clear to me, that since The Bahamas inherited this Constitution, they have only made copies of it; and have not made an effort to certify it or make it a Bahamian legislation. I could be wrong, but because the printed copy of the Bahamian Constitution is still sold as the aforementioned document, without reference to the Parliament of The Bahamas, I have unequivocally concluded, that the Bahamian Constitution is still only a Statutory Instrument of the British Parliament – as previously stated.

Setting the Stage for Constitutional Reform

In order for Constitutional reform to take root in the heart of a people, it must begin with the process of creating a new political atmosphere and culture in the country. To create a new political culture requires shared national values. You can only create new culture by articulating core values and creating in the people a need to change or renew their established value system. If the people can buy into this idea, then the breaking of the 'fallow ground' will begin. Following up on that, the nation can in actuality begin this most important and sacred process.

In view of the above, a return to the 'original intent' of the nation's core values are important in finding a new 'revolution-ized', yet old political culture. Many of the founding fathers and mothers in the nation, including the former Governor General, Her Excellency Dame Marguerite Pindling, have noted, that during the days leading up to the attainment of Majority Rule in 1967, and the process towards Independence 1973; the Bahamian people were full of hope and unified for the creation of the new Bahamas. She said that the people were filled with Purpose and Identity.

These desires and aspirations were penned by Sir Arthur Foul-kes, in a few verses that were included as the Preamble in the Inde-pendence Constitution. These aspirations articulated a set of core values that were expected to be kept before the Bahamian people, as a sense of where the founding fathers of the new Bahamas wanted to take the nation, and the kind of nation they intended to create.

Some of the other items used to create a National Identity were the National Anthem, the Pledge, the Flag, the Coat of Arms, and the Motto, among other national symbols. These important items spoke volumes regarding the spirit of the Bahamian people, which had caused their spirit to soar during the years between the 1967 General Election victory, up to the 1973 Declaration of Independence, and thereafter. Therefore, it is necessary that we recognize and articulate all the core-values in these items, in order to identify a new spirit, or a renewed national personality and national culture of the Commonwealth of The Bahamas.

Based on all my research and planning, I have come to the conclusion that the intrinsic worth of the core values articulated in the Preamble of the Constitution, despite the inherent difficulties of the Westminster system, if we followed after those values in a precise way, we would have attained our objective of good governance, and achieved the creation of a righteous nation, as we had set out to achieve.

New Political Agenda for The Bahamas

The primary aim of The Bahamas Constitution Party is to highlight the Preamble of the Constitution and the core values contained therein, as the basis of a system of good governance in all institutions in the nation, and particularly, the creation of criteria for national leadership.

From the early days of the Bahamas Constitution Party, we have always articulated that we will be in pursuit of the creation of a new Constitution for the Commonwealth of the Bahamas; to facilitate the creation of a truly sovereign Bahamian state, free from the Executive management of Her Majesty Queen Elizabeth II and the Westminster system.

The creation of this new Bahamian Constitution is expected to bring about Constitutional democracy, and the change of the nation's status to a Republic system of Governance; a political system based on accountability and popular sovereignty, meaning Government for the people, by the people. This new status will produce Institutional Integrity in all systems of governance, providing for a more 'equitable and just' process, and the sharing of power in the nation among all stakeholders and political parties involved. It is our hope that ideas for the new Constitution, along with these I have included, will be garnered and discussed widely by all stakeholders, all political parties and citizens, before being placed before the Bahamian people, and the Parliament in a Referendum for approval.

Since the BCP's inception in 1998, I have written and published numerous articles and press statements via the mainstream media, online social media, and via our websites, on matters of Constitutional reform. Those editorial contributions have brought to light many irregularities perpetrated by successive PLP and FNM administrations, highlighting the need for 'righteous' mandates for governance, like Campaign Funding Reform, the Freedom of Information Act, among many others, which can only take 'root' with significant Constitutional reform.

During the discussions I had with the late Sir Lynden Pindling during 1998 - 2000, I asked him why the PLP government's twenty-five (25) year tenure in office did not seek any kind of 'constitutional changes. He indicated that they were too busy creating institutions like the Defense Force, College of The Bahamas, Central Bank, the building of schools, and other national institutions. He noted that initially, it was not a priority, because they had already obtained the 'franchise' from England to govern the nation; and that was all they needed to empower the Bahamian people.

While that may have been a reasonable excuse initially, it is clear that successive administrations have shirked the legislation of any significant changes to that Constitution, for real accountability and transparency, at every level of governance in the nation. As is now clear, over the years, there has not been any pursuit of Constitutional changes to the status of our political machinery. It appears that the Westminster system works well for the 'government of the day' to maintain the entrenchment of the 'absolute power of the regime'.

Therefore, if a government is to pursue real Constitutional reform, it must first have a unilateral commitment to the Rule of Law – an 'Abiding Respect' as the Preamble has articulated. And thus, I believe that it will be a travesty to leave the very delicate process of Constitutional Reform in the hands of any government whose pursuit does not include 'all stakeholders and political parties' in the process of the discussion. Therefore, I am suggesting that The Bahamas Constitution Party and other political parties, must be included at any table advocating Constitutional amendments or reform. This is what has been intentionally denied over the past twenty-years by successive administrations, despite my requests for inclusion.

Why The Need for Constitutional Change

HRH Her Majesty, Queen Elizabeth II (Head of State)

Many Bahamians have asked the following questions, 'Do we have Full Independence from Britain or are we just a more autonomous form of Internal Self-Governance?' 'Why do we need full independence from Britain?' 'What will that full Independence mean?' We are still seeking answers to these old-age questions. I will attempt to answer some.

The Bahamas Is A Constitutional Monarchy Or Parliamentary Democracy. (Judging from the Wikipedia Dictionary explanation of the same, The Bahamas fits into this form of government.)

A Constitutional Monarchy is a form of democratic government in which a Monarch acts as a non-party political head of state within the boundaries of a Constitution, whether written or unwritten. While the Monarch may hold formal reserve power and government may officially take place in the Monarch's name, they do not set public policy or choose political leaders.

Political scientist Vernon Bogdanor, paraphrasing Thomas Macaulay, has defined a Constitutional Monarch as 'a sovereign who reigns but does not rule.' This form of government differs from absolute monarchy, in which the Monarch controls political decision-making and is not effectively restricted by constitutional constraints.

Constitutional monarchies are sometimes referred to as limited monarchies, crowned republics, or parliamentary monarchies. The United Kingdom and fifteen of its former colonies are constitutional monarchies with a Westminster system of government.

In addition to acting as a visible symbol of national unity, a Constitutional Monarchy may hold formal powers such as dissolving Parliament or giving Royal Assent to legislation. However, the exercise of such powers is generally a formality rather than an opportunity for the Sovereign to enact personal political preference.

In *The English Constitution*, British political theorist Walter Bagehot identified three main political rights that a Constitutional monarchy could freely exercise:

1. The right to be consulted
2. The right to advise
3. The right to warn.

Let's look at The Bahamas' present system of governance, and who controls the culture of power in The Bahamas, according to the Constitution:

- The Executive Authority of The Bahamas is vested in Her Majesty (Constitution Ch. 5 -Article 71 (1))

- The Governor-General is Head of State, On behalf of Her Majesty (Constitution Ch. 5 -Article 71 (2) & 79 (1))

- The Prime Minister is appointed by the Governor-General, (the Prime Minister is the Leader of the party who has the support of the Majority of elected members in the House of Assembly (Constitution Ch. 5 - Article 73 (1))

- The Cabinet of The Bahamas (Constitution Ch. 5 - Article 72 (1)) – Provides General Direction and Collective responsibility to Parliament

- The Leader of the Opposition is Her Majesty's Loyal Opposition (Constitution Ch. 5 -Article 82 (1)), appointed by the Governor-General, who is the Leader of the Opposition party. (Provides Consultation for most Appointments by the government)

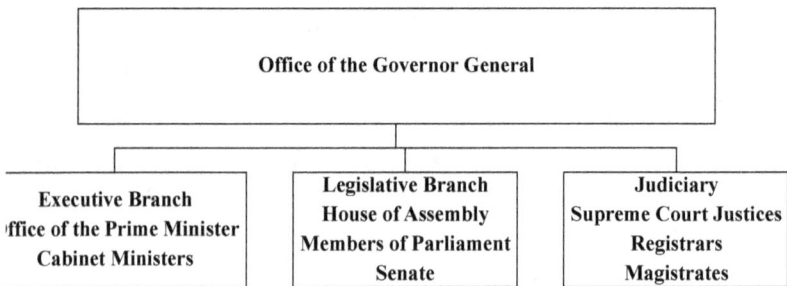

Office of the Governor General		
Executive Branch Office of the Prime Minister Cabinet Ministers	Legislative Branch House of Assembly Members of Parliament Senate	Judiciary Supreme Court Justices Registrars Magistrates

Bahamas Government Structure

As you can note from the above, it is Her Majesty's government. However, the greatest concern I have regarding politics in The Bahamas is the overwhelming powers of the Office of the Prime Minister. While it is essential for the Chief Executive of the nation to have Executive Authority to govern the nation and get their political agenda accomplished, the protection of the 'State' is still more critical. Thus, the Office of the Prime Minister requires streams of accountability to the people to ensure against corruption. This overwhelming power of the Prime Minister has led to 'elected' dictatorship, tyranny, corruption, and malfeasance, which are all considered misbehavior in public office by elected officials.

Despite accusations of misbehavior in the Office of the Prime Minister, we the people have not been able to successfully sanction or bring to trial, the conduct of any person who has ever held that office. While the law implies accountability to Parliament, alleged abuses that occurred in the Office of the Prime Minister, under any administrations, have not been able to be reprimanded or prosecuted, during or after the holder's tenure.

Benefits of Constitutional Democracy (Republic System of Government)

What is it? And how important it is to future National Development?

A Constitutional Democracy is a government system that is based on popular sovereignty. In a constitutional democracy, the structures, powers as well as limits of government are set forth in a Constitution. Most rights within a Constitutional democracy are also balanced by responsibilities and order. It is a government of, by, and for the people. It is the government of a community in which all citizens, rather than favoured individuals or groups, have the right and opportunity to participate. In a democracy, the people are sovereign. The people are the ultimate source of authority.

In a Constitutional Democracy, the authority of the majority is limited by legal and institutional means, so that the rights of individuals and minorities are respected. This is the form of democracy practiced in Germany, Israel, Japan, the United States of America, and several other countries.

The essential characteristics and principles of Constitutional Democracy are:

1. Popular Sovereignty
2. Majority Rule and Minority Rights
3. Limited Government
4. Institutional and Procedural Limitations on Powers

There are certain institutional and procedural devices that limit the powers of government.

These may include:

1. Separated and Shared Powers
2. Checks and Balances
3. Due Process of Law
4. Leadership Succession Through Elections

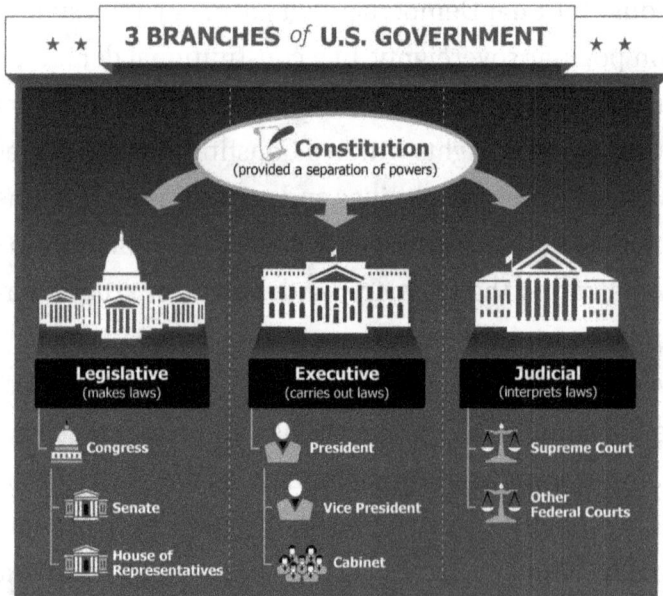

3 BRANCHES *of* **U.S. GOVERNMENT**

Constitution
(provided a separation of powers)

| Legislative (makes laws) | Executive (carries out laws) | Judicial (interprets laws) |

Congress — President — Supreme Court
Senate — Vice President — Other Federal Courts
House of Representatives — Cabinet

United States Government Structure

What Constitutional Democracy Would Entail For The Bahamas

The following points are simply provided to create a discussion on where The Bahamas should be headed in Creating & Developing National Legislation and Revising Public Policies for the various platform issues:

The BCP recommendations are for the Bahamas to transition from Parliamentary Monarchy to Constitutional Democracy. These are some of the beneficial attributes:

- Creating Real National Sovereignty - So that The Bahamas will have autonomy to create, select and manage its own Treaties alone, if necessary, and not as a block with other Caribbean nations
- Creating Accountability & Transparency among all power structures of Governance
- The sharing of Political Power between all stakeholders in society towards the creation and control of public policy
- Creating a new Constitution, approved by Parliament and by the Bahamian people in Constitutional Referendum

Political and Election Reform

The following points are provided to create a discussion and provide suggestions for Reform:

- Set fixed Dates & Times for General Elections & Midterm Elections
- General Elections for national leadership (Includes House of Parliament / Senators / The Presidency)
- Mid-term elections for Local government leaders & personnel
- Establish Independent & Permanent Constituency Boundaries Commission

- Establish Electoral & Integrity Commission to Examine and Pre-clear Electoral Candidates)
- Remove Restraint & Expand time Frame for the Nomination of Candidates,
- Establish Independent Parliamentary / Elections Commissioner & Deputy Commissioner (Must have Security of Tenure - Suggested oversight of Constituency Boundary Commission, and Electoral Integrity Commission)
- The Candidates – Qualifications – The right to Recall - Access to the Process
- Term Limits (Consecutive and Non-Consecutive terms)
- Voter Participation (Mandatory Registration & Continuous Register of Voters, Absentee Ballots, Advance Polling, Qualifications for Overseas Voting, Access to Voters Lists, etc.)
- Campaign Funding Policies & Reform (Legislate principles & tenants punishable by law)

Bill of Rights - Creating & Securing Righteous Mandates
- The struggle for Equality (Social, Economic, and Gender)
- Protection of the Fundamental Rights and Freedoms of Individual Citizens

The Executive

The following points are provided to create a discussion and provide suggestions for Reform on the portfolio items listed:

The Election & Role of the Presidency / The President

The following points are simply provided to create a discussion:

- The Role of the President – Provide leadership for all Bahamians
- Leading the nation and Chief Administrator of the government

- What is the President's Constituency? All Bahamians
- Election of the President – By all Bahamians
- The Role of the Vice President – Assist the President with leadership/Elected by all Bahamians
- Staffing the Presidency – (Both Civil Service and political appointments)
- The Cabinet – (Selected by the Presidency, Ratified by both Parliament and the Senate)
- The Independence of the President and Access to the President
- Accountability of the office of the President – To both Houses of Parliament
- The Candidate – Their Qualifications (Specified)
- The right to recall the holder of the Office of President or Vice-President
- Term Limits for The President (Consecutive and Non-Consecutive terms)

The Legislature

The following points are simply provided to create a discussion on the portfolio items listed:

Parliament / The House of Assembly/ Representatives (Elected)

BCP Recommendations

Leadership of the House of Assembly (Proposed)

Speaker, Deputy Speaker, Majority Leader, Minority leader, Backbenchers

The Senate / Representatives (Propose to be Elected)

BCP Recommendations

Leadership of the Senate (Proposed)

President, Vice President, Members - All senators are politically independent.

- The re-organizing of electoral districts, so that Senators can be elected on the configuration of their seats in restructured districts across The Bahamas (e.g. A portion of an island, a constituency or a group of islands.)
- Persons being nominated and subsequently elected to the Senate will not be drawn on party lines, but independent individuals seeking to be elected.
- The purpose of electing Senators is to draw further and deeper from an independent pool and from more divergent interests across the nation.

Local Government Councils
(Midterm elections on local community levels)

The Federal System - Reinventing Government Bahamian Style / An Imperative for national development & diversification

- The Central (Federal) and Local Government – Administering the Bureaucracy in all Constituencies
- Local Government over the entire country including New Providence
- The Power of Legislative Approval (Local Government Assemblies and Councils)
- Balancing Power / Sharing Power, and Setting Boundaries for Power Sharing
- National Goals versus Local Interests (All National Stakeholders and Local government participation)

An Independent Judiciary

The following points are provided to create a discussion and provide suggestions for Reform on the portfolio items listed:
- Office of Attorney General (Not elected Official – Appointed and Ratified by Both Houses of Parliament)

- Office of The Chief Justice, approved by both Houses of Parliament
- The Supreme Court and Court of Appeal, approved by both Houses of Parliament
- Her Majesty Privy Council eliminated in this Jurisdiction for Criminal Cases (No leave to be given to appeal for Criminal cases)
- Bahamas Appeals Court - Highest Court (Last resort and access to Criminal Justice in The Bahamas)
- The Prerogative of Mercy (by Executive Order)
- Legal and Judicial Service Commission members must be approved by both Houses of Parliament – Subsequent Recruitments and Appointment by Parliamentary approval by both Houses
- The Doctrine of Judicial Restraint Versus Judicial Activism defined
- The Penal Code Revised
- Capital Punishment Implemented (Methods Revised & Options: Lethal Injection or Electric Chair – Legislated)

The Media - The Fourth Estate

The following points are provided to create a discussion and provide suggestions for Reform on the portfolio items listed:

- The Protection of the Press
- Preserving authentic Public Opinions (Increase facilities for access to the public)
- Endorsement of political Candidates and political ideologies
- Developing or communicating political opinion during and between elections (Legislation)

The People's Access to Government

The following points are provided to create a discussion and provide suggestions for Reform on the portfolio items listed:

- Establish The Ombudsman – Independent Office for Citizens Review & Appeal against Government Misconduct
- Establish & Legislate the Freedom of Information Act (FOIA)
- Activism – Public Pressure on / Effective Lobbying for, influence in government of all stakeholders and the citizenry
- The Role of the Church in Influencing Government Actions / and the participation in the creation of Public Policies and Legislation
- The role of Non-Government Organizations (NGO's) and Civil Society, access to and in influencing government policies

Independent Consumer Protection Agency

- Partially Funded by Government (Public - Private Partnership)
- Legislation for Corporation of quasi-government Agency

National Defense Policy (A Reformed Constitutional Imperative)

The following points are provided to create a discussion and provide suggestions for Reform on the portfolio items listed:

- Commissioner of Police – Approved by Both House of Parliament with Security of Tenure
- Deputy Commissioner of Police – Approved by Both House of Parliament with Security of Tenure
- Defense Force Commodore / Deputy Approved by Both House of Parliament with Security of Tenure
- All Military / Armed Force Service Commissions must be approved by both Houses of Parliament

- A Joint Chiefs Commission to include all the Armed Forces
- A National Guard - A Restructured Military (Reserved Military - Recruitment of twenty to thirty (20-30%) percent of eligible population)
- A National Youth Service to include all students and adults under twenty-five (Military and Non-Military Components)
- Defending the Borders and National Sovereignty – A national priority for all citizens.
- Redefining Citizenship & Developing an effective Legal and Illegal Immigration policies

The Government's Role in Economic Stability

The following points are provided to create a discussion and provide suggestions for Reform on the portfolio items listed:

Government Contributing to Prosperity or Managing It? Redefining the Role of the government in Economic Policies. What should it be?
- Government as a Generator of the Economy
- Government as a Manager of the Economy
- Government as a Promoter of Economic interests
- Government as a Protector of the Environment for Economic growth

Environmental Policies and Renewable Energy Sources

What should the Government do?

The following points are provided to create a discussion and provide suggestions for Reform on the portfolio items listed:
- Natural Resources are the People's Inheritance. (Must be minimized in the hands of Foreign elements)
- Nationalized the Natural Resources. such as Sand, Oolitic Aragonite, Salt, Minerals, Oil, Natural Gases, Discovered

Treasures, Marine Life & the abundance of Sea vegetables and life-saving algae.

- Create Industries with Natural Resources such as Sand, Oolitic Aragonite, Salt, Minerals, Oil, Natural Gases
- Create & Implement Sovereign Wealth Fund for disbursement of Funding from the sales of Natural Resources
- Solar Power & Technology and other Renewable Energy sources - A National Imperative for Immediate response
- Convert Waste Products to Energy Initiative in Mass Scale
- The Launch of a National Recycling Initiative (Explore All Options)

Education Philosophy – The Re-education & Training of Bahamian Society

The following points are provided to create a discussion and provide suggestions for Reform on the portfolio items listed:

- The new Curriculum – Empowering the future (Evaluating each child's specific learning type and needs)
- Re-constructing education with a specific plan for a new socialization of Bahamian children (Primary education to high school education)
- Tertiary Education – A free one-year post-high school education; a must for all Bahamians
- Free two and four tertiary level education for all Bahamians who qualify or desire
- Home-schooling versus public education, creating a mutual collaborative imperative
- New revenue streams to fund tertiary education

The Politics of Social Welfare

The following points are provided to create a discussion and provide suggestions for Reform on the portfolio items listed:

- Addressing the needs of the Poor – How should the government respond?
- Unemployment & Entitlement Programs (protecting the future)
- National Insurance (NIB), National Prescription Benefits, National Unemployment Benefits, National Health Insurance, etc.

National Economic Recovery Plans

The following points are provided to create a discussion and provide suggestions for Reform on the portfolio items listed:

- New philosophy for Budgeting and Money Management – Biblical Principles
- Budget Reallocation and Restructuring
- Tithing of National Revenue and Income
- Creation of New Revenue Streams from Industries of Natural Resources
- National Investment Corporation (to generate projects and funding locally and overseas)
- Debt Reduction and Remediation
- Temporary Austerity Measures, where needed

Biblical Principles for Money Management & Budgeting

In order for the nation to exercise good stewardship and upright money management, we must explore new biblical strategies to bring the nation out of severe debt and onto the road to prosperity. Among many other biblical references for good stewardship, Malachi

3:7-9 articulates both the nation's fault and the solution to it. The implementation of this Biblical principle of Tithing & Offering will compensate for the charge of robbing God, from a national perspective; and will bring financial matters back in order for the nation.

Therefore, I am recommending the Tithing of the National Recurrent Revenue and Income of the Government. Tithing is the allocation of Ten percent (10%) of all financial gains coming to the nation in Revenue, Taxes, and other Income including Gifts. An additional Ten percent (10%) of the National Recurrent Revenue and Income will also be allocated as an automatic National Savings Fund for Recession and Disasters such as Hurricanes. This will mandate a Debt-Ceiling to the government's budgetary planning at eighty percent (80%) of government Revenue for Recurrent Expenditures.

If these biblical principles for good stewardship are not taken into consideration and implemented, the present covetous philosophy of 'Borrow, Tax and Spend' will overtake the nation's desire to achieve a Debt-Free status in the medium to long term.

In order to produce new streams of Recurrent Revenue in the nation, the government must initiate new Legislation and new stringent policy measures, to collect, utilize and maximize Taxable Income from all the Natural Resources exported out of the country. This can also be realized by increasing Industries with the natural resources that will grow the economy and add new streams for government income. These Natural Resources are God's gifts to the Bahamian nation, as the inheritance for all the people, not a selected few. So, these resources must benefit all the people of The Bahamas and build the nation for the future.

Strong Leadership For Change

Strong leadership and political will are required for change of this magnitude. And strong leadership needs personal force of character to be adequately maintained. The place of leadership is a very narrow and lonely one. It is a place where the leader will encounter his or her greatest test of character, and the place where the potency of that character will be most challenged.

As a leader, if you have no strength of character for real change, everybody will eventually know. Decisions will or not be made for those hard choices. In fact, the leader's entire life would have been preparing them for the place of leadership. And whenever the leader arrives in that place, whatever is in them will be revealed. The pressures of leadership will prove who they truly are. And it may even be a surprise to the leader what is actually in them, whether they can stand the test of such pressure, and not slide into peer pressure.

In the governance process, there are times when major changes and strong decisions are required. During that time, you will experience people that are 'cutthroats, backbiters, radicals and sell-outs', as participants or disciples around the table. In fact, around every table, there is seated a Judas, the betrayer; a Thomas, the doubter; a Peter, a strong personality; and a John, a trusted, beloved, and loyal friend. However, as a leader, you will have to stand up and deal with any one of them, even if it means confronting and exposing them. And then, there are times that you must sit humbly and let everyone say their peace and give their ideas and advice. It is not always to incorporate it all into the agenda or try to please everybody, but it is to simply know who sits at your table and what is in them, and what they are thinking.

However, as the leader, you are given a vision to organize, the ability to articulate it, the charisma to mobilize people after it, and the character to defend it. All of these tasks are necessary if you are going to succeed. As a leader, you must have faith in the agenda for real change. It is what leadership is about. As the leader, you are responsible, not only to people but to God.

Accountability in leadership is not just about what you can tell the public, but what you can live in public and private; and whether your personal character can withstand the challenges of governing a society in crisis, one needing drastic changes.

When attempting to govern a nation, the ability to 'walk the talk' and 'talk the walk', brings front and center, the leader's character and strength, which should involve both visionary and pragmatic concepts of good governance all in one place.

As we reflect on Open Governance & the Freedom of Information, as I see it, sometimes when negotiations and interchanges are done in the public, it creates an entirely different resolution, to that which happens behind closed doors, in the comfort of internal organizational diplomacy. Leaders are allowed to speak their true minds, and eventually, reach the position of what is best for all the people. This idea of governance transpiring before the Media is not entirely what I fully consider the 'public right to know'. It is often an exercise in futility and sometimes has created disingenuous results. It causes politicians to be superficial, for the sake of political expediency. This form of governance has to be reconsidered for the United States of America; where all of the national security issues are aired for the world to see. This sometimes compromises the nation's security. And contrary to what some may consider is transparency or open government, this is not where I believe the Bahamian nation must go towards either.

Although, governing behind closed doors does not negate the concept and responsibility of accountability and transparent governance. People still have the right to know what the result of the government's discussion is, and what led them there. This is the responsibility of the State, which includes all three Arms of the government, and the Media, the Fourth estate; if the nation is going to be protected and guarded from the forces who wish to destroy it, both from within and without.

This is imperative in any nation, with the re-building of strong bi-partisan and autonomous institutions like the Office of the Ombudsman and an independent Consumer Protection Agency; with strong moral stakeholders committed to a strong democracy, holding political leaders accountable to their actions, whether in public and private.

Regarding Diplomacy

The United States of America is the closest in proximity to The Bahamas, and strategically The Bahamas' closest neighbor. I believe we want some of the very same things, regarding the securing of our borders.

Figuratively speaking, when a country's back door is your front door, like America is to The Bahamas: when your properties border each other as ours do, and when what happens in your country may affect theirs: you need to have at least some commonalities and many civilities. And you want to make sure you at least see eye to eye on most things that are important to the security of both nations. The Bahamas depend strongly on the United States, as most of our Imports, including Food and consumable items, are imported from there. Many of our children attend college and universities there, and many close family ties are maintained there. The Bahamas also seek assistance from the U.S. government with logistical support, Border control, and many tactical issues, relating to national security and the defense of our nation. I believe our relationships should be strong, and tacitly maintained, and indeed always cordial and amenable for both countries.

The United States of America needs the strongest alliance with The Bahamas as its closest neighbor, and The Bahamas need the same. I believe that the maintenance of this alliance must be our most urgent consideration, and it should be given priority over some economic considerations like our ominous relationship with the People's Republic of China and its agencies.

While it is important for strong alliances and cooperation between our nations, it is also equally important that a nation as big and powerful as the United States; always takes into consideration the Sovereignty of our small nation, to honor and respect our wishes, our leadership, and our need to be accepted as an equal in the league of nations.

My concern as a future leader, in The Bahamas, is always, who is leading, the United States of America, that is the President; and who is representing the United States to us, meaning, Ambassador to The Bahamas. These positions of our neighboring country, always affect and influence our country's leadership, either in a positive or negative way, in relation to the overall quality of life for every single citizen and resident of the Commonwealth of The Bahamas.

In closing, the introduction of a new style of governance in The Bahamas is necessary for the real empowerment of the Bahamian masses. The task of building new national institutions and producing new initiatives through the restructuring of the financial and economic arenas, social, religious, and political spheres, are also necessary for a commencement towards developing a better nation for the next generation of Bahamians. The work of reconstruction through the building of core values and networks of people across the country will bring this society closer to where we should be heading as a nation.

—————— CHAPTER TWENTY-FOUR ——————

Summary / Reflections

n order to bring a conclusion to my opinion on the subject of
The Bahamas' need for Reconstruction, Order, and Revival, I
wish to borrow some words from a political essay *The American
Democrat* written by American Republican author James Fenimore
Cooper, which was published initially in New York State in 1838,
and currently available on Amazon.com. He quoted:

> 'It is the intention of this book to make a commencement
> towards a more just discrimination between truth and
> prejudice. With what success the task has been accom-
> plished, the honest reader will judge for himself.'

As I complete this work, I am indeed relieved and grateful that
the tedious process of his project and the venomous fight against
its publication is finally concluded. This project has been in the
making for almost twenty (20) years, which ambitiously began as
a research paper I wrote on the subject of 'Criteria for National
Leadership and Governance' in the Fall of 2001 at the American

University in Washington, D.C. The opinions contained therein are mine alone, and it gives me profound contemplation as to whether I have accurately articulated what I believe you needed to hear on the subject.

The Bahamas needs revival of both Church and State regarding our regretful state of affairs. Needless to say, it is we the people, God's people, who will have to take up the task to seek revival and renewal of the Bahamaland. In this regard, I am reminded of the scripture:

> 'If My people, which are called by my name shall humble themselves and pray and seek my face, and turn from their wicked ways; then will I hear from Heaven, and forgive their sins and heal their land.' 2 Chronicles 7:14

So, if we want national reconstruction and renewal and order, then the people of God must lead the way. Thus, the agenda and call of the Bahamas Constitution Party for righteous men and women to join the work as leaders and candidates, to take on the fight in the Bahamas towards the attainment of a new government for a new Bahamas.

In this regard, and in consideration of my open request for leaders and servants, I wish to refer you to some interesting commentary in a most enlightening book, *The Family Under Siege* by George Grant, who poses a question, regarding who will rule the nations. He identifies Satan's plot and strategy for total rulership over mankind when he noted that:

> 'If Satan can attain the rule of nations, his strategy for the rule of citizens is just as surely accomplished. A moral decline of a people (nation), thus precedes the moral decline of a person in the overarching plot.'

George Grant in his book, *The Family Under Siege*, asks the following questions: What is Satan doing? What is his overall strategy? What does he hope to accomplish?

In a comprehensive response, he provides the answers:

> 'Simply put, his grand design seems to include possessing the heart and souls of individual men, in part, by remaking their nations into his own image. Disingenuously, he seems to believe that if he can somehow win the much-disputed culture wars, he can end-run God's Providence and at last enthrone himself. Not surprisingly then, the assaults on the Christian foundations of Western and democratic culture are very real, very powerful and very calamitous.'

George Grant concludes that God has called us to engage in spiritual warfare on behalf of our nations. Pure and simple! We are admonished again and again 'to put on the whole armour of God' because it is inevitable that we will have to 'wage war' to 'demolish strongholds' and to 'tear down fortresses and principalities' in this present world system, in order to win.

Satan's desire to rule the nations through mankind is an attempt to mimic God's desire to rule the nations through transformed men and women, who will submit and commit themselves to His Lordship. This is the Bahamas Constitution Party's mandate as a divinely ordered, counterstrategy, to Satan's ongoing tactics against good governance in the Commonwealth of The Bahamas.

I wish to concur with George Grant's concept because it is my solemn belief that it is God's ultimate desire for The Bahamas to rise up as a nation, that is a Beacon of Light and an Ensign of Hope in troubled times; and that this nation reflects His purpose in the earth. God's desire is to rule this nation, and to be the God in the Commonwealth of The Bahamas; and in turn, the people of the Islands of The Bahamas shall be 'His' people'.

That sounds pretty simple to me, but how that is accomplished will require much more than mere wishful thinking. It will require much prayer, and the commitment to change, by the people of God – the Bahamian people.

Tommy Tenney in his book, *The God Chasers* describes a conversation with the author of Cry for Me Argentina, Dr. Edward Miller, about how revival broke out in Argentina in the 1950s. He said students in a Bible seminary in Argentina prayed day after day in repentant weeping until God showed up. They had to suspend classes because of the continued prayer meetings held by the weeping students for fifty days. While Dr. Miller only knew about 600 Christians in Argentina at the time, consequent to the student's prayers, eighteen months later, the people of the country were flocking to revival services in the thousands; even the largest stadium could not hold them.

Author Tommy Tenney noted that Dr. Edward Miller alleged:

'If God can get enough people in an area to reject the rulership and the dominion of satan; if enough of His people will reject satan's dominion in the right way – with humility, with brokenness, and in repentant intercession; then God will slap an eviction notice on the doorway of the ruling demonic power of that area. And when He does that, then there is light and glory that begins to come.'

I certainly do concur with the above sentiments, and I am more than elated to see that, finally, after twenty years of my advocating, the people of The Bahamas are beginning to find their voices regarding Righteous Leadership, Good Governance, and Economic Justice for the masses of Bahamian people.

Due to my advocacy towards this end, I have lived under threat of my life and economic welfare for a very long time. It is only because none of my adversaries' tactics, shenanigans, monitoring, threats of intimidation, multitudes of sorceries, and assassination attempts have been successful, that I am still alive today in the Commonwealth of The Bahamas. They simply could not break the protective barrier surrounding my life. And there were times, and I am sometimes still bewildered why I have lasted this long, with an agenda that most men would have abandoned within the first few years. Only the grace of God in my life has seen me through.

You see, if you have started and failed as many times as I have, you would often wonder if it is indeed God who is leading you. When you have worked for good, and have been resisted with the magnitude of force and hatred that I have had to endure, sometimes, you question the direction that you are going in. When you have been used and abused, and your talents, gifts, and work stolen by people of power, and then rebutted and shunned like you have no intrinsic worth, there are reasons to concern yourself about your continued viability. When you have been betrayed by friends and colleagues, overlooked and pushed aside as I have been, there is a level of doubt that comes back every so often, about whether you should continue working for change.

And when it seems that the only opportunity you will have to prosper in your own country, is to sell your soul, or forget both your integrity and what God has said to you; because there seems to be nothing there for you – as I have been pushed and forced to consider – you will always question God as I have.

And finally, when God speaks to you, and you are so ahead of the crowd, that you have to sit and wait it out for months and years, and in this case, two decades – and yet, you are still being divinely pressed to go on: you must know and be certain, that it is God who is in control of your life. For whatever it is worth, I am called for purpose in the Commonwealth of The Bahamas. And since guns and knives cannot kill purpose, 'I will not Die until I am Done.' Therefore, the battles that lay before me and the ones I have attempted to engage, are not my own – 'The battle is the Lord's!'

Therefore, in conclusion of all this, I wish to now make a clarion call to men and women who believe that they have been called to leadership in this generation for this Bahamas, to stand up and prepare yourself for the task that confronts us now. It doesn't matter where you live in the world, if you are a Bahamian and you feel so impressed, I wish to pose the following questions to you,

Are you one of the leaders of the next generation of Bahamians? Are you ready to lead in the quest for accountable governance and the commitment of new national leadership in the Bahamas? Are you ready to take a stand and represent the cries of the Bahamian people for better representation on the principles of the Preamble of the Constitution? Are you ready to make the wealth common in the Commonwealth of The Bahamas, to the benefit of the Bahamian masses?

If so, if any of your answers are YES... Then I wish to invite you to stand now! This is your Time. This is your Clarion Call. 'The People have a Choice, but God has a Plan.'

The Final Charge for Change

And indeed, I am encouraged that despite our present dilemma and the imminent adjudication of both the PLP and the FNM Administrations as part and parcel of our failed state; the Almighty God, Yahweh Elohim - the Creator of Heaven and Earth has great plans for the nation of the Commonwealth of The Bahamas. I leave you now with God's sincerest recommendation and admonishment to the Bahamian nation as a whole, and for the consideration of every single Bahamian for their own individual life:

'If you fully obey the LORD your God and carefully follow all his commands, I give you today, the LORD our God will set you high above all the nations on earth. All these blessings will come on you and accompany you if you obey the LORD your God: You will be blessed in the city and blessed in the country. The fruit of your womb will be blessed, and the crops of your land and the young of your livestock—the calves of your herds and the lambs of your flocks. Your basket and your kneading trough will be blessed. You will be blessed when you come in and blessed when you go out. The LORD will grant that the enemies who rise up against you will be defeated before you. They will come at you from one direction but flee from you in seven. The LORD will send a blessing on your barns and on everything you put your hand to. The LORD your God will bless you in the land he is giving you. The LORD will establish you as his holy people, as he promised you on oath, if you keep the commands of the LORD your God and walk in obedience to him. Then all the peoples on earth will see that you are called by the name of the LORD, and they will fear you. The LORD will grant you abundant prosperity—in the fruit of your womb, the young of your livestock and the crops of your ground—in the land he swore to your ancestors to give you. The LORD will open the heavens, the storehouse of his bounty, to send rain on your land in season and to bless all the work of your hands. You will lend to many nations but will borrow from none. The LORD will make you the head, not the tail. If you pay attention to the commands of the LORD your God that I give you this day and carefully follow them, you will always be at the top, never at the bottom. Do not turn aside from any of the commands I give you today, to the right or to the left, following other gods and serving them. However, if you do not obey the LORD your God and do not carefully follow all his commands and decrees I am giving you today, all these curses will come on you and overtake you. Deuteronomy 28:1-15.

In conclusion

'I call Heaven and Earth to record this day against you, that I have set before you, Life and Death, Blessings and Cursing: Therefore, choose Life, that both you and your seed shall live. That thou may love the Lord thy God, that thou may obey his voice, and thou may cleave unto him, for he is thy life, and the length of thy days: That thou may dwell in the land which he promised to your fore-fathers, to give them.' Deuteronomy 30:19-20

THIS IS MY HOPE FOR MY BAHAMALAND! MAY GOD BLESS AND KEEP SAFE THE COMMONWEALTH OF THE BAHAMAS.

Bibliography

Section One

Aristotle - *Nicomachean Ethics*, Dover Publications Inc., 1998

Cleary, Robert E. (Editor) - *The Role of Government in the United States*, University Press of America, 1985

Dogan, Mattei - *The Concept of Legitimacy, Encyclopedia of Government and Politics, Volume One*

Fawkes, Sir Randol - *The Faith that Moved the Mountain*, The Nassau Guardian Ltd., 1988/1997

Grant, George - *The Family Under Siege*, Bethany House Publishers, 1994

Locke, John - *The Second Treatise on Civil Government*, Prometheus Books, 1986

Maxwell, John C. - *Leadership 101 Inspirational Quotes*, Honor Books, 1994

Maxwell, John C. - *21 Irrefutable Laws of Leadership*, Thomas Nelson, 1998/2007

Munroe, Myles - *Becoming a Leader*, Pneuma Life Publishing, 1993

Peck, Robert S. - *The Bill of Rights and the Politics of Interpretation*, West Publishing Company, 1992

Reshon, Stanley (Editor) - *One America? – National Identity*, Georgetown University Press, 2001

Vincent, Andrew - *The Concept of the State, Encyclopedias of Government and Politics, Vol. 1*

Greenleaf, Robert K. - *The Power of Servant Leadership* (Edited by Larry C. Spears), Publishers (The Greenleaf Centre for Servant Leadership) Berrett (BK) Koehler

Tenney, Tommy - *The God Chasers*, Destiny Image Publishers, 2001

Patterson, Thomas E. - *We the People – A Concise Introduction to American Politics*, McGraw Hill Higher Education, 2006

Research Department, Central bank of The Bahamas, A. Gabriella Frazier - *The Monetary & Fiscal Implication of Achieving Debt Sustainability* – Appendix #3 - Chart of Government Operations & Financing, 1975 - 1998

Research Department, Central Bank of The Bahamas, A. Gabriella Frazier - *The Monetary & Fiscal Implication of Achieving Debt Sustainability* - Appendix #4 – Chart of National Debt of 1975 – 1998

Section Two

Bahamas Independence Order 1973 – The Bahamas Constitution

King James Version, The Holy Bible, Thomas Nelson Publishers

Oxford On-line Dictionary, American University Library

Roger 21st Century Thesaurus, Thomas Nelson Publishers, 1992

S. A. DeSmith, *Constitutional and Administrative Law*, 1971

The Parliamentary Act, 1992, Government Publication, 15th January, 1992 (Nassau)

Webster 21st Century Dictionary, Thomas Nelson Publishers, 1993

Webster Classic Reference Library Dictionary & Thesaurus, Landoll Inc., 1999

Matthew Henry Commentary of the Entire Bible (Hendrickson Publishers 1991)

Articles and Leaflets (Online & Printed)

Foster, Dr. Gregory D. - *Ethics, Government and Security - The Democratic Imperative*, "The Humanist" – Buffalo – Volume 61 - May/June 2001

McIntosh, S. Ali - *The News Spectator Magazine* (Bahamas) - August 2000

Moxey, Pastor J. Mario - *The Role of Leadership in Society*, "The News Spectator Magazine" (Bahamas) - August 2000

Duncan, Neville Professor - *University of West Indies*, UNIFEM TL Conference October 2002

Narcisse, Carol - *Women Working For Transformation*, UNIFEM TL Conference October 2002

Talma, Grace - Grace Talma & Associates, UNIFEM TL Conference October 2002

UNIFEM Caribbean Secretariat, *TL Learning Community Manual*, TL Conference October 2002

Women' Media Watch (WMW) - *Understanding Gender* – Jamaica

Online Resources

www.scientificamerican.com Unconscious Reactions Separate Liberals and Conservatives by Emily Laber-Warren

www.Studentnewsdaily.com Views on Liberal and Conservative Beliefs

http://en.wikipedia.org Wikipedia On-line Free Dictionary

https://tradingeconomics.com/bahamas/government-debt-to-gdp Trading Economics.com

Interviews

Foulkes, Sir Arthur - Interview, September 2000

Pindling, The Late Rt. Honourable Sir Lynden Oscar - Exclusive Interview, June 13th, 2000

My photo - Cover and Inside (Photography by Rodger D. Sands – Rodger D Photography, Nassau, Bahamas)

About The Author

harell Ali McIntosh was born in St. Matthew's Parish on the island of New Providence in April 1966, just nine months before the attainment of Majority Rule in January 1967.

Enjoying the privilege of being raised in a Post-Colonized Bahamas, S. Ali McIntosh, as she is professionally known, is a student of history and a first-generation product of an Independent Bahamas and a Government Educational system, graduating in 1983 from the renowned R.M. Bailey Senior High School in Nassau.

Brought up in a home with two talented pastoral parents, Ali is an avid reader, and has been involved in leadership in Church work all of her life, spending the last 27 years as a Prayer Intercessor and Lay Preacher & Lay Administrator, in the Bahamas Conference of Seventh-day Adventists.

Trained as a newspaper Journalist, and a Radio & News broadcaster with the Government-Owned Broadcasting Corporation of The Bahamas since the 1980s; Ali is a well-sought-after Radio and TV talk-show guest, bringing a fresh perspective to national and topical issues facing the nation.

Her community work with the youth advocacy organization she founded in 1995, the National Committee for Youth Renewal & Revival, has landed her a 'Humanitarian Award' in 1997, and a 'Changing A Generation Award' in 2001 by The Bahamas National Gospel Excellence Awards.

Her work with civil society spans more than two decades as a voluntary Strategic Planner and Consultant in Urban Development; the Royal Bahamas Police Force Consultative Committee; the Bureau of Women's Affairs, now the Department of Gender and Family Services; and an Executive Officer of the National Organization of Women's Association of The Bahamas (NOWAB); among other ongoing Children Rights, Women Rights, Gender-Based Violence Legislation, and Community Enrichment Projects she still participates in.

She has authored her own syndicated weekly newspaper column *Answering the Call* for several years in the 1990-the 2000s and has drafted several working documents for youth and urban development; have contributed to several Bahamian Consultative Reports on Youth, Crime, and Urban Development; and drafted a private legislation for Parliament in 2016 on Electoral Reform.

She is the founder of the 22-year-old Bahamas Constitution Party, in which she serves as its Servant Leader. This has created many firsts for her becoming the first woman in The Bahamas to ever organize and found a political party; the first woman to lead a political party into General Elections, in May 2012 and 2017 respectively; and the first woman to contest a Bye-election in the Bahamas, when she ran in North Abaco in October 2012.

She has attended numerous United Nations-sponsored conferences, in addition to representing The Bahamas on three occasions, at the United Nations General Assembly on the Commission on the Status of Women in New York, including in 2019 at the 63rd CSW; when she was introduced to HRH Sophie Duchess of Wessex, who represented the Commonwealth on behalf of Her Majesty HRH Queen Elizabeth, Head of The Commonwealth.

In 2018, Ali received the 'Sir Lynden Pindling Nation Building Award' in January from The Grace Centre (Bahamas) for her effort to keep the work of the founding fathers before the nation; and was honoured in December by The Esther's Ball Network for Outstanding Women in Ministry, in the area of Politics.

Currently, she serves as the Chairman of the Josiah Institute for Leadership & Public Policy (Bahamas / U.S.A), a Leadership Development & Training School, she formally established in 2018; and is the President & CEO of S. Ali McIntosh & Associates Leadership Consultants, a consultancy firm she created, which provides a fresh perspective and focus to leaders in business, civic organizations, political and governmental institutions, in the areas of human development, productivity specialists, and ethical wisdom.

Author Contact

S. Ali McIntosh & Associates Leadership Consultants
Corporate Office in Nassau, The Bahamas
(242) 423-2709 / (242) 524-1798 Mobile
In the United States – (470) 909-1140

Websites

www.samcintoshassociates.com
www.thejosiahinstitute.com
www.bcpparty.org
Email - ali@samcintoshassociates.com
Email - sambahamasbusiness@gmail.com